AFTER HOUDINI

AFTER HOUDINI

Written by
Jeremy Holt

Illustrated by
John Lucas

Colors by
Adrian Crossa

Lettered by
A Larger World Studios

INSIGHT COMICS

San Rafael, California

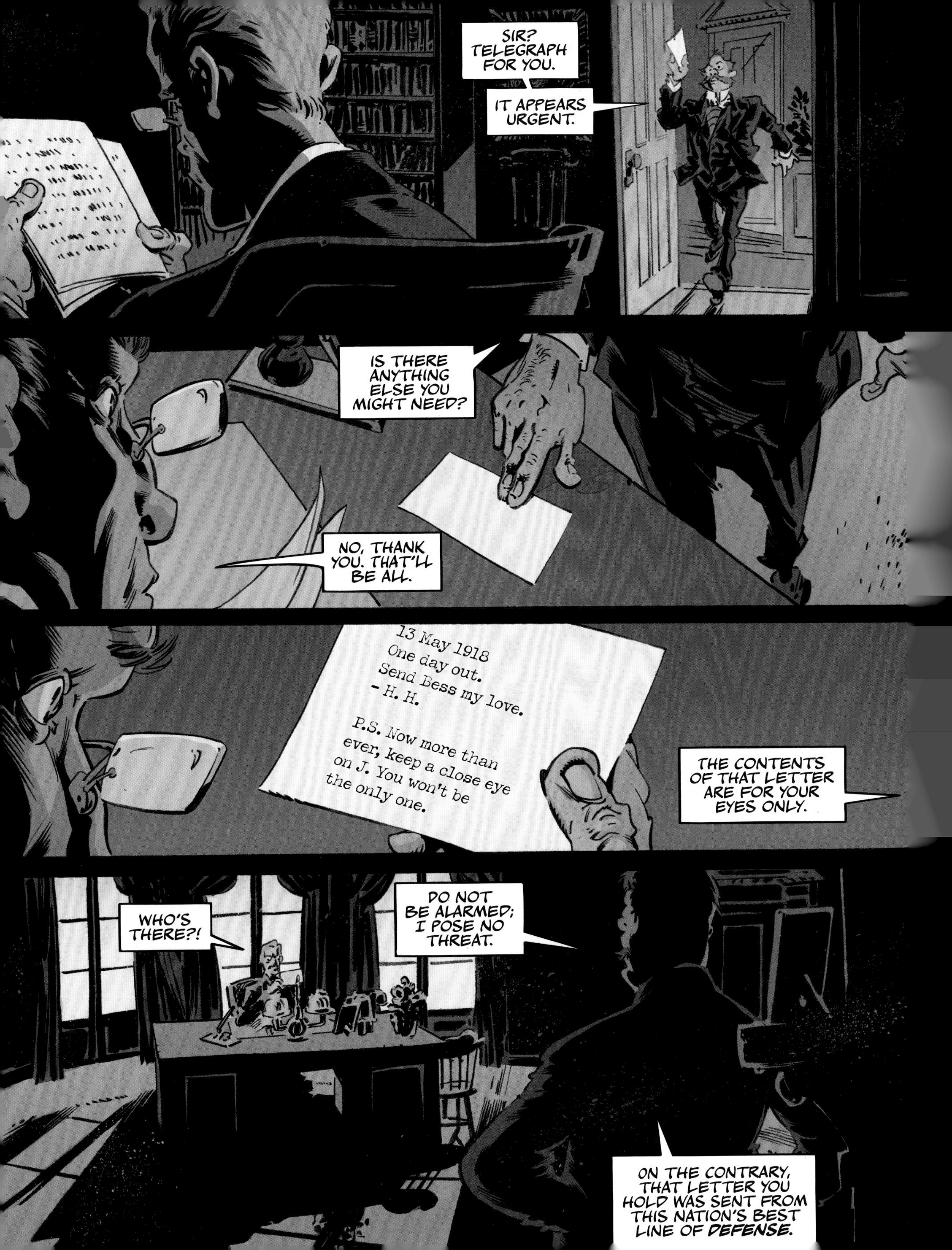

SIR? TELEGRAPH FOR YOU.
IT APPEARS URGENT.
IS THERE ANYTHING ELSE YOU MIGHT NEED?
NO, THANK YOU. THAT'LL BE ALL.
13 May 1918
One day out.
Send Bess my love.
- H. H.
P.S. Now more than ever, keep a close eye on J. You won't be the only one.
THE CONTENTS OF THAT LETTER ARE FOR YOUR EYES ONLY.
WHO'S THERE?!
DO NOT BE ALARMED; I POSE NO THREAT.
ON THE CONTRARY, THAT LETTER YOU HOLD WAS SENT FROM THIS NATION'S BEST LINE OF DEFENSE.

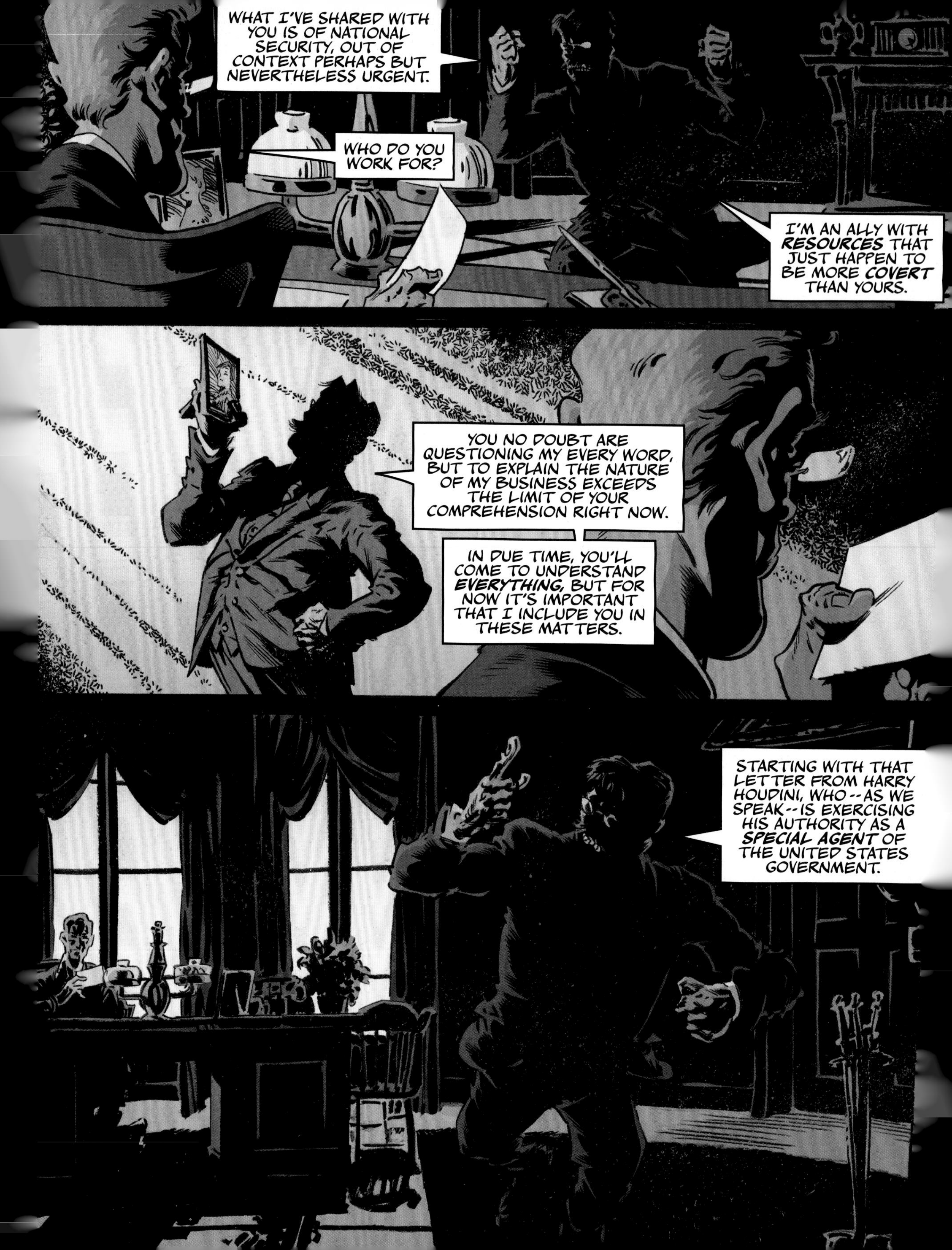
WHAT I'VE SHARED WITH YOU IS OF NATIONAL SECURITY, OUT OF CONTEXT PERHAPS BUT NEVERTHELESS URGENT.
WHO DO YOU WORK FOR?
I'M AN ALLY WITH RESOURCES THAT JUST HAPPEN TO BE MORE COVERT THAN YOURS.
YOU NO DOUBT ARE QUESTIONING MY EVERY WORD, BUT TO EXPLAIN THE NATURE OF MY BUSINESS EXCEEDS THE LIMIT OF YOUR COMPREHENSION RIGHT NOW.
IN DUE TIME, YOU'LL COME TO UNDERSTAND EVERYTHING, BUT FOR NOW IT'S IMPORTANT THAT I INCLUDE YOU IN THESE MATTERS.
STARTING WITH THAT LETTER FROM HARRY HOUDINI, WHO--AS WE SPEAK--IS EXERCISING HIS AUTHORITY AS A SPECIAL AGENT OF THE UNITED STATES GOVERNMENT.

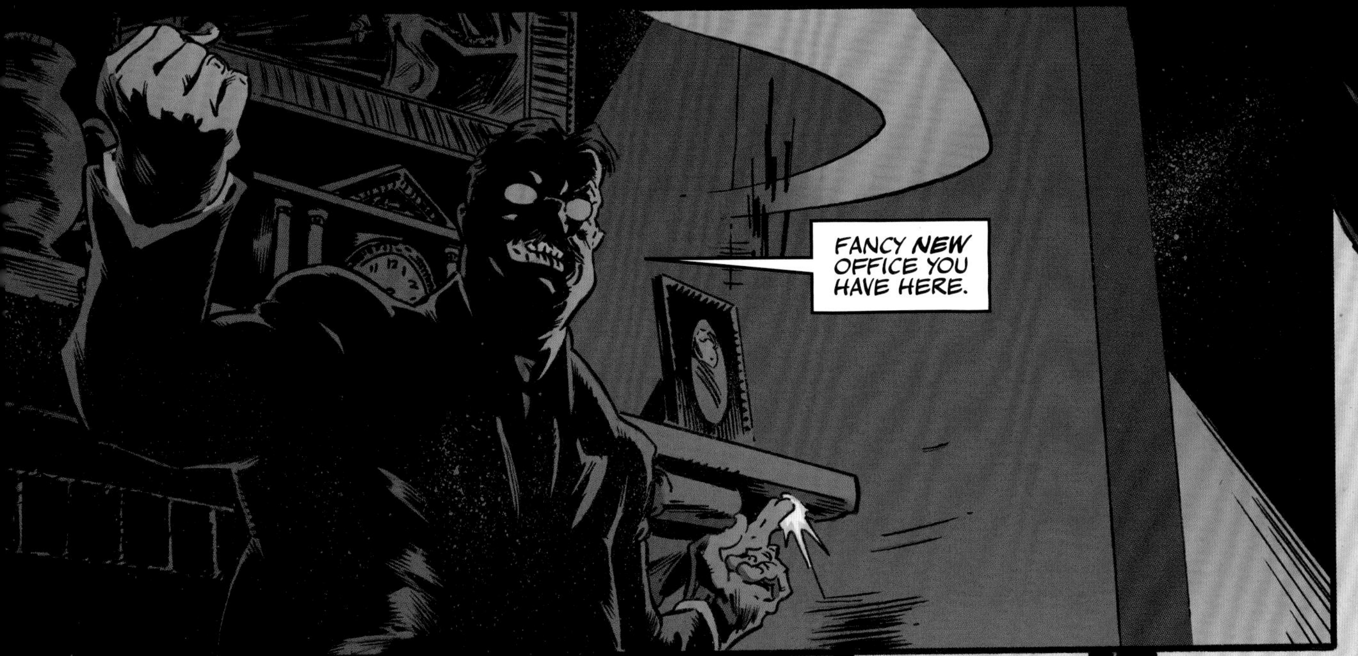
FANCY NEW OFFICE YOU HAVE HERE.

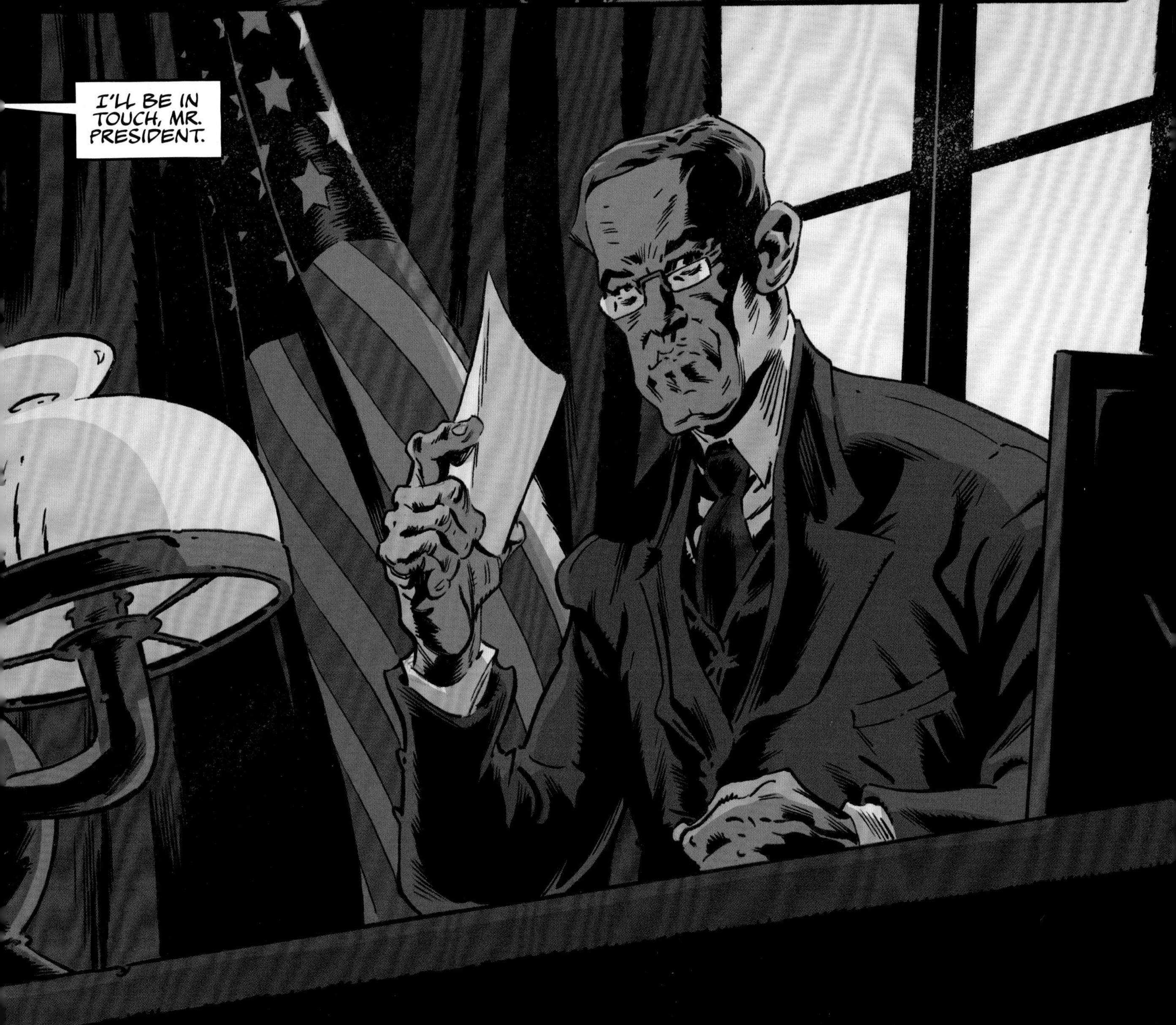
I'LL BE IN TOUCH, MR. PRESIDENT.

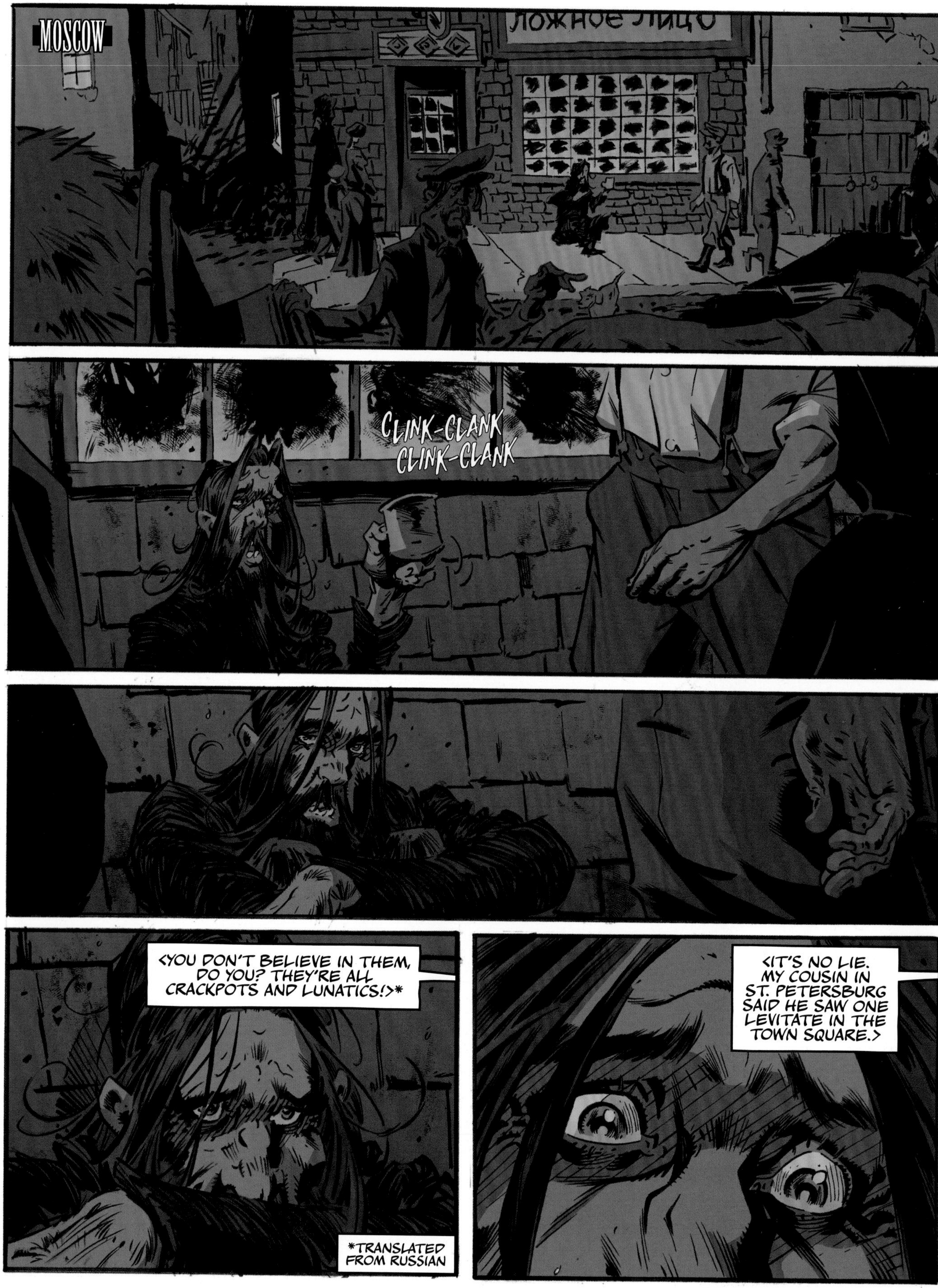
MOSCOW
ложное лицо
CLINK-CLANK
CLINK-CLANK
<YOU DON'T BELIEVE IN THEM, DO YOU? THEY'RE ALL CRACKPOTS AND LUNATICS!>*
*TRANSLATED FROM RUSSIAN
<IT'S NO LIE. MY COUSIN IN ST. PETERSBURG SAID HE SAW ONE LEVITATE IN THE TOWN SQUARE.>

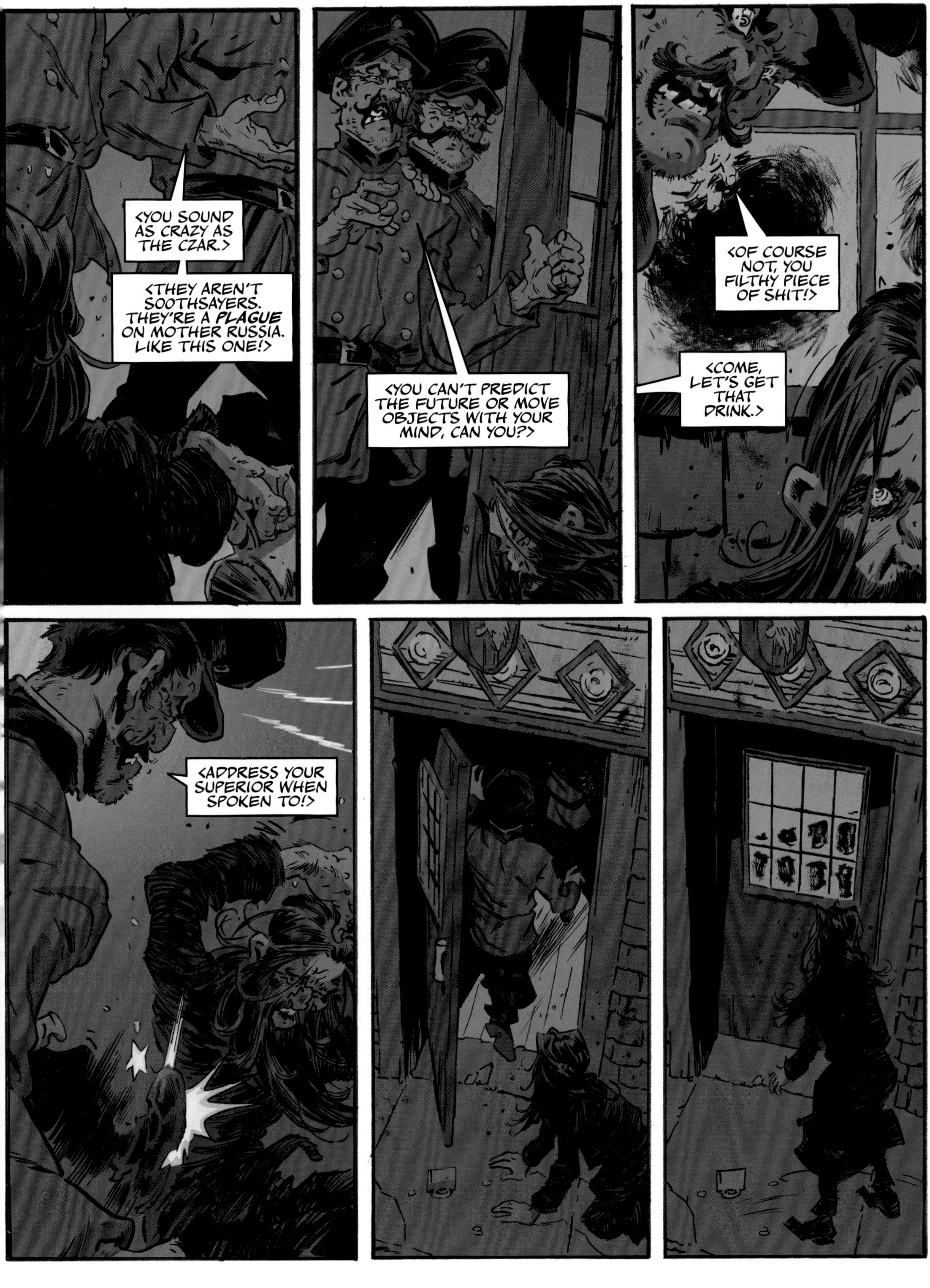
<YOU SOUND AS CRAZY AS THE CZAR.>
<THEY AREN'T SOOTHSAYERS. THEY'RE A *PLAGUE* ON MOTHER RUSSIA. LIKE THIS ONE!>
<YOU CAN'T PREDICT THE FUTURE OR MOVE OBJECTS WITH YOUR MIND, CAN YOU?>
<OF COURSE NOT, YOU FILTHY PIECE OF SHIT!>
<COME, LET'S GET THAT DRINK.>
<ADDRESS YOUR SUPERIOR WHEN SPOKEN TO!>

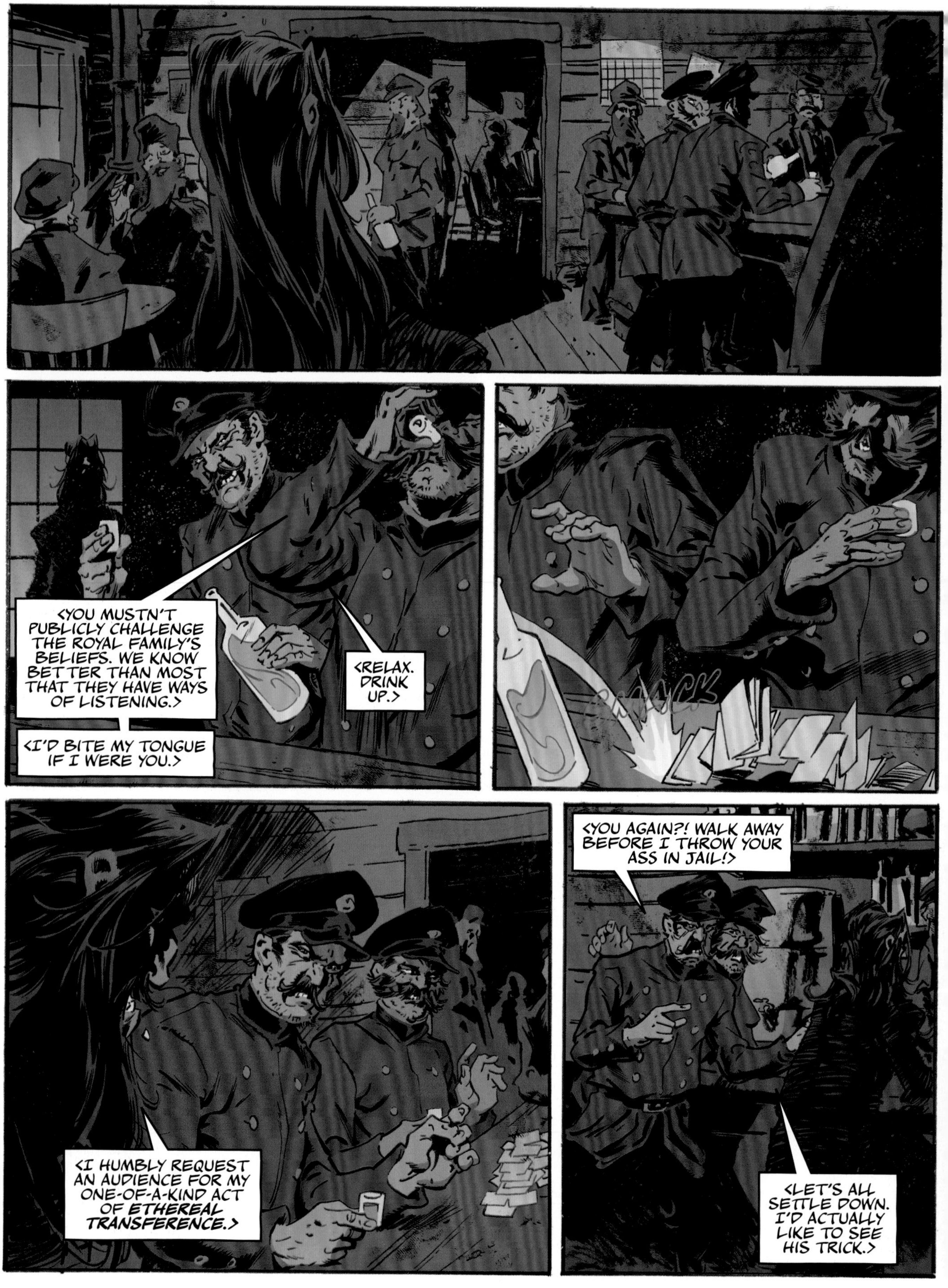
<YOU MUSTN'T PUBLICLY CHALLENGE THE ROYAL FAMILY'S BELIEFS. WE KNOW BETTER THAN MOST THAT THEY HAVE WAYS OF LISTENING.>
<I'D BITE MY TONGUE IF I WERE YOU.>
<RELAX. DRINK UP.>
<I HUMBLY REQUEST AN AUDIENCE FOR MY ONE-OF-A-KIND ACT OF ETHEREAL TRANSFERENCE.>
<YOU AGAIN?! WALK AWAY BEFORE I THROW YOUR ASS IN JAIL!>
<LET'S ALL SETTLE DOWN. I'D ACTUALLY LIKE TO SEE HIS TRICK.>

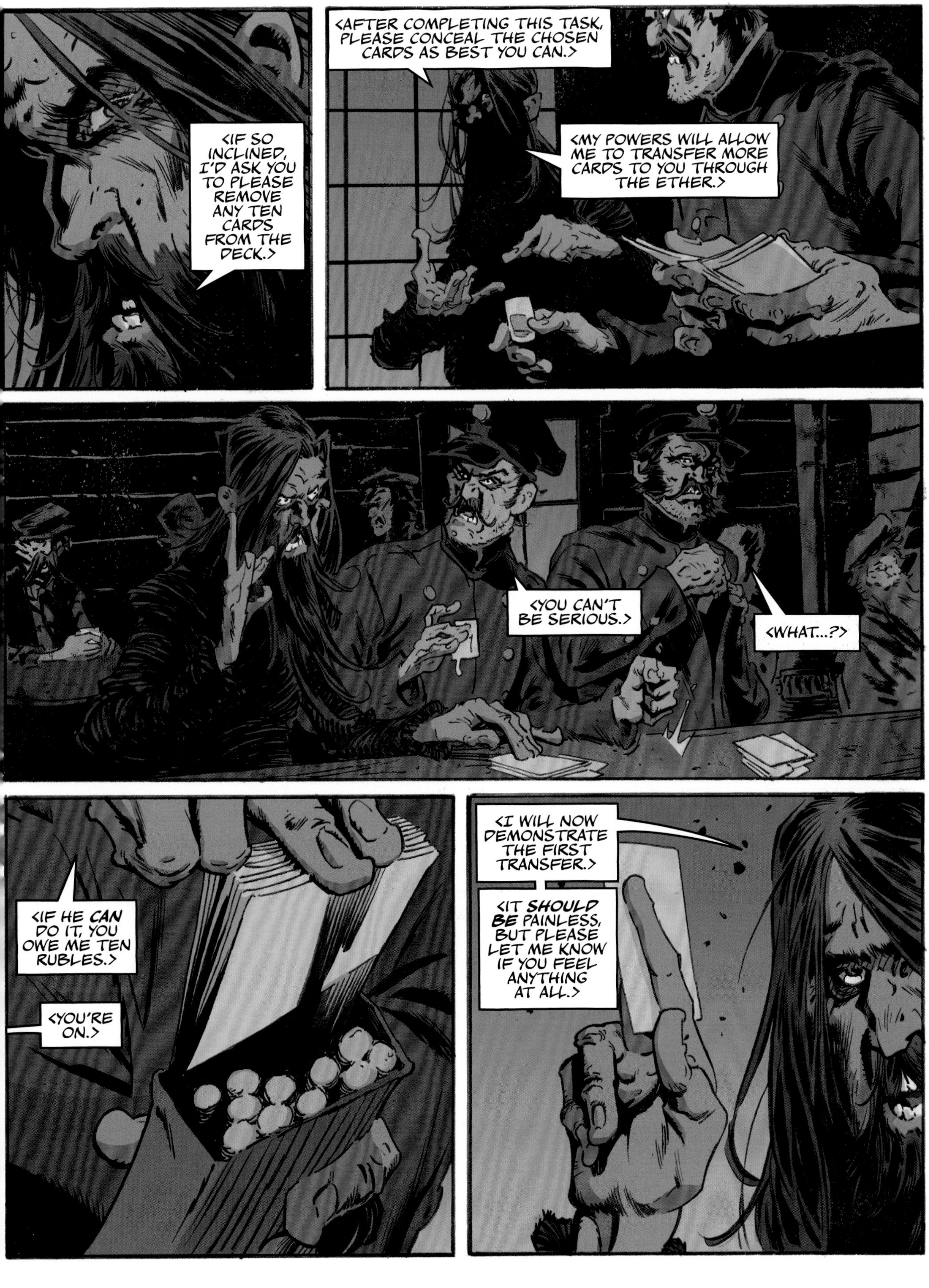
<IF SO INCLINED, I'D ASK YOU TO PLEASE REMOVE ANY TEN CARDS FROM THE DECK.>
<AFTER COMPLETING THIS TASK, PLEASE CONCEAL THE CHOSEN CARDS AS BEST YOU CAN.>
<MY POWERS WILL ALLOW ME TO TRANSFER MORE CARDS TO YOU THROUGH THE ETHER.>
<YOU CAN'T BE SERIOUS.>
<WHAT...?>
<IF HE *CAN* DO IT, YOU OWE ME TEN RUBLES.>
<YOU'RE ON.>
<I WILL NOW DEMONSTRATE THE FIRST TRANSFER.>
<IT ***SHOULD BE*** PAINLESS, BUT PLEASE LET ME KNOW IF YOU FEEL ANYTHING AT ALL.>

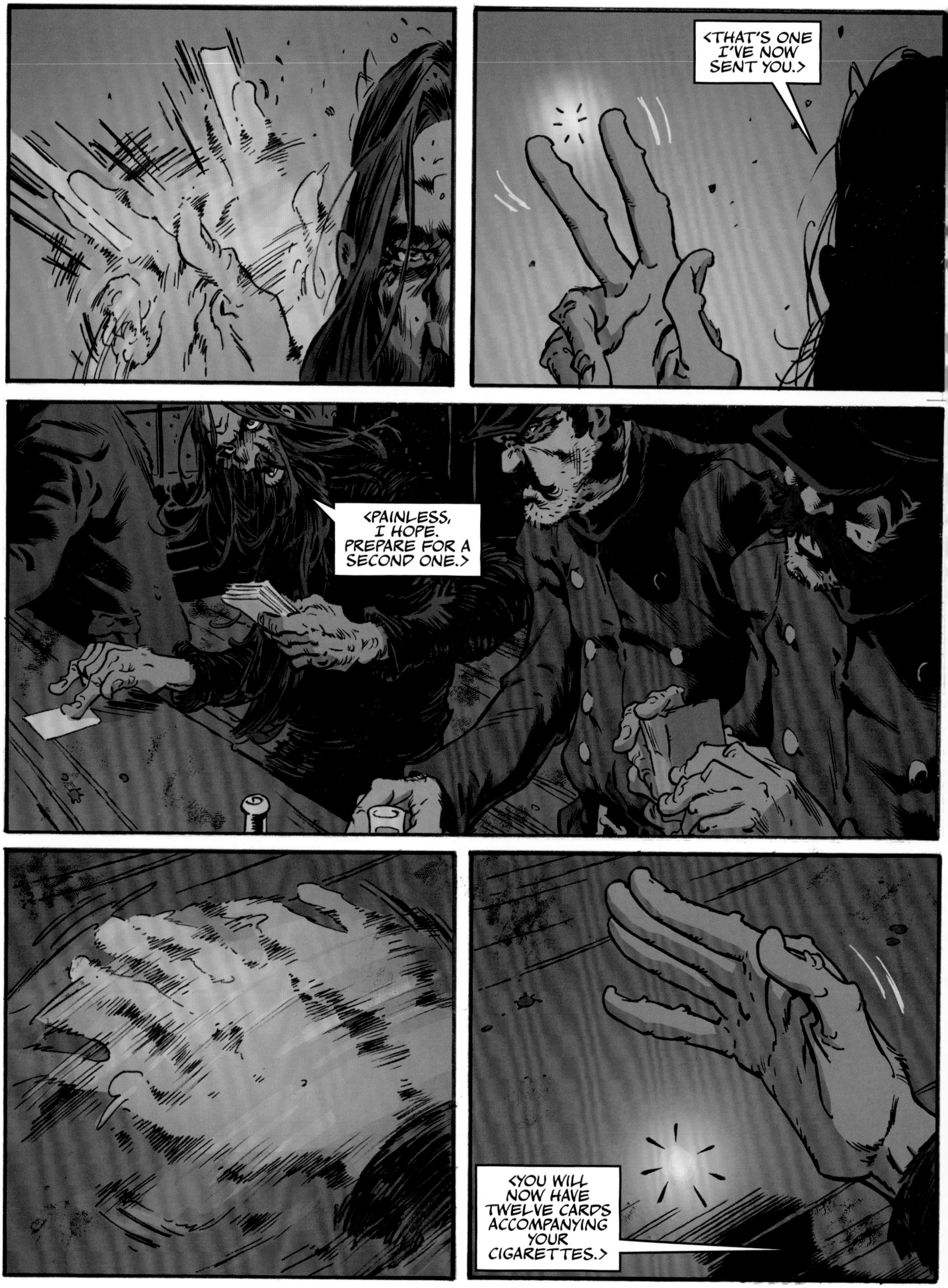
<THAT'S ONE I'VE NOW SENT YOU.>
<PAINLESS, I HOPE. PREPARE FOR A SECOND ONE.>
<YOU WILL NOW HAVE TWELVE CARDS ACCOMPANYING YOUR CIGARETTES.>

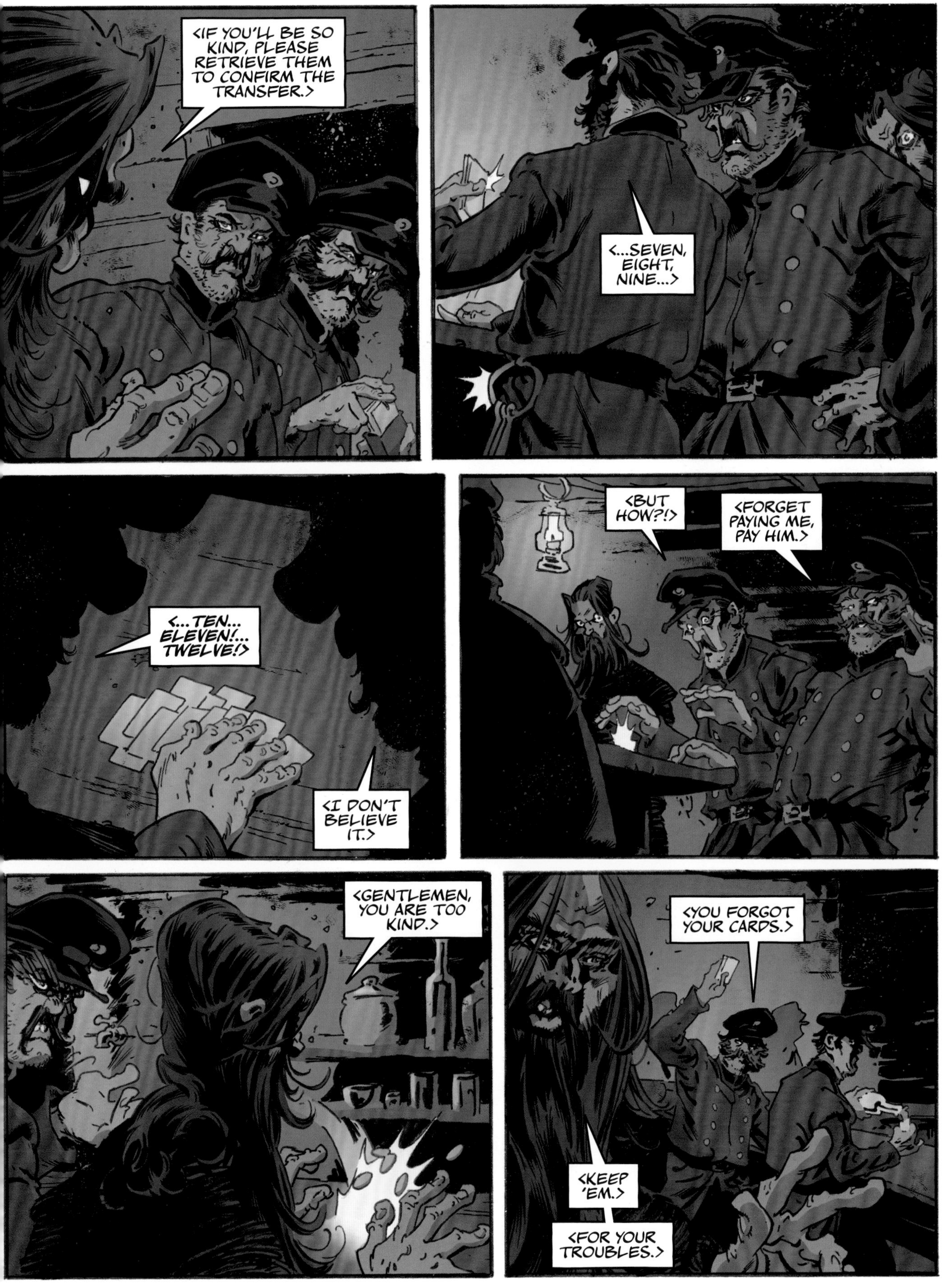
<IF YOU'LL BE SO KIND, PLEASE RETRIEVE THEM TO CONFIRM THE TRANSFER.>
<...SEVEN, EIGHT, NINE...>
<...TEN... ELEVEN!... TWELVE!>
<I DON'T BELIEVE IT.>
<BUT HOW?!>
<FORGET PAYING ME, PAY HIM.>
<GENTLEMEN, YOU ARE TOO KIND.>
<YOU FORGOT YOUR CARDS.>
<KEEP 'EM.>
<FOR YOUR TROUBLES.>

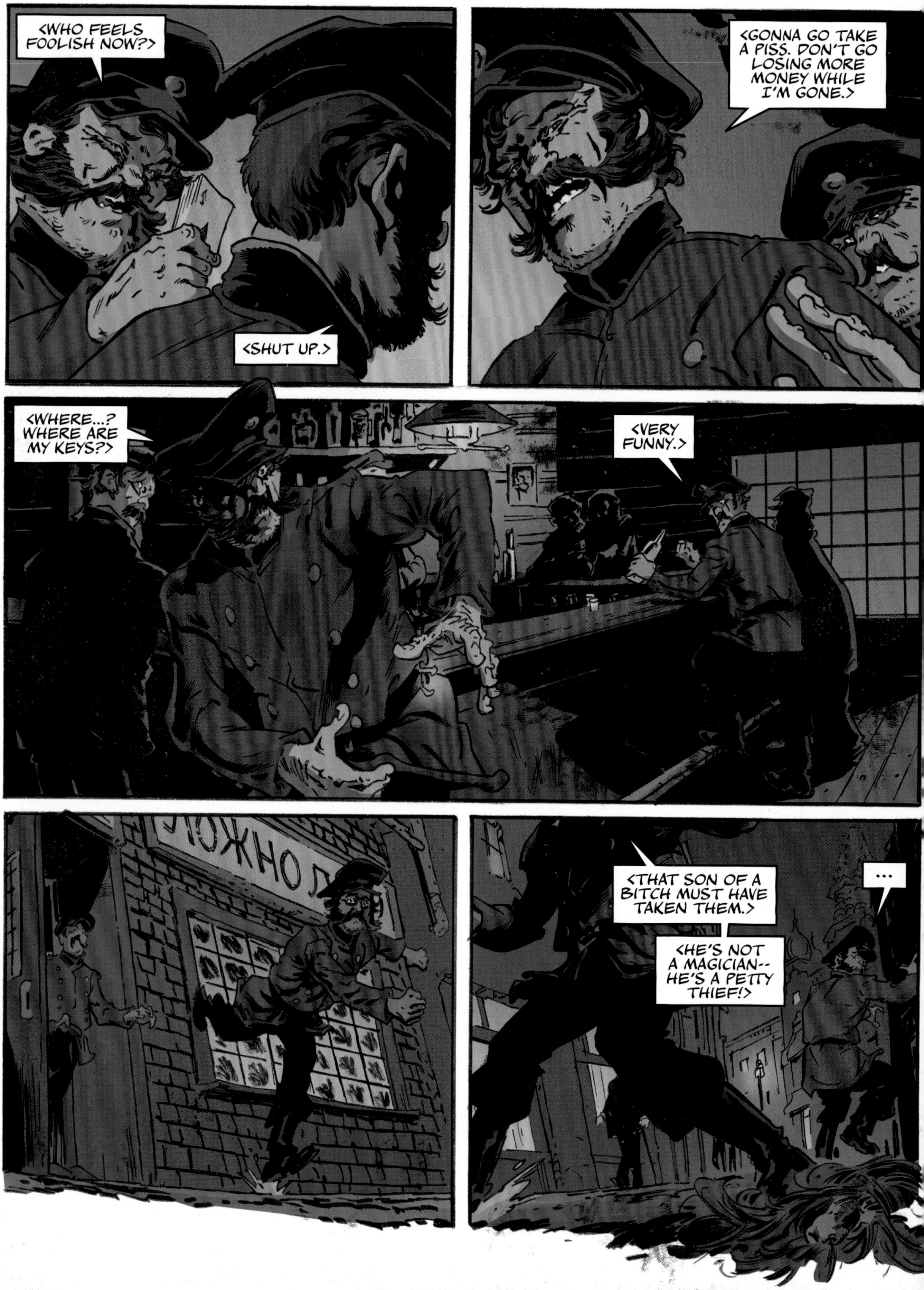
<WHO FEELS FOOLISH NOW?>
<SHUT UP.>
<GONNA GO TAKE A PISS. DON'T GO LOSING MORE MONEY WHILE I'M GONE.>
<WHERE...? WHERE ARE MY KEYS?>
<VERY FUNNY.>
<THAT SON OF A BITCH MUST HAVE TAKEN THEM.>
<HE'S NOT A MAGICIAN-- HE'S A PETTY THIEF!>
...

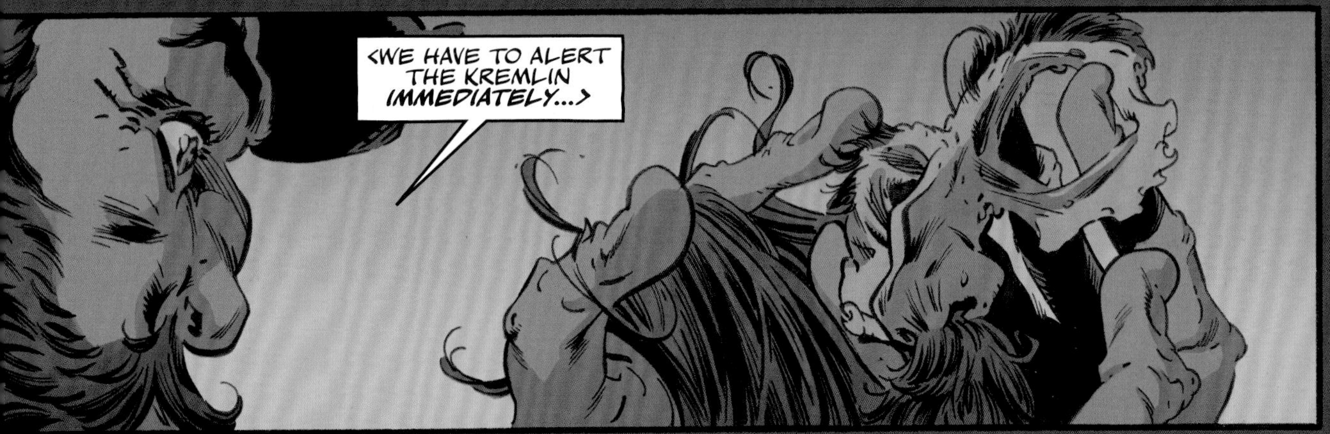
<WE HAVE TO ALERT THE KREMLIN IMMEDIATELY...>

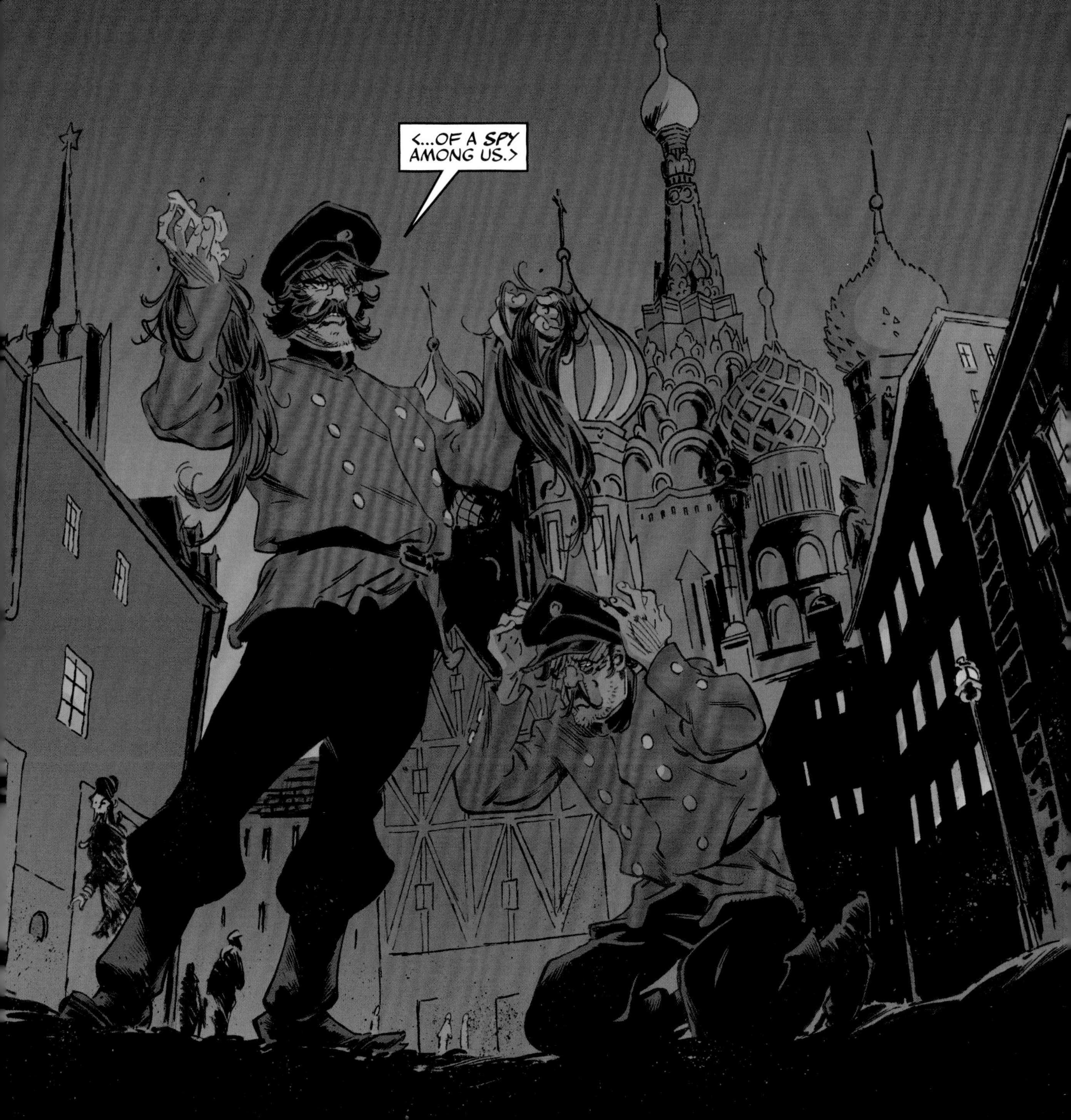
<...OF A SPY AMONG US.>

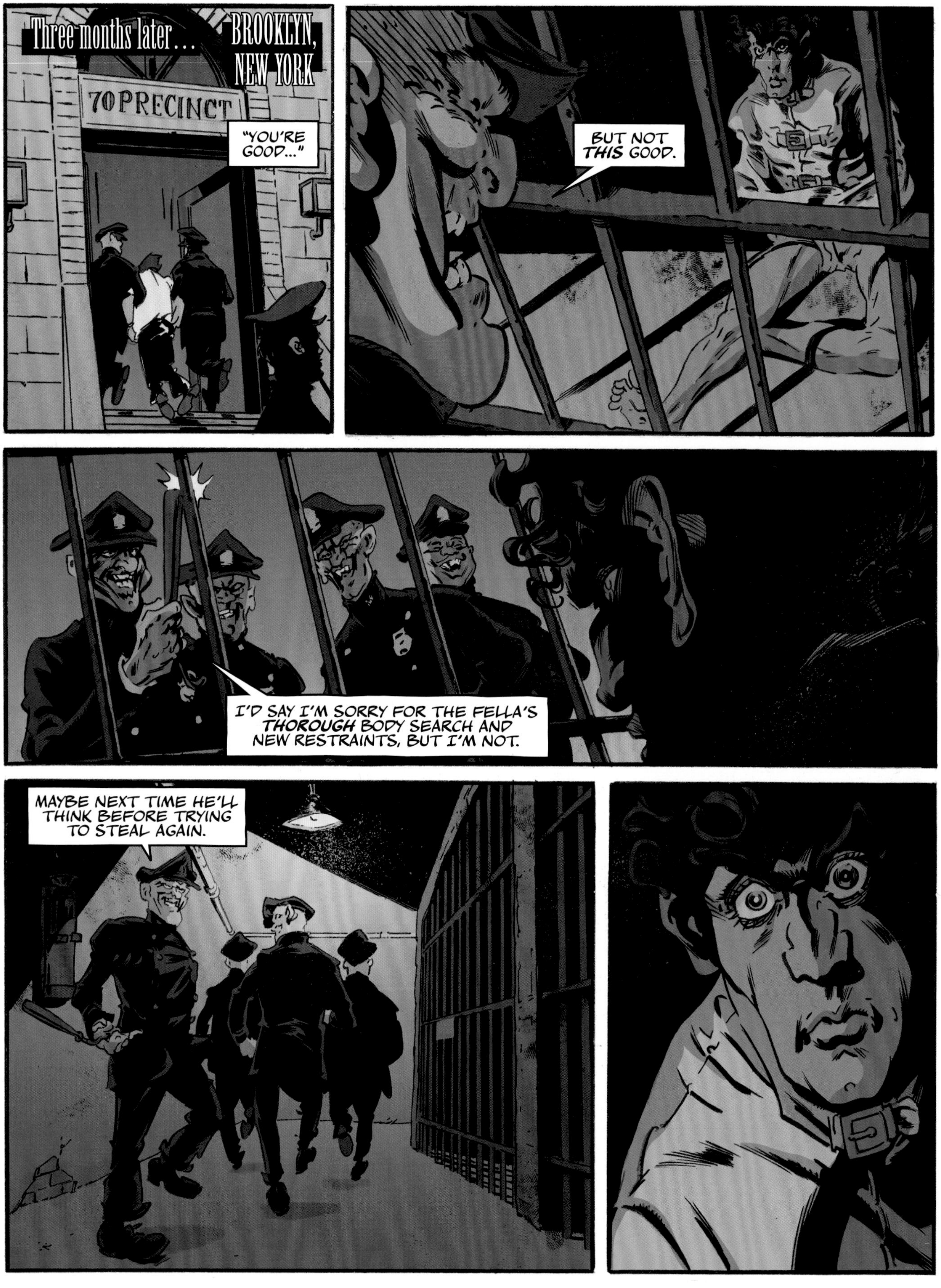
Three months later...
BROOKLYN, NEW YORK
70 PRECINCT
"YOU'RE GOOD..."
BUT NOT THIS GOOD.
I'D SAY I'M SORRY FOR THE FELLA'S THOROUGH BODY SEARCH AND NEW RESTRAINTS, BUT I'M NOT.
MAYBE NEXT TIME HE'LL THINK BEFORE TRYING TO STEAL AGAIN.

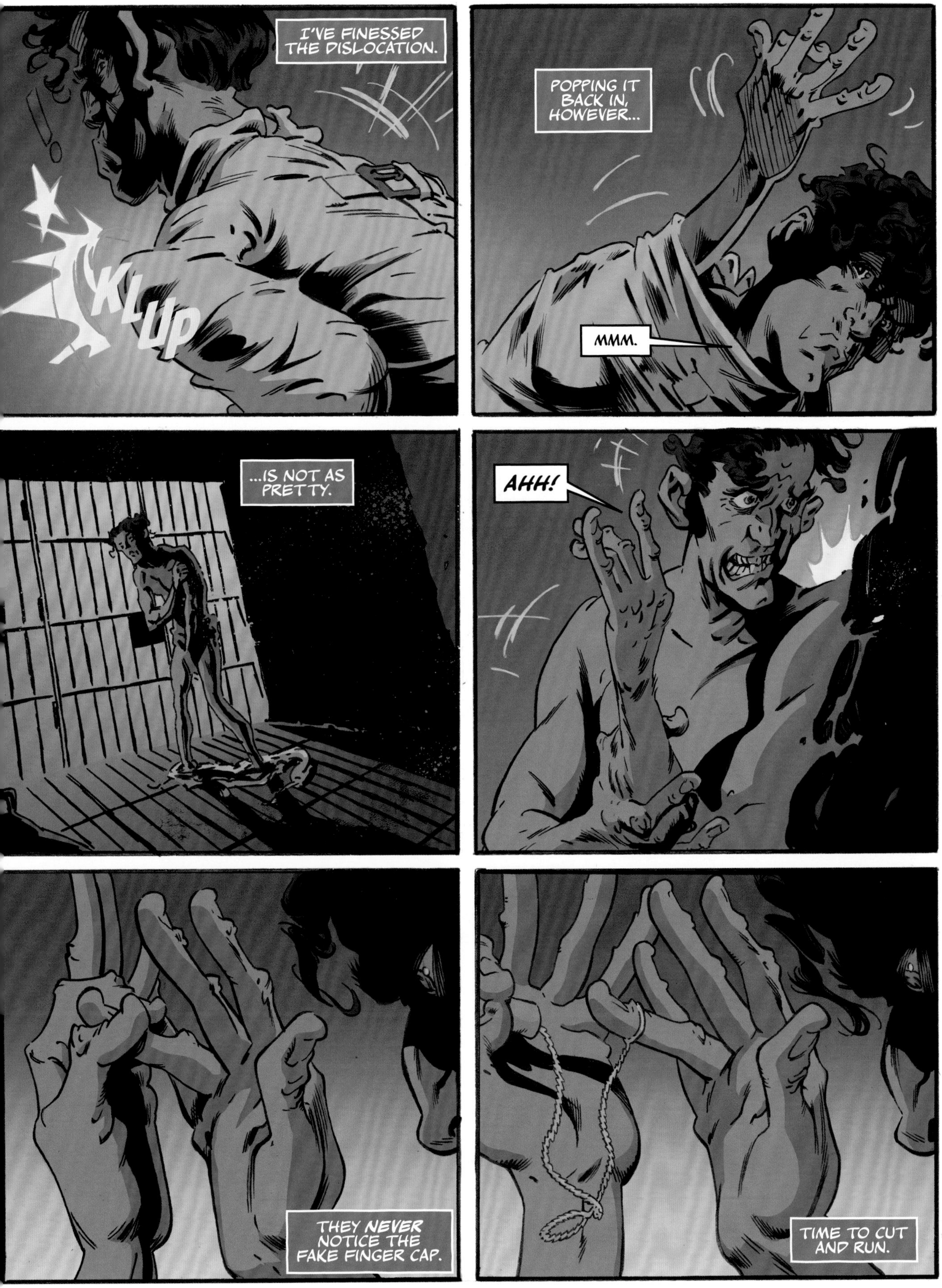
I'VE FINESSED THE DISLOCATION.
KLUP
POPPING IT BACK IN, HOWEVER...
MMM.
...IS NOT AS PRETTY.
AHH!
THEY *NEVER* NOTICE THE FAKE FINGER CAP.
TIME TO CUT AND RUN.

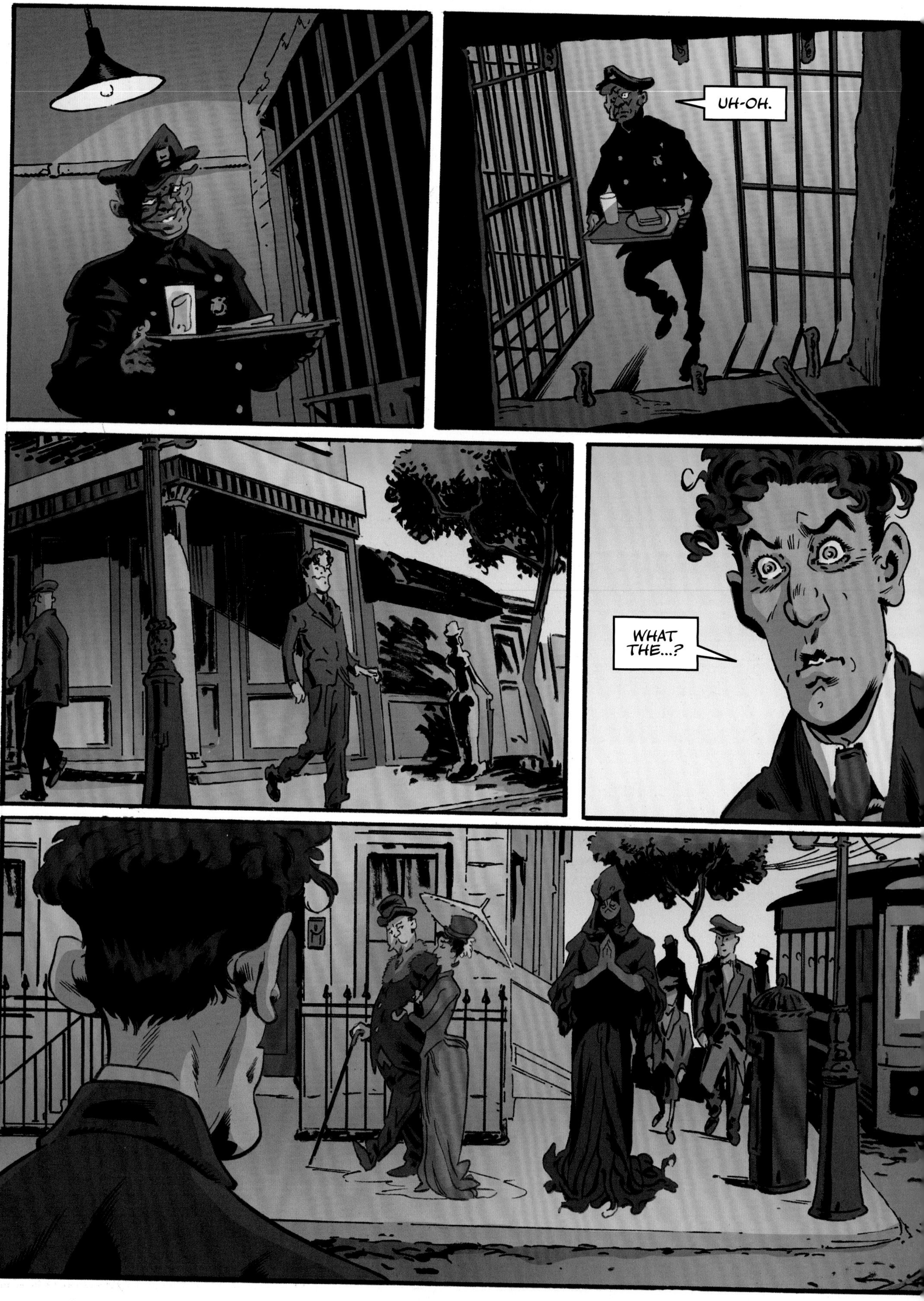
UH-OH.
WHAT THE...?

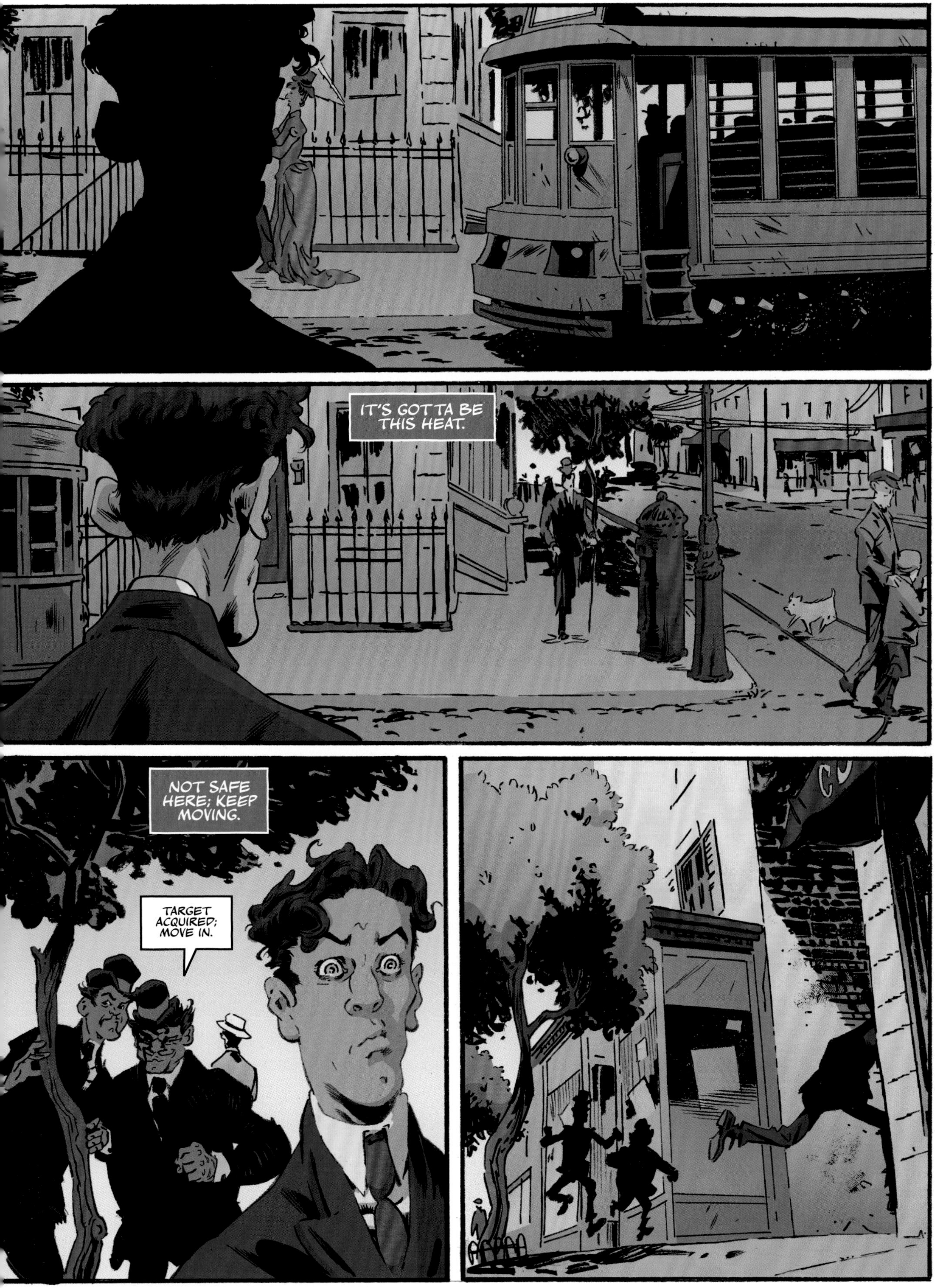
IT'S GOTTA BE THIS HEAT.
NOT SAFE HERE; KEEP MOVING.
TARGET ACQUIRED; MOVE IN.

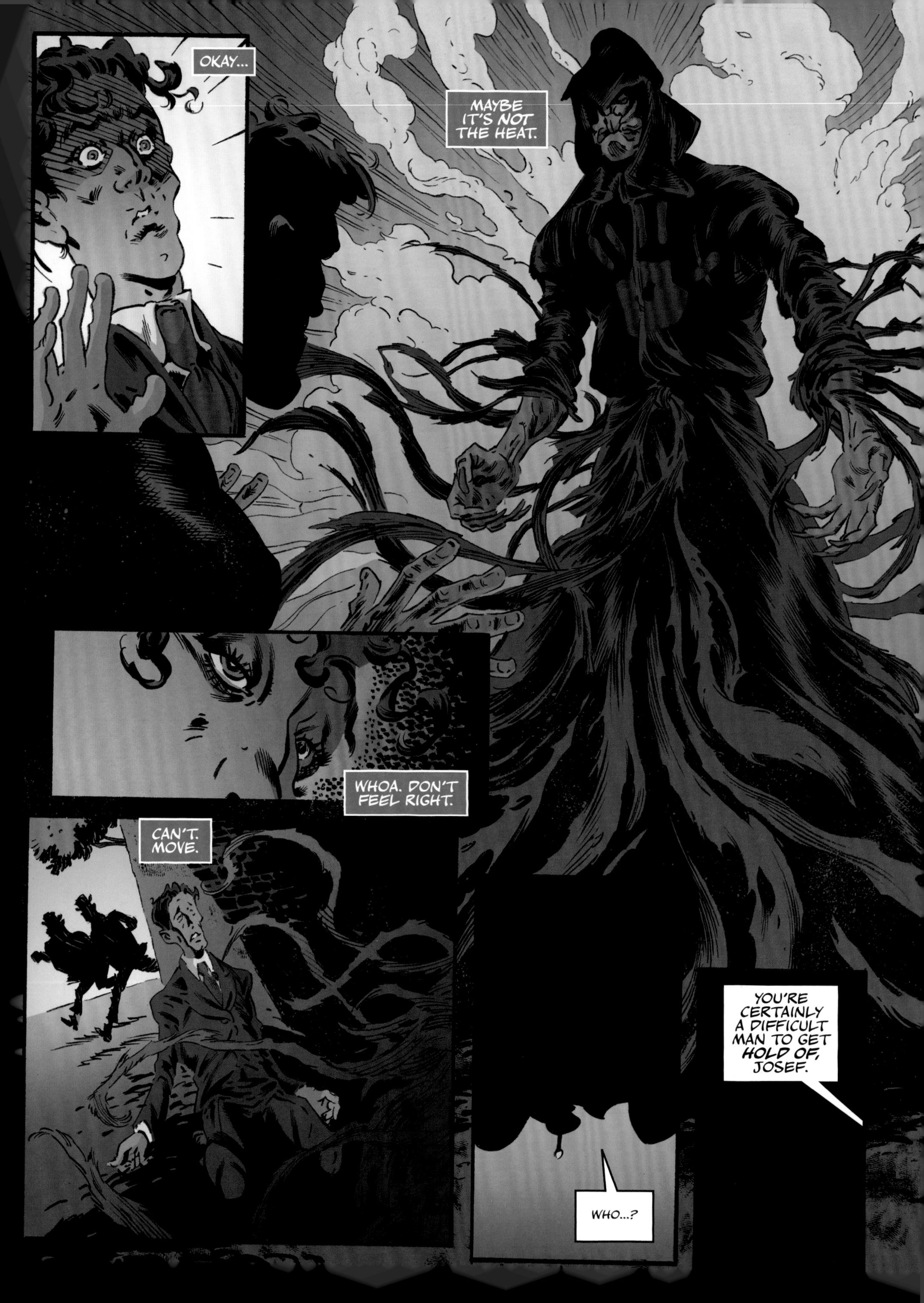
OKAY...
MAYBE IT'S NOT THE HEAT.
WHOA. DON'T FEEL RIGHT.
CAN'T. MOVE.
YOU'RE CERTAINLY A DIFFICULT MAN TO GET HOLD OF, JOSEF.
WHO...?

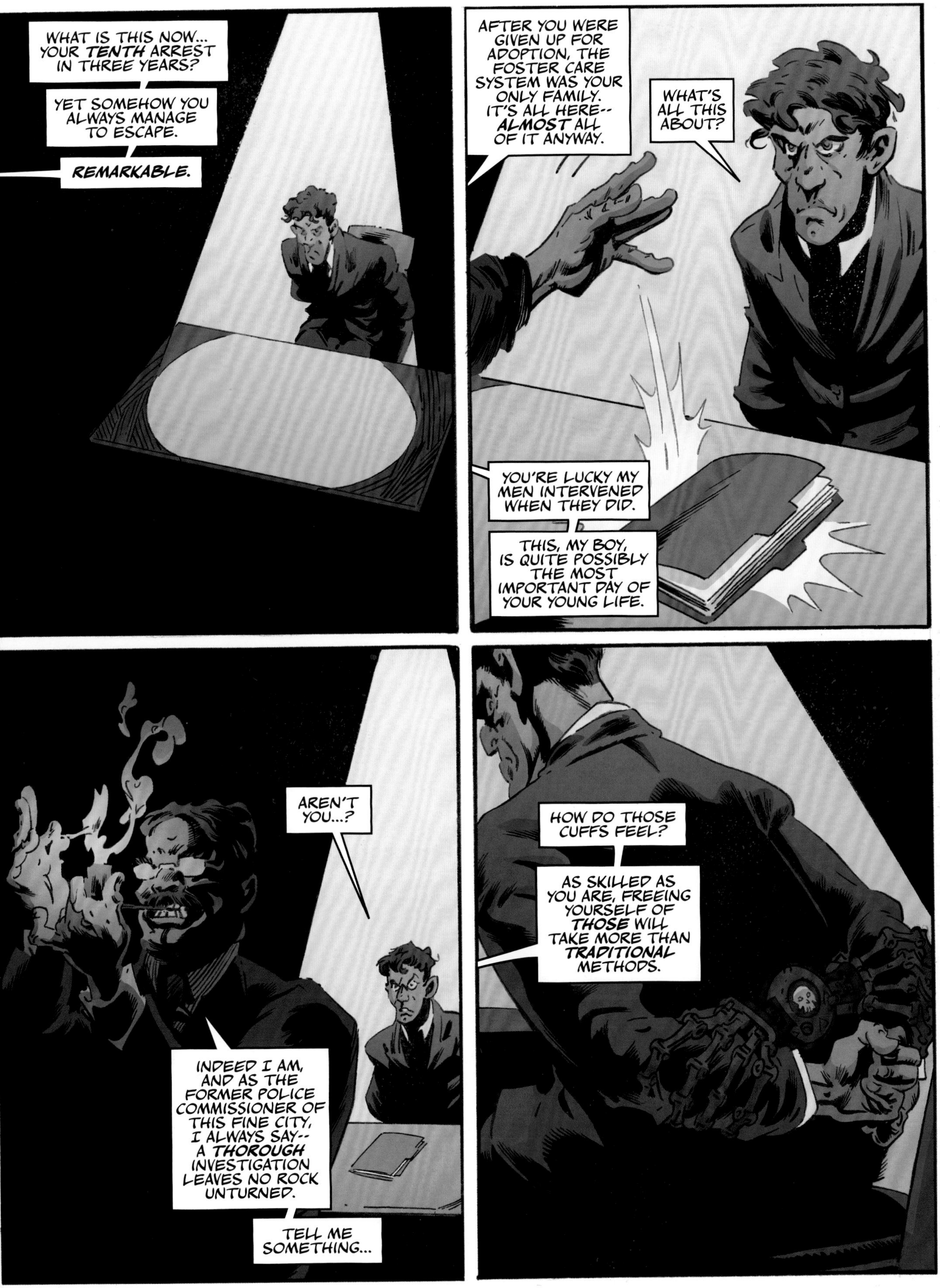
WHAT IS THIS NOW... YOUR TENTH ARREST IN THREE YEARS?
YET SOMEHOW YOU ALWAYS MANAGE TO ESCAPE.
REMARKABLE.
AFTER YOU WERE GIVEN UP FOR ADOPTION, THE FOSTER CARE SYSTEM WAS YOUR ONLY FAMILY. IT'S ALL HERE-- ALMOST ALL OF IT ANYWAY.
WHAT'S ALL THIS ABOUT?
YOU'RE LUCKY MY MEN INTERVENED WHEN THEY DID.
THIS, MY BOY, IS QUITE POSSIBLY THE MOST IMPORTANT DAY OF YOUR YOUNG LIFE.
AREN'T YOU...?
INDEED I AM, AND AS THE FORMER POLICE COMMISSIONER OF THIS FINE CITY, I ALWAYS SAY-- A THOROUGH INVESTIGATION LEAVES NO ROCK UNTURNED.
TELL ME SOMETHING...
HOW DO THOSE CUFFS FEEL?
AS SKILLED AS YOU ARE, FREEING YOURSELF OF THOSE WILL TAKE MORE THAN TRADITIONAL METHODS.

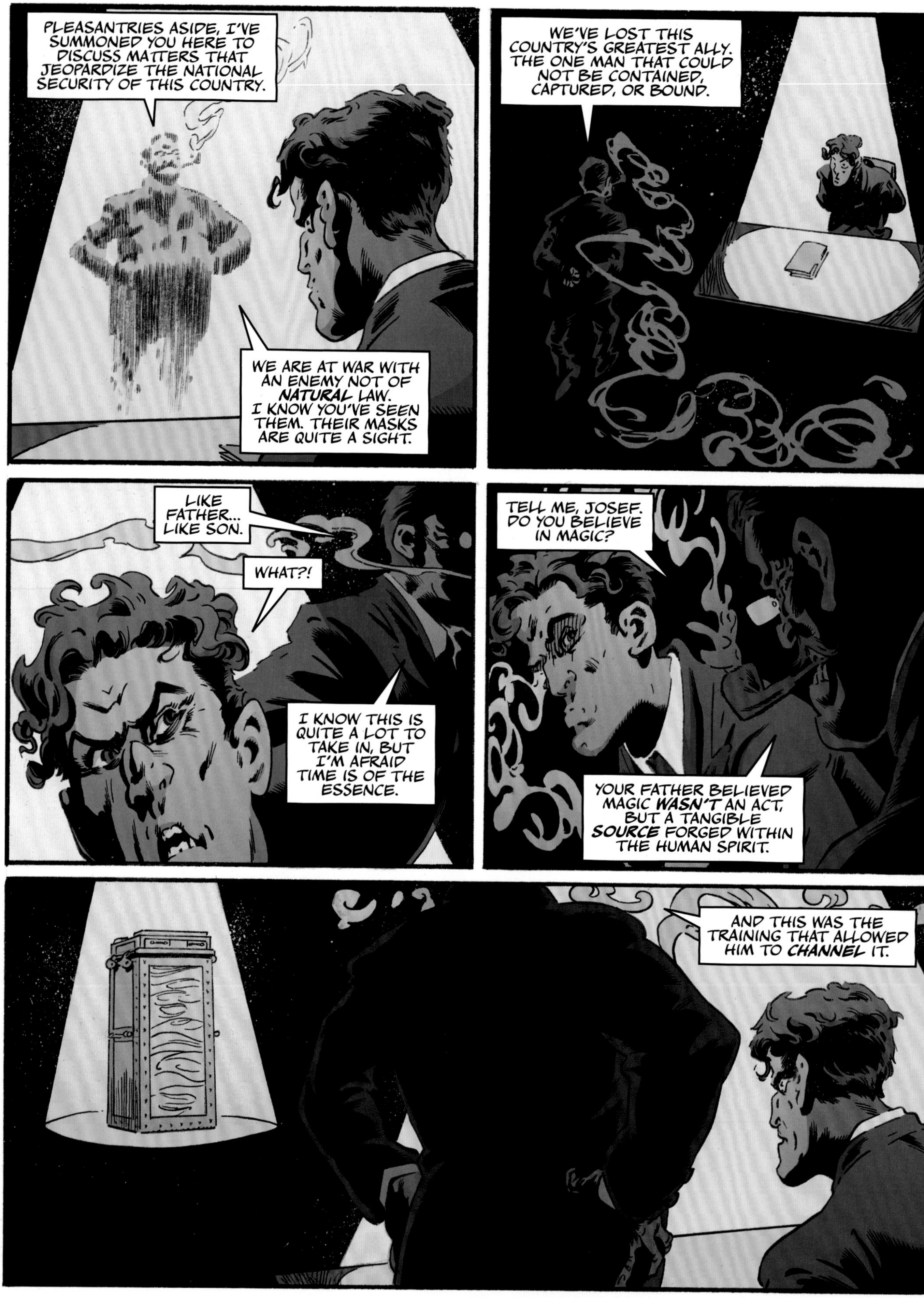

PLEASANTRIES ASIDE, I'VE SUMMONED YOU HERE TO DISCUSS MATTERS THAT JEOPARDIZE THE NATIONAL SECURITY OF THIS COUNTRY.
WE ARE AT WAR WITH AN ENEMY NOT OF NATURAL LAW. I KNOW YOU'VE SEEN THEM. THEIR MASKS ARE QUITE A SIGHT.
WE'VE LOST THIS COUNTRY'S GREATEST ALLY. THE ONE MAN THAT COULD NOT BE CONTAINED, CAPTURED, OR BOUND.
LIKE FATHER... LIKE SON.
WHAT?!
I KNOW THIS IS QUITE A LOT TO TAKE IN, BUT I'M AFRAID TIME IS OF THE ESSENCE.
TELL ME, JOSEF. DO YOU BELIEVE IN MAGIC?
YOUR FATHER BELIEVED MAGIC WASN'T AN ACT, BUT A TANGIBLE SOURCE FORGED WITHIN THE HUMAN SPIRIT.
AND THIS WAS THE TRAINING THAT ALLOWED HIM TO CHANNEL IT.

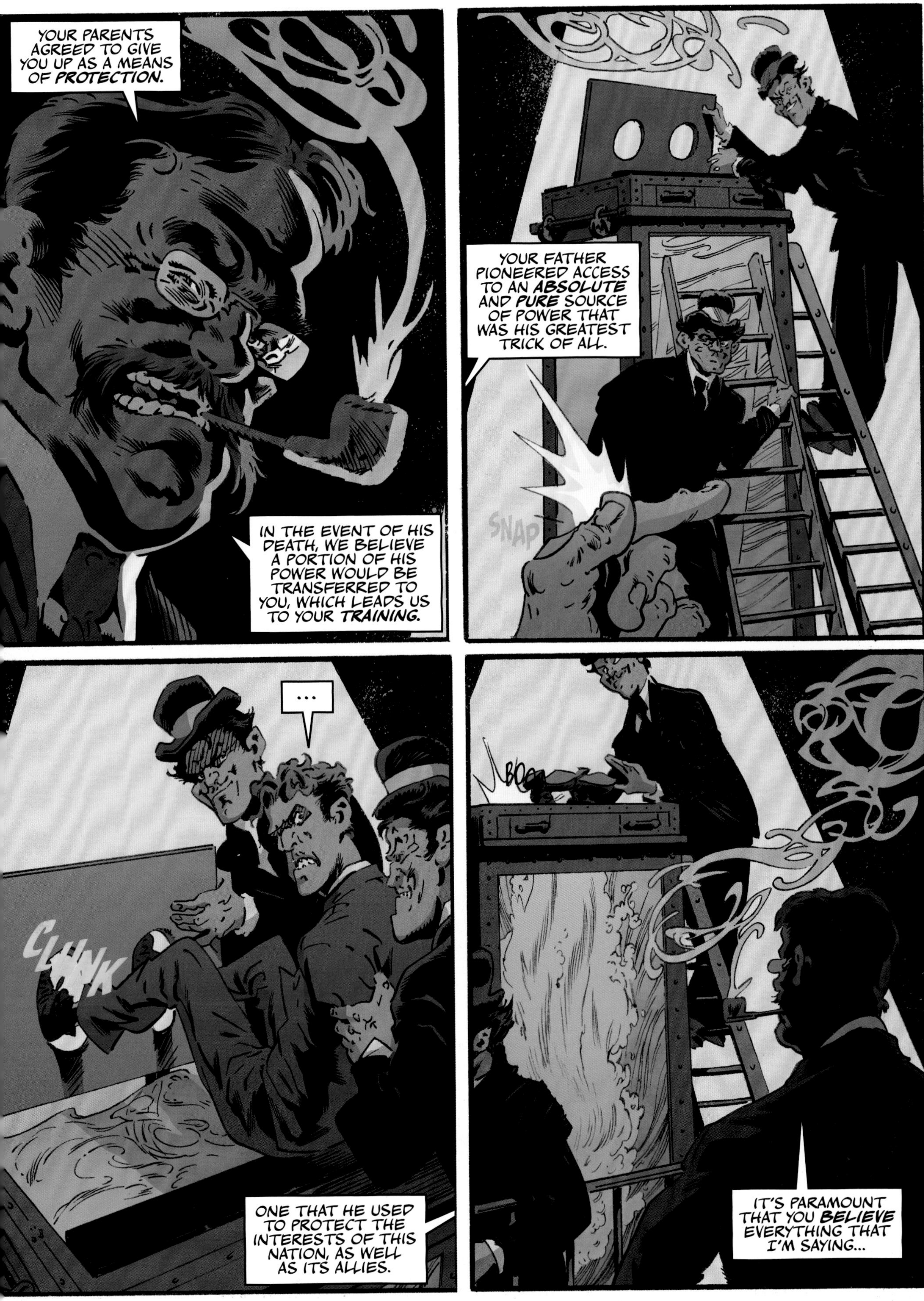
YOUR PARENTS AGREED TO GIVE YOU UP AS A MEANS OF PROTECTION.
IN THE EVENT OF HIS DEATH, WE BELIEVE A PORTION OF HIS POWER WOULD BE TRANSFERRED TO YOU, WHICH LEADS US TO YOUR TRAINING.
YOUR FATHER PIONEERED ACCESS TO AN ABSOLUTE AND PURE SOURCE OF POWER THAT WAS HIS GREATEST TRICK OF ALL.
SNAP
...
CLUNK
ONE THAT HE USED TO PROTECT THE INTERESTS OF THIS NATION, AS WELL AS ITS ALLIES.
IT'S PARAMOUNT THAT YOU BELIEVE EVERYTHING THAT I'M SAYING...

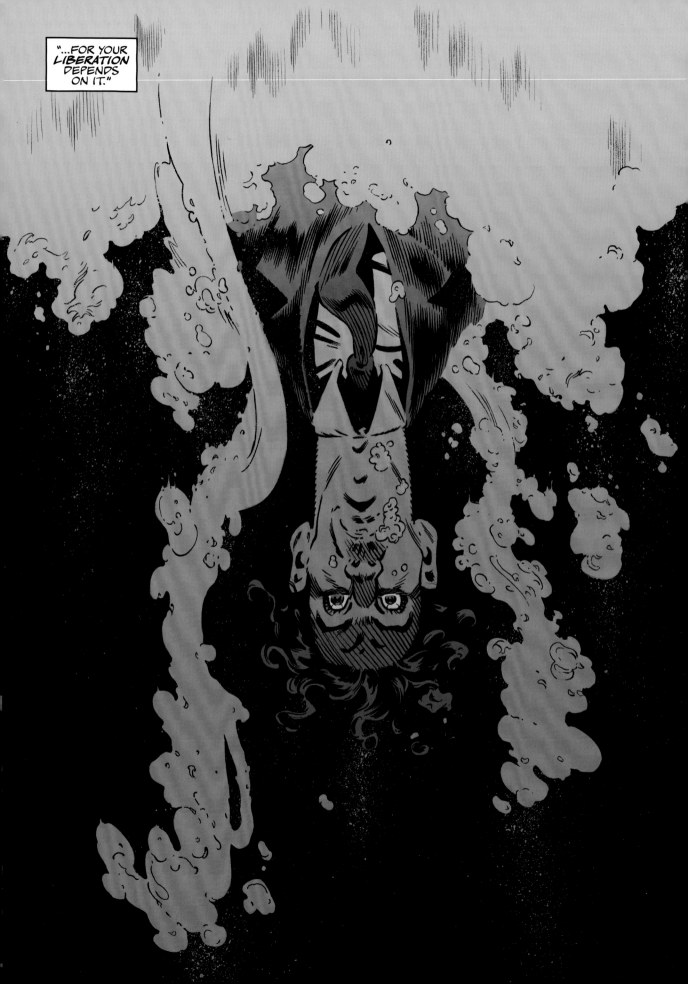

"...FOR YOUR LIBERATION DEPENDS ON IT."

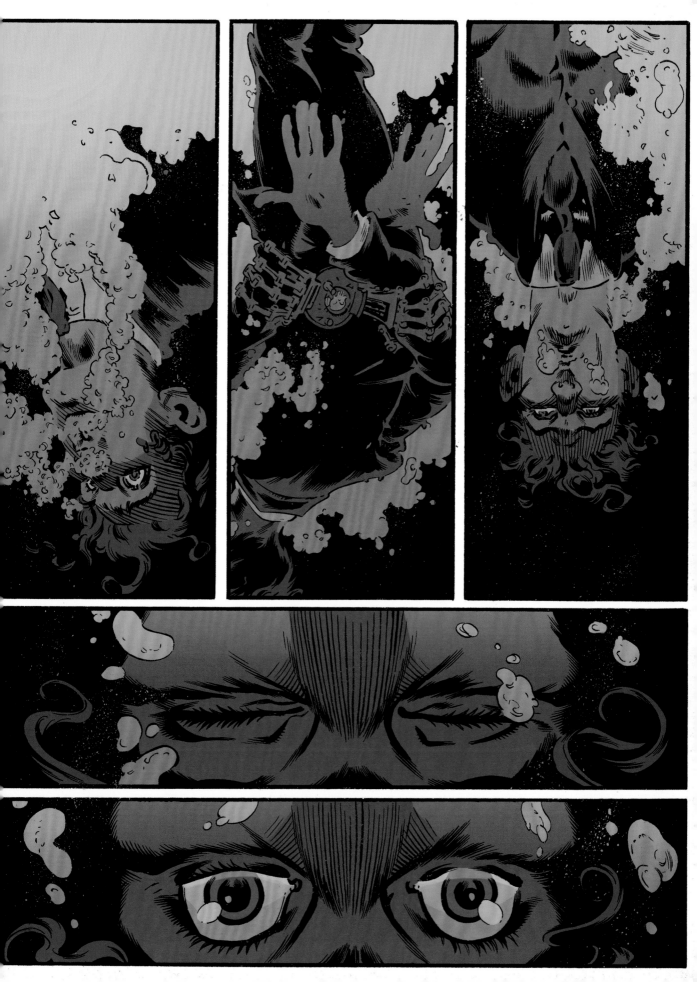

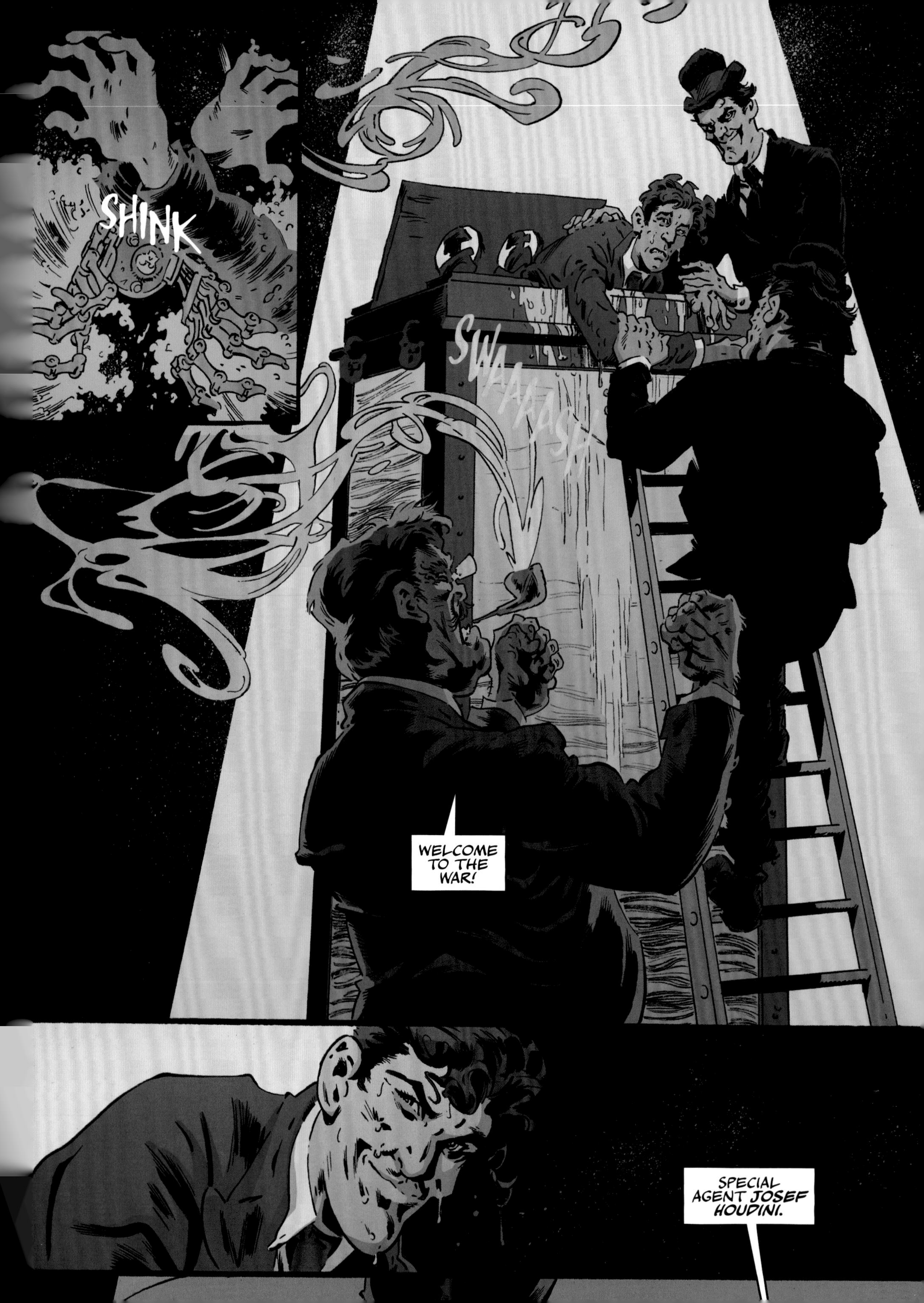
SHINK
SWAAAASH
WELCOME TO THE WAR!
SPECIAL AGENT JOSEF HOUDINI.

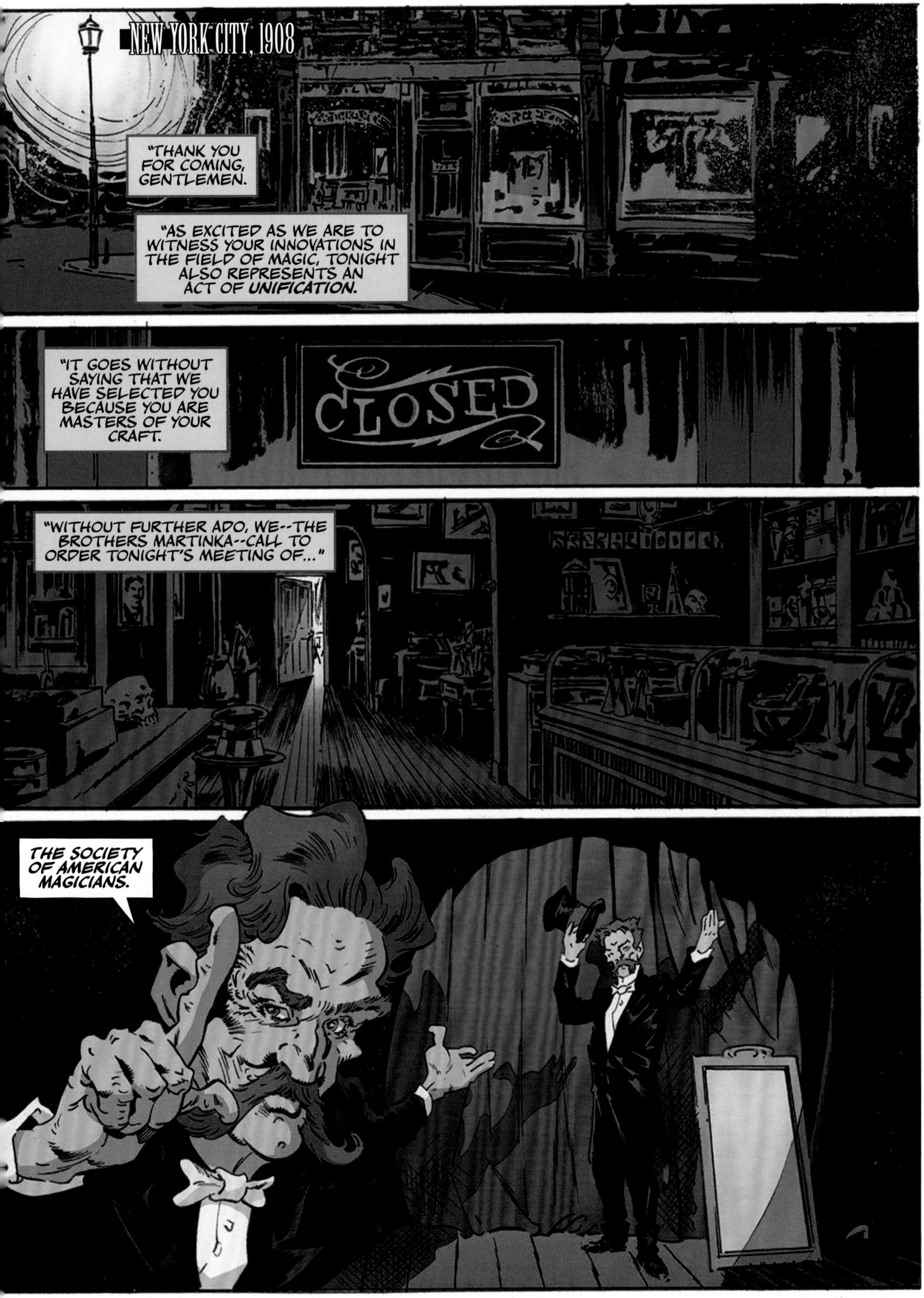
NEW YORK CITY, 1908
"THANK YOU FOR COMING, GENTLEMEN.
"AS EXCITED AS WE ARE TO WITNESS YOUR INNOVATIONS IN THE FIELD OF MAGIC, TONIGHT ALSO REPRESENTS AN ACT OF *UNIFICATION*.
"IT GOES WITHOUT SAYING THAT WE HAVE SELECTED YOU BECAUSE YOU ARE MASTERS OF YOUR CRAFT.
CLOSED
"WITHOUT FURTHER ADO, WE--THE BROTHERS MARTINKA--CALL TO ORDER TONIGHT'S MEETING OF..."
THE SOCIETY OF AMERICAN MAGICIANS.

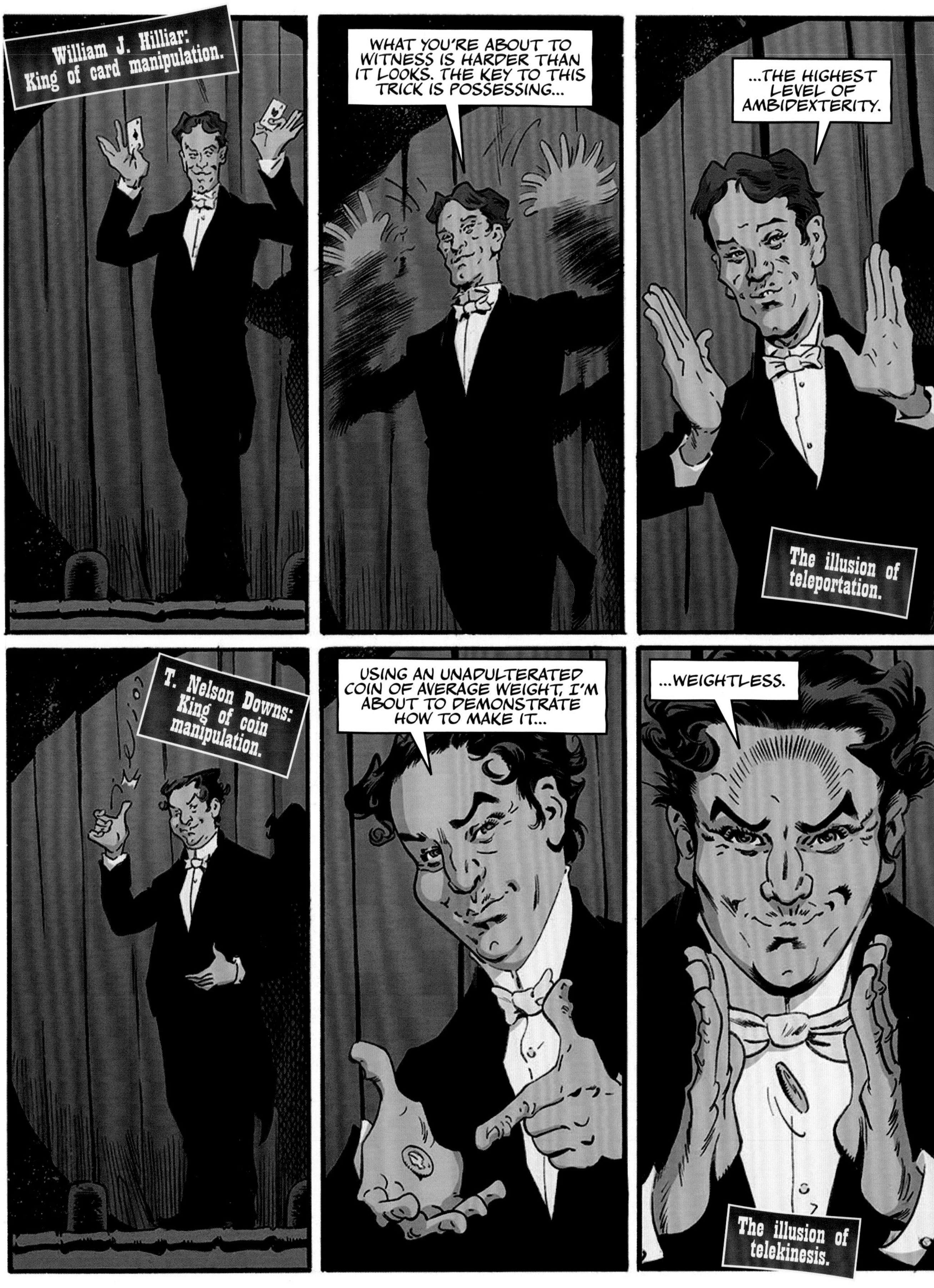
William J. Hilliar: King of card manipulation.
WHAT YOU'RE ABOUT TO WITNESS IS HARDER THAN IT LOOKS. THE KEY TO THIS TRICK IS POSSESSING...
...THE HIGHEST LEVEL OF AMBIDEXTERITY.
The illusion of teleportation.
T. Nelson Downs: King of coin manipulation.
USING AN UNADULTERATED COIN OF AVERAGE WEIGHT, I'M ABOUT TO DEMONSTRATE HOW TO MAKE IT...
...WEIGHTLESS.
The illusion of telekinesis.

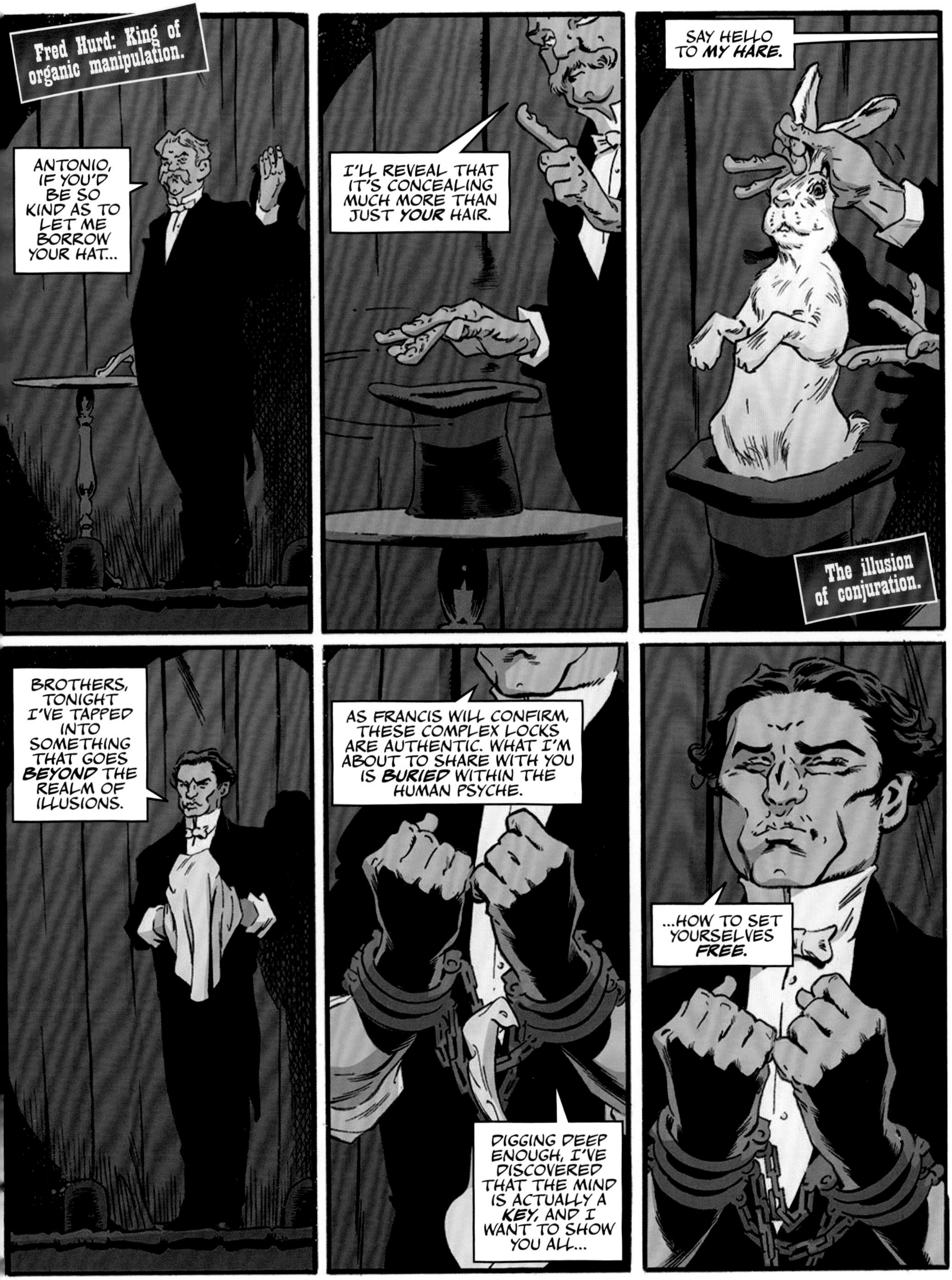
Fred Hurd: King of organic manipulation.
ANTONIO, IF YOU'D BE SO KIND AS TO LET ME BORROW YOUR HAT...
I'LL REVEAL THAT IT'S CONCEALING MUCH MORE THAN JUST YOUR HAIR.
SAY HELLO TO MY HARE.
The illusion of conjuration.
BROTHERS, TONIGHT I'VE TAPPED INTO SOMETHING THAT GOES BEYOND THE REALM OF ILLUSIONS.
AS FRANCIS WILL CONFIRM, THESE COMPLEX LOCKS ARE AUTHENTIC. WHAT I'M ABOUT TO SHARE WITH YOU IS BURIED WITHIN THE HUMAN PSYCHE.
DIGGING DEEP ENOUGH, I'VE DISCOVERED THAT THE MIND IS ACTUALLY A KEY, AND I WANT TO SHOW YOU ALL...
...HOW TO SET YOURSELVES FREE.

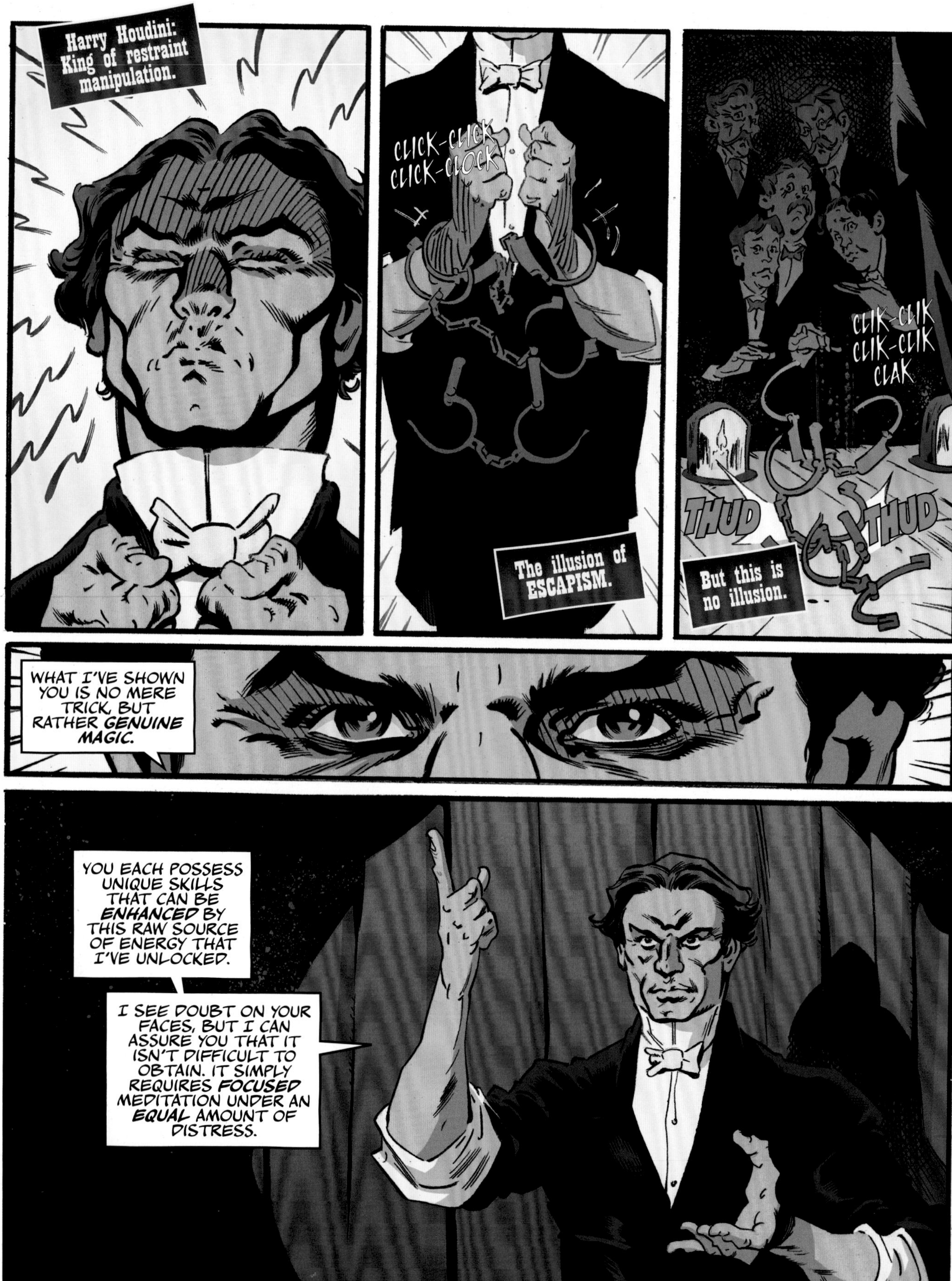

Harry Houdini: King of restraint manipulation.
CLICK-CLICK CLICK-CLOCK
The illusion of ESCAPISM.
CLIK-CLIK CLIK-CLIK CLAK
THUD THUD
But this is no illusion.
WHAT I'VE SHOWN YOU IS NO MERE TRICK, BUT RATHER GENUINE MAGIC.
YOU EACH POSSESS UNIQUE SKILLS THAT CAN BE ENHANCED BY THIS RAW SOURCE OF ENERGY THAT I'VE UNLOCKED.
I SEE DOUBT ON YOUR FACES, BUT I CAN ASSURE YOU THAT IT ISN'T DIFFICULT TO OBTAIN. IT SIMPLY REQUIRES FOCUSED MEDITATION UNDER AN EQUAL AMOUNT OF DISTRESS.

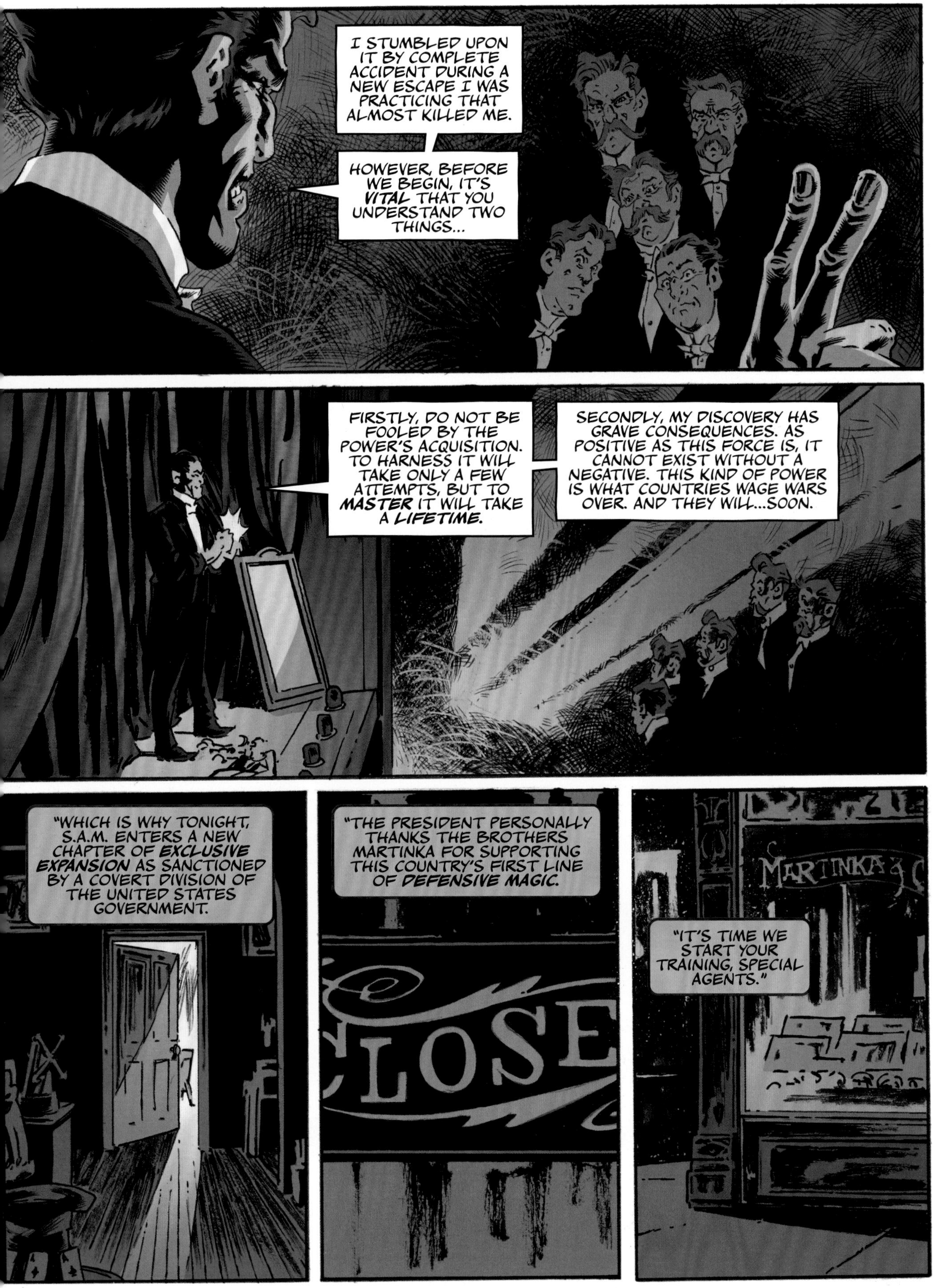
I STUMBLED UPON IT BY COMPLETE ACCIDENT DURING A NEW ESCAPE I WAS PRACTICING THAT ALMOST KILLED ME.
HOWEVER, BEFORE WE BEGIN, IT'S VITAL THAT YOU UNDERSTAND TWO THINGS...
FIRSTLY, DO NOT BE FOOLED BY THE POWER'S ACQUISITION. TO HARNESS IT WILL TAKE ONLY A FEW ATTEMPTS, BUT TO MASTER IT WILL TAKE A LIFETIME.
SECONDLY, MY DISCOVERY HAS GRAVE CONSEQUENCES. AS POSITIVE AS THIS FORCE IS, IT CANNOT EXIST WITHOUT A NEGATIVE. THIS KIND OF POWER IS WHAT COUNTRIES WAGE WARS OVER. AND THEY WILL...SOON.
"WHICH IS WHY TONIGHT, S.A.M. ENTERS A NEW CHAPTER OF EXCLUSIVE EXPANSION AS SANCTIONED BY A COVERT DIVISION OF THE UNITED STATES GOVERNMENT.
"THE PRESIDENT PERSONALLY THANKS THE BROTHERS MARTINKA FOR SUPPORTING THIS COUNTRY'S FIRST LINE OF DEFENSIVE MAGIC.
CLOSE
MARTINKA & C
"IT'S TIME WE START YOUR TRAINING, SPECIAL AGENTS."

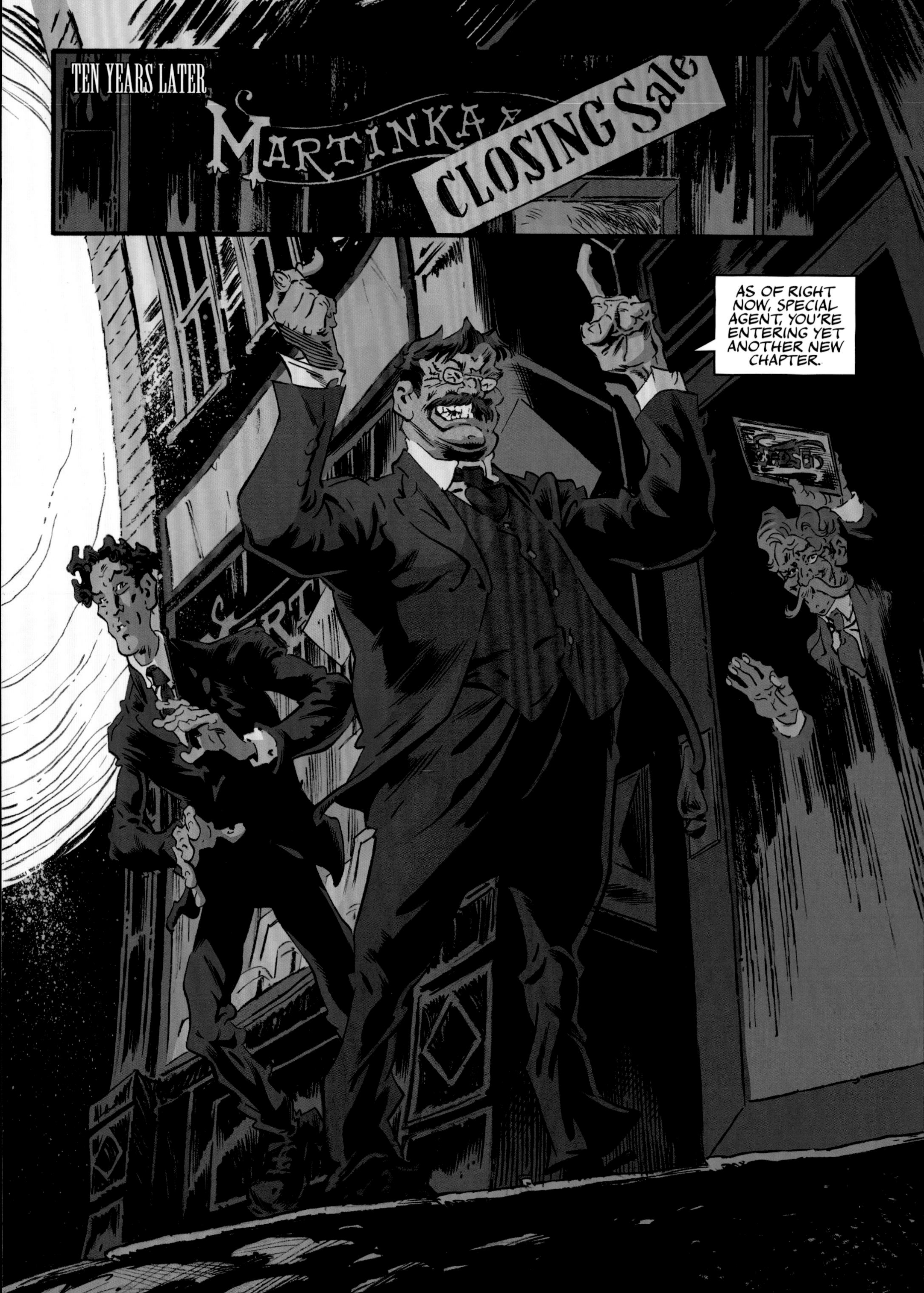
TEN YEARS LATER
MARTINKA
CLOSING Sale
AS OF RIGHT NOW, SPECIAL AGENT, YOU'RE ENTERING YET ANOTHER NEW CHAPTER.

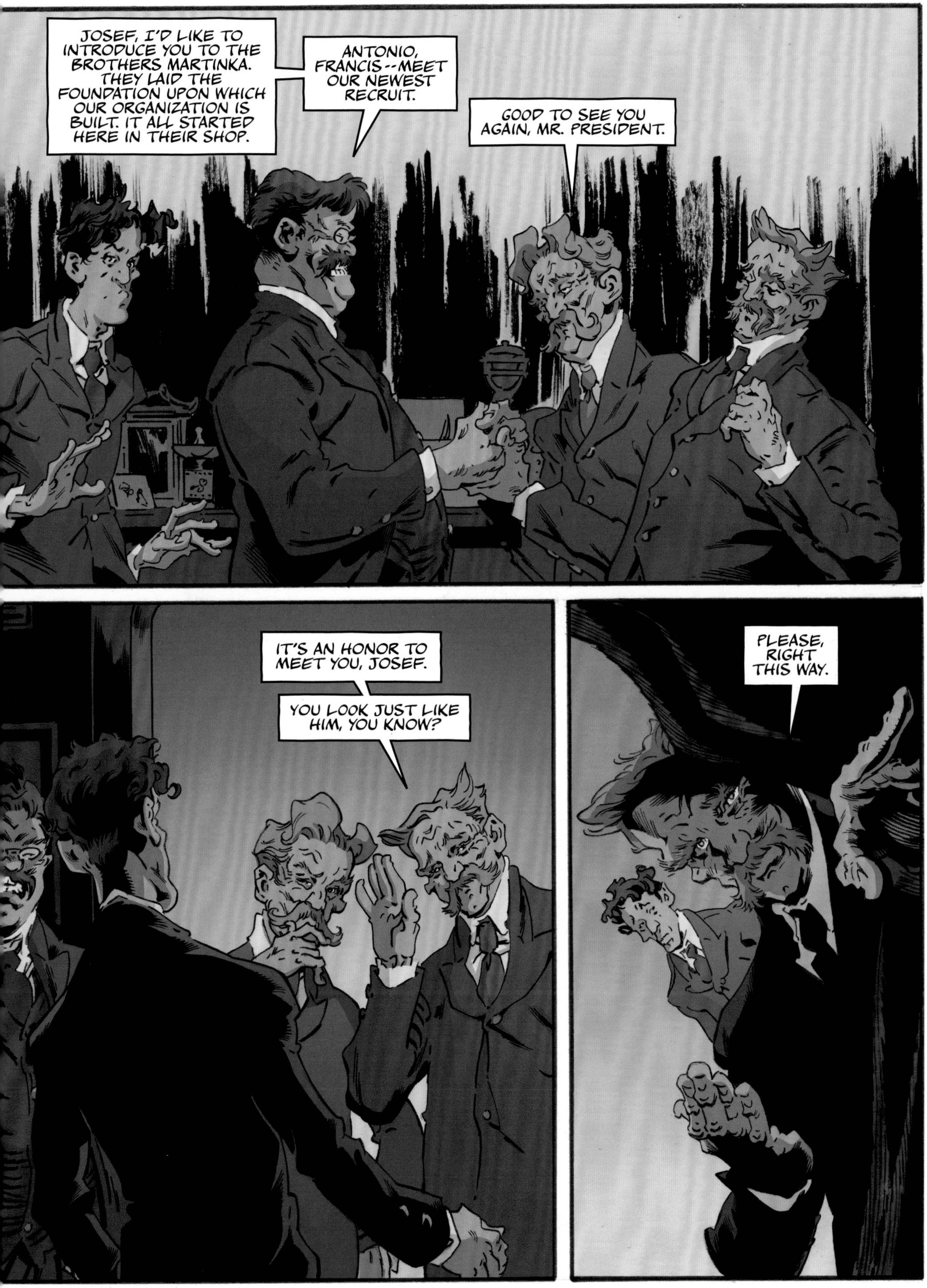
JOSEF, I'D LIKE TO INTRODUCE YOU TO THE BROTHERS MARTINKA. THEY LAID THE FOUNDATION UPON WHICH OUR ORGANIZATION IS BUILT. IT ALL STARTED HERE IN THEIR SHOP.
ANTONIO, FRANCIS--MEET OUR NEWEST RECRUIT.
GOOD TO SEE YOU AGAIN, MR. PRESIDENT.
IT'S AN HONOR TO MEET YOU, JOSEF.
YOU LOOK JUST LIKE HIM, YOU KNOW?
PLEASE, RIGHT THIS WAY.

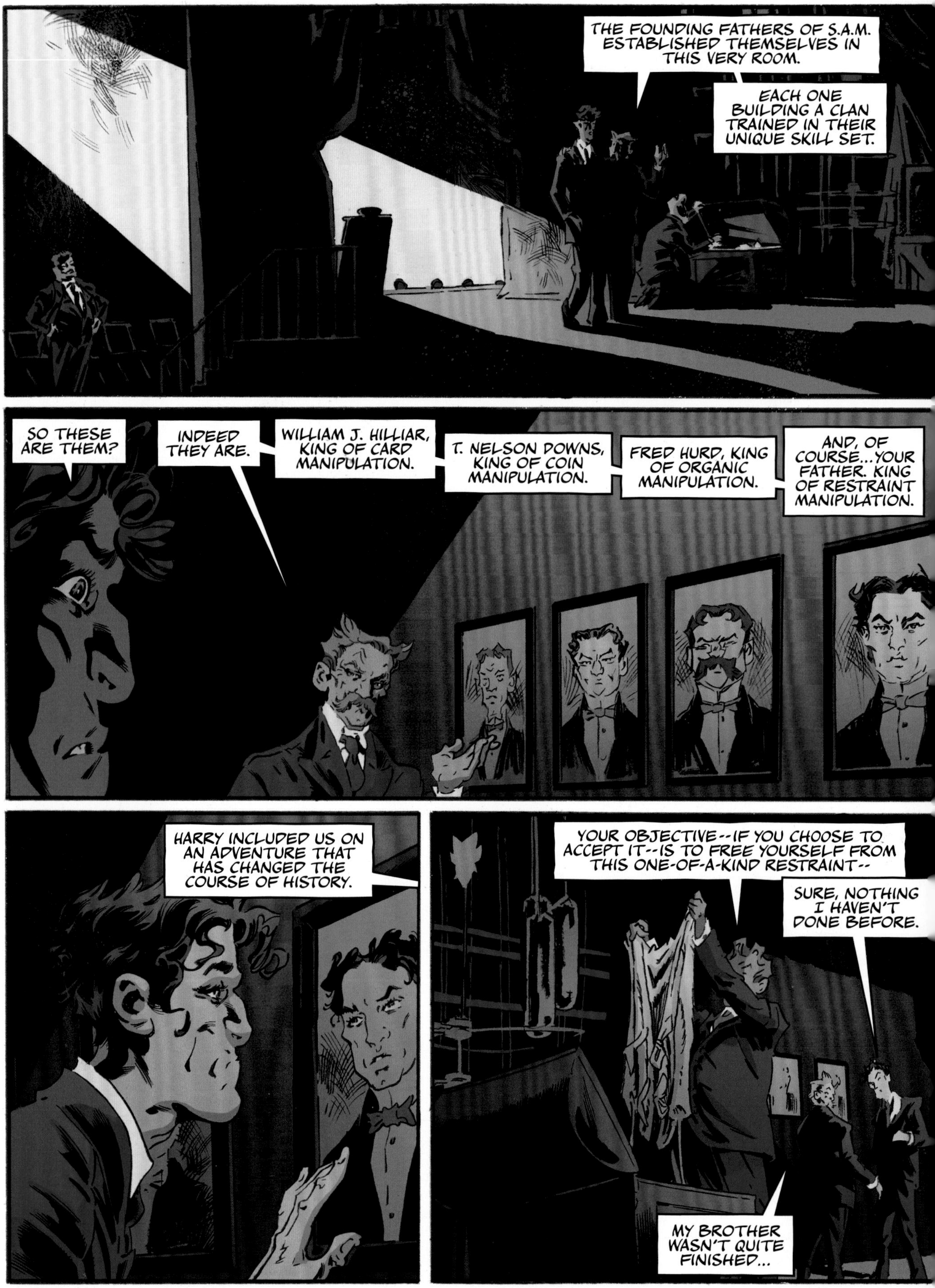
THE FOUNDING FATHERS OF S.A.M. ESTABLISHED THEMSELVES IN THIS VERY ROOM.
EACH ONE BUILDING A CLAN TRAINED IN THEIR UNIQUE SKILL SET.
SO THESE ARE THEM?
INDEED THEY ARE.
WILLIAM J. HILLIAR, KING OF CARD MANIPULATION.
T. NELSON DOWNS, KING OF COIN MANIPULATION.
FRED HURD, KING OF ORGANIC MANIPULATION.
AND, OF COURSE...YOUR FATHER. KING OF RESTRAINT MANIPULATION.
HARRY INCLUDED US ON AN ADVENTURE THAT HAS CHANGED THE COURSE OF HISTORY.
YOUR OBJECTIVE--IF YOU CHOOSE TO ACCEPT IT--IS TO FREE YOURSELF FROM THIS ONE-OF-A-KIND RESTRAINT--
SURE, NOTHING I HAVEN'T DONE BEFORE.
MY BROTHER WASN'T QUITE FINISHED...

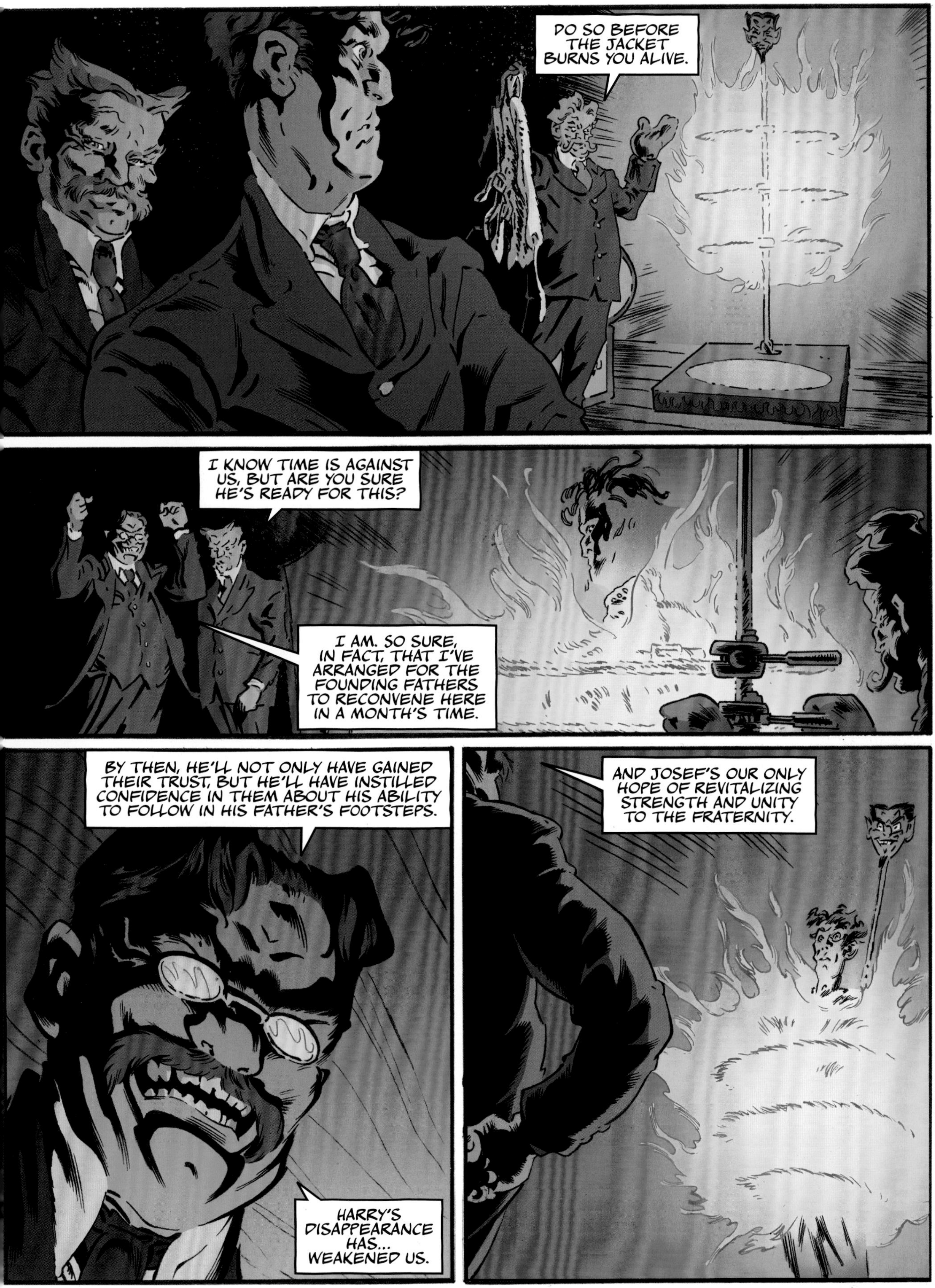
DO SO BEFORE THE JACKET BURNS YOU ALIVE.
I KNOW TIME IS AGAINST US, BUT ARE YOU SURE HE'S READY FOR THIS?
I AM. SO SURE, IN FACT, THAT I'VE ARRANGED FOR THE FOUNDING FATHERS TO RECONVENE HERE IN A MONTH'S TIME.
BY THEN, HE'LL NOT ONLY HAVE GAINED THEIR TRUST, BUT HE'LL HAVE INSTILLED CONFIDENCE IN THEM ABOUT HIS ABILITY TO FOLLOW IN HIS FATHER'S FOOTSTEPS.
HARRY'S DISAPPEARANCE HAS... WEAKENED US.
AND JOSEF'S OUR ONLY HOPE OF REVITALIZING STRENGTH AND UNITY TO THE FRATERNITY.

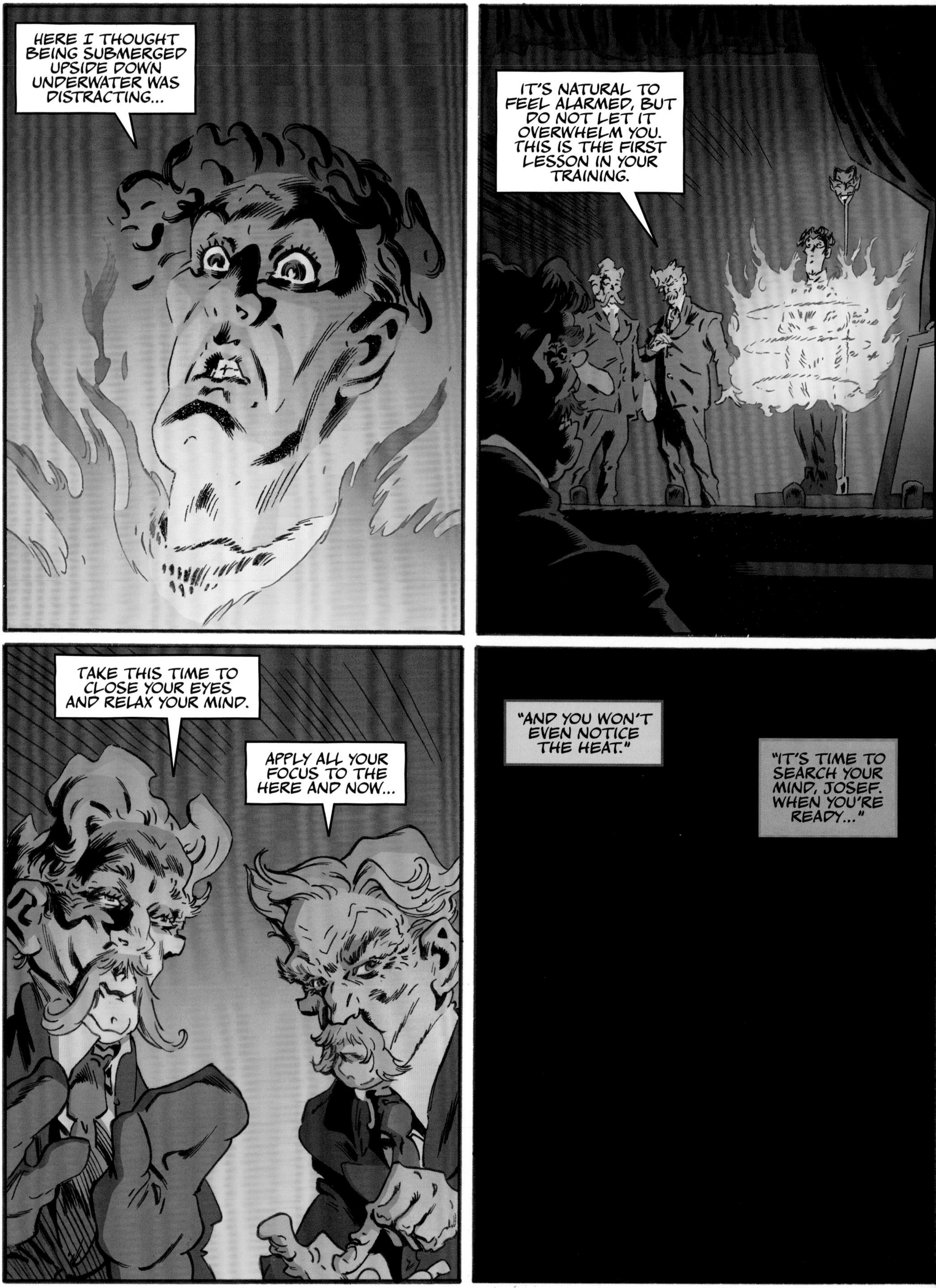
HERE I THOUGHT BEING SUBMERGED UPSIDE DOWN UNDERWATER WAS DISTRACTING...
IT'S NATURAL TO FEEL ALARMED, BUT DO NOT LET IT OVERWHELM YOU. THIS IS THE FIRST LESSON IN YOUR TRAINING.
TAKE THIS TIME TO CLOSE YOUR EYES AND RELAX YOUR MIND.
APPLY ALL YOUR FOCUS TO THE HERE AND NOW...
"AND YOU WON'T EVEN NOTICE THE HEAT."
"IT'S TIME TO SEARCH YOUR MIND, JOSEF. WHEN YOU'RE READY..."

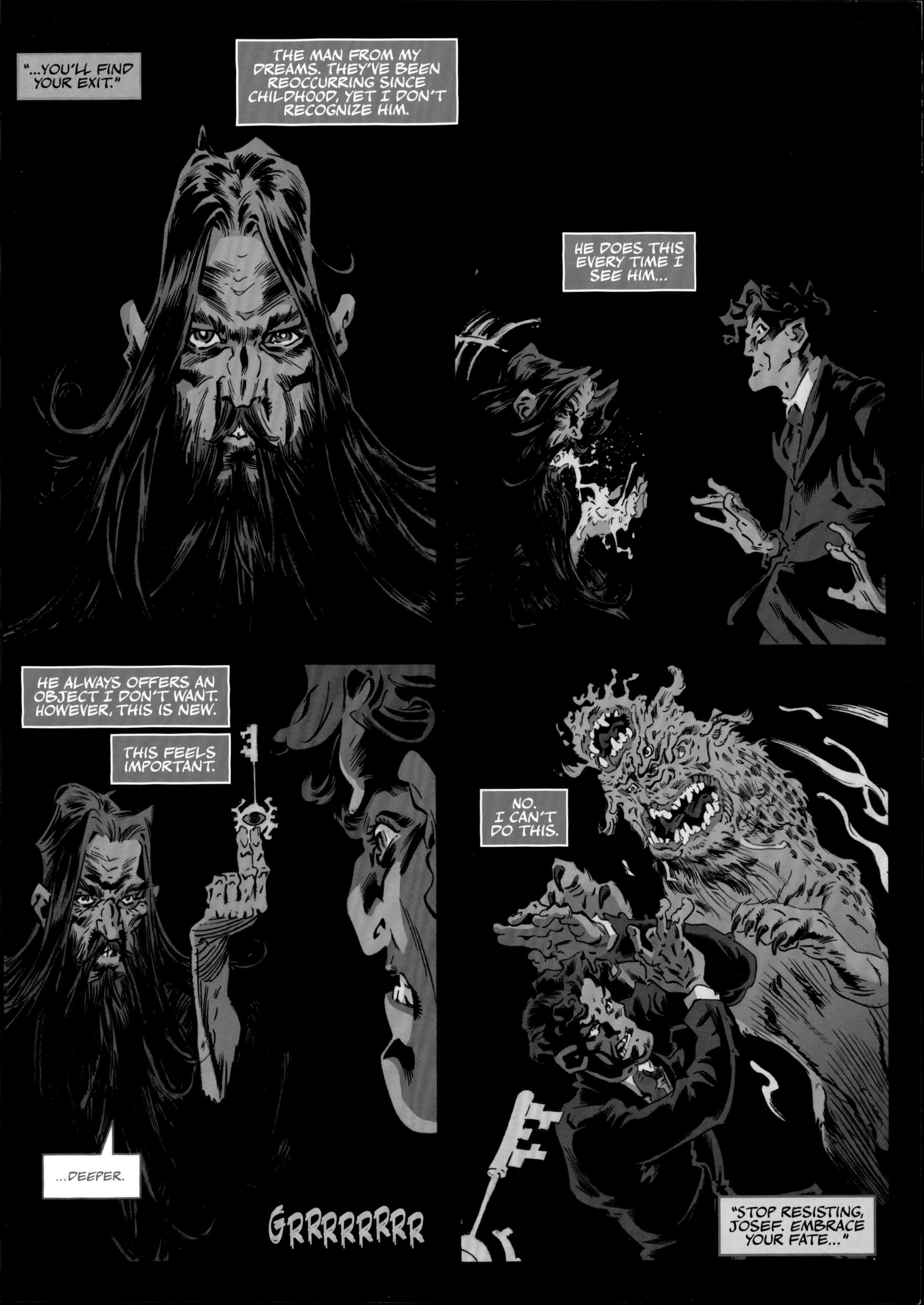
"...YOU'LL FIND YOUR EXIT."
THE MAN FROM MY DREAMS. THEY'VE BEEN REOCCURRING SINCE CHILDHOOD, YET I DON'T RECOGNIZE HIM.
HE DOES THIS EVERY TIME I SEE HIM...
HE ALWAYS OFFERS AN OBJECT I DON'T WANT. HOWEVER, THIS IS NEW.
THIS FEELS IMPORTANT.
...DEEPER.
GRRRRRRRR
NO. I CAN'T DO THIS.
"STOP RESISTING, JOSEF. EMBRACE YOUR FATE..."

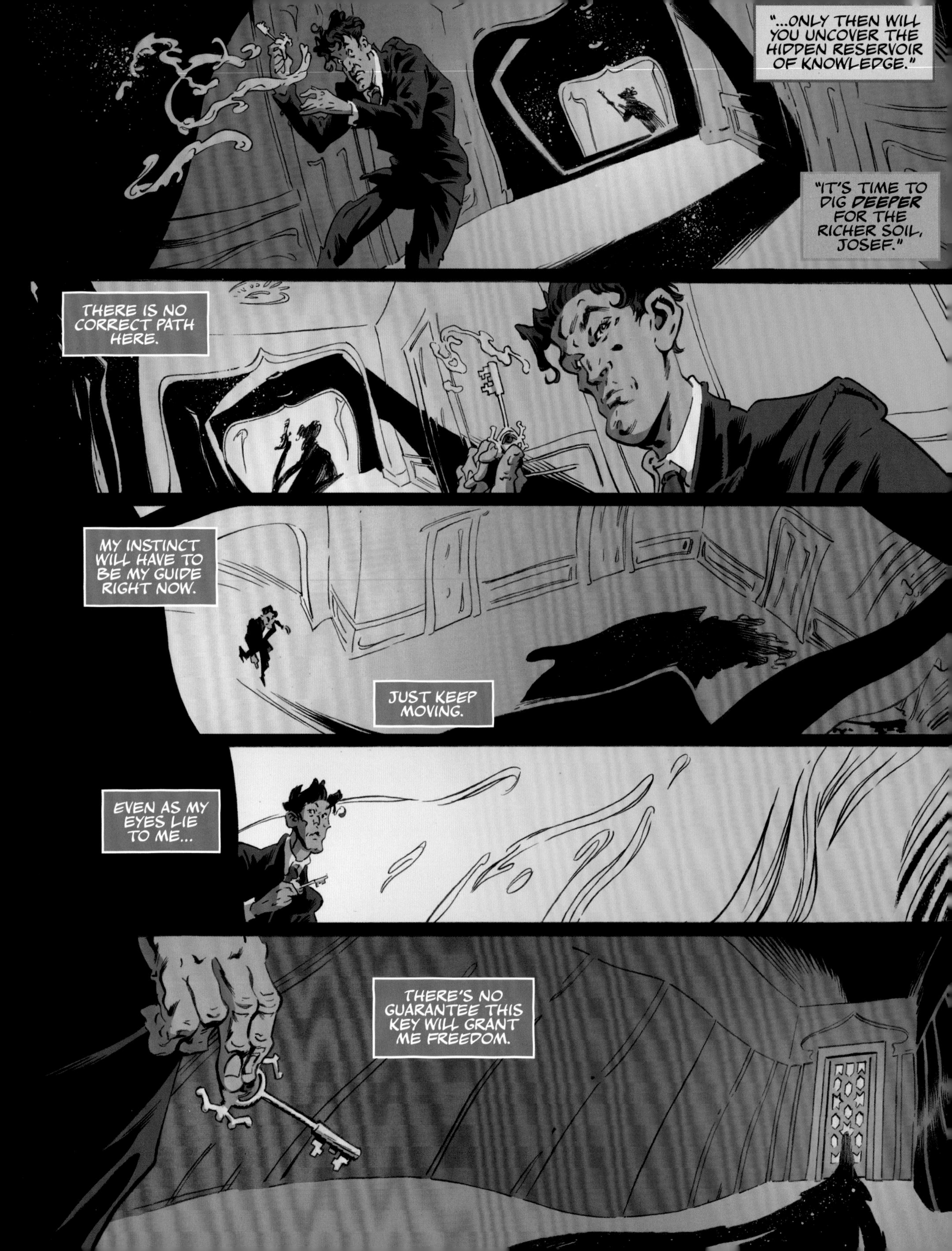
"...ONLY THEN WILL YOU UNCOVER THE HIDDEN RESERVOIR OF KNOWLEDGE."
"IT'S TIME TO DIG *DEEPER* FOR THE RICHER SOIL, JOSEF."
THERE IS NO CORRECT PATH HERE.
MY INSTINCT WILL HAVE TO BE MY GUIDE RIGHT NOW.
JUST KEEP MOVING.
EVEN AS MY EYES LIE TO ME...
THERE'S NO GUARANTEE THIS KEY WILL GRANT ME FREEDOM.

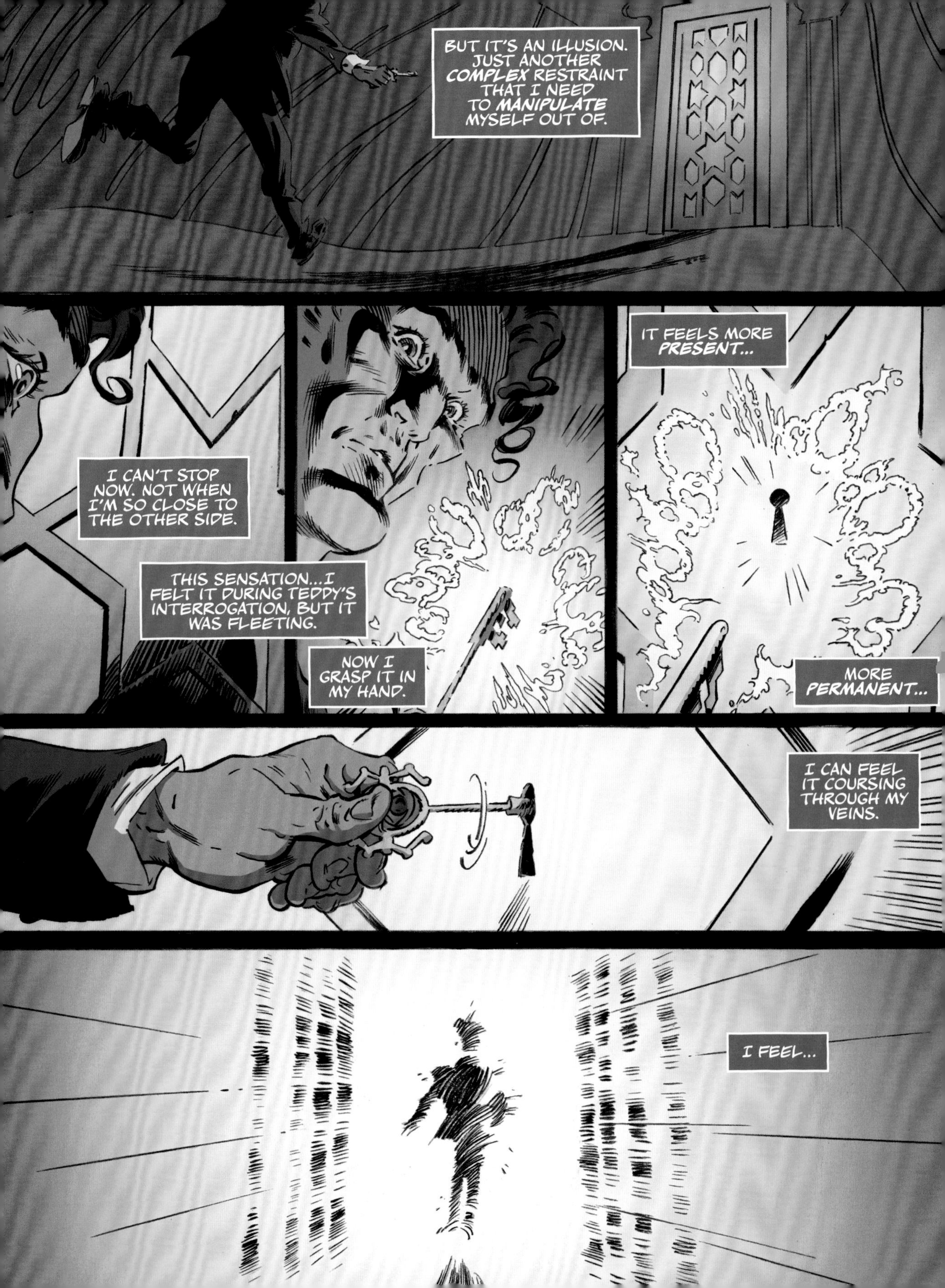

BUT IT'S AN ILLUSION. JUST ANOTHER COMPLEX RESTRAINT THAT I NEED TO MANIPULATE MYSELF OUT OF.
I CAN'T STOP NOW. NOT WHEN I'M SO CLOSE TO THE OTHER SIDE.
THIS SENSATION...I FELT IT DURING TEDDY'S INTERROGATION, BUT IT WAS FLEETING.
NOW I GRASP IT IN MY HAND.
IT FEELS MORE PRESENT...
MORE PERMANENT...
I CAN FEEL IT COURSING THROUGH MY VEINS.
I FEEL...

FREE.

CLANG

CLANG

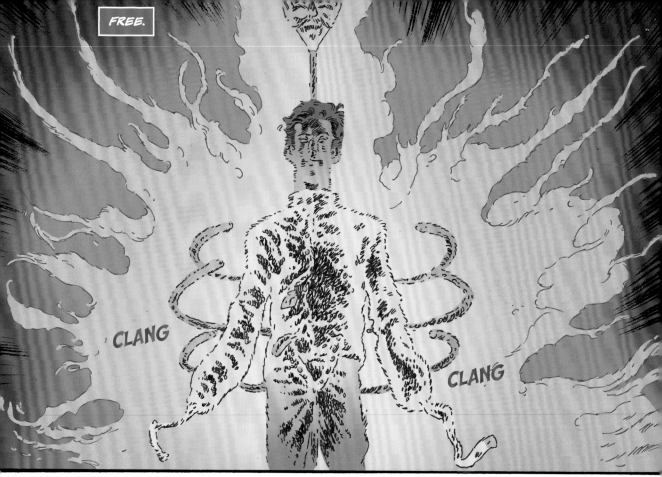

THE APPLE CLEARLY HASN'T FALLEN FAR FROM THE TREE.

I AGREE, YOU'RE A NATURAL.

THUNK

PARDON THE INTERRUPTION. IT APPEARS THAT ANOTHER ESTEEMED MEMBER OF S.A.M. HAS DECIDED TO GRACE US WITH HIS PRESENCE.

MEMBER IS A STRONG WORD; I PREFER CONSULTANT.

REGARDLESS, I'D LIKE TO INTRODUCE EDGAR CAYCE-- A PSYCHIC WITH UNMATCHED ABILITIES THAT CONTINUE TO AID THE FRATERNITY.

MEANING...?

I LOCATE PEOPLE AMONG OTHER THINGS, AND TONIGHT

...I'VE MADE CONTACT WITH HARRY.

HE'S--

ALIVE, YES. I KNOW. BELIEVE ME, I DO NOT BEAR SUCH NEWS LIGHTLY.

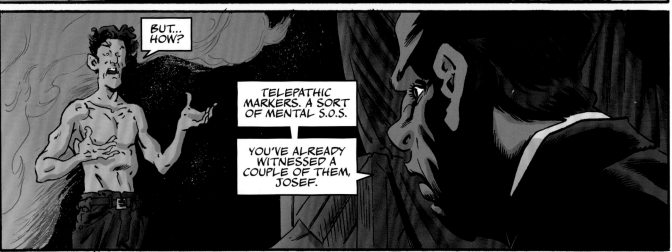

BUT... HOW?

TELEPATHIC MARKERS. A SORT OF MENTAL S.O.S.

YOU'VE ALREADY WITNESSED A COUPLE OF THEM, JOSEF.

THE MARKERS CERTAINLY HELPED START MY SEARCH...

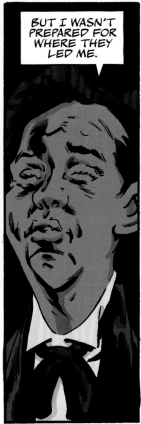

BUT I WASN'T PREPARED FOR WHERE THEY LED ME.

THIS PLACE...

IT'S COLD AND DARK, AND I CAN BARELY...

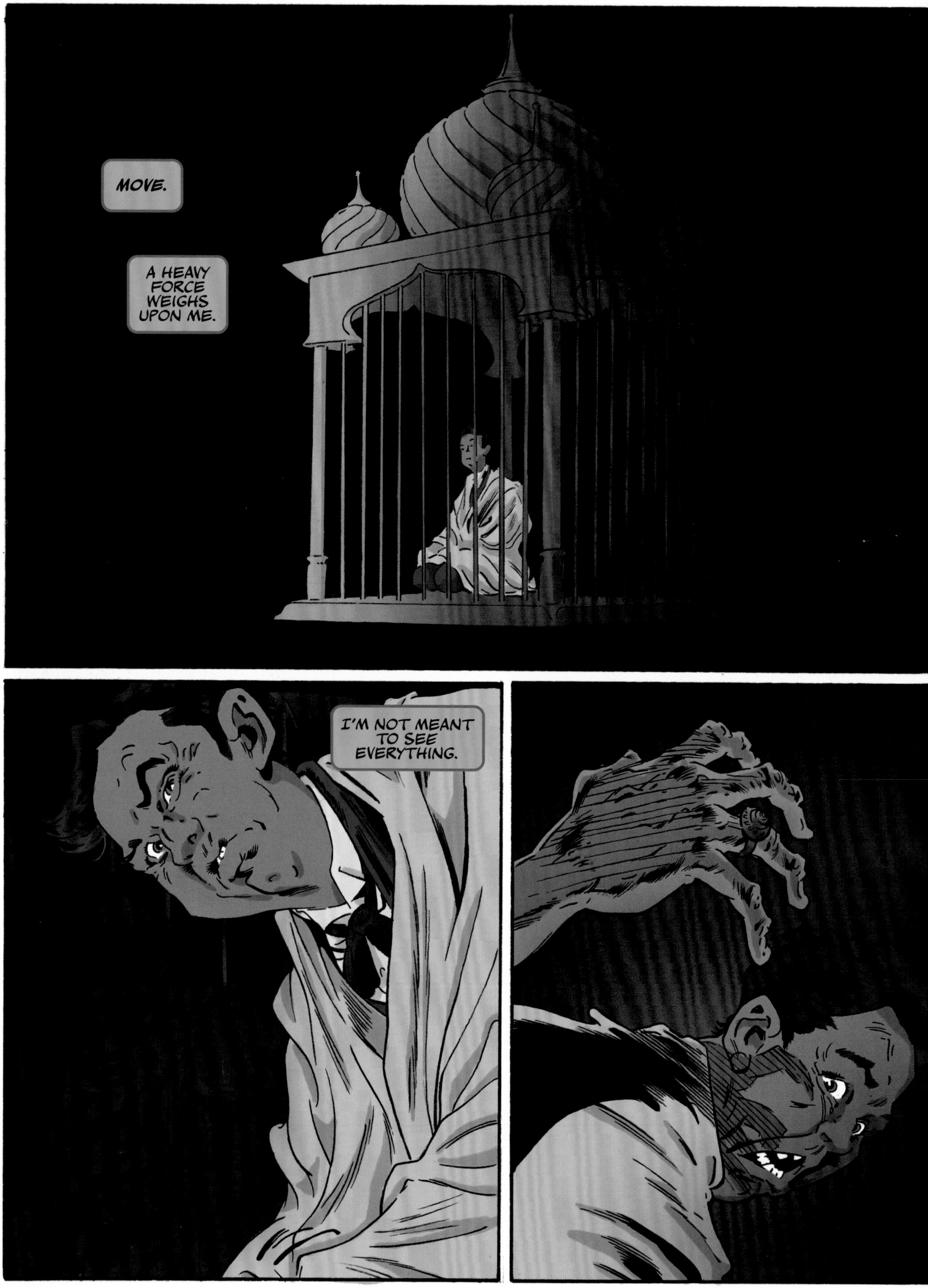
MOVE.
A HEAVY FORCE WEIGHS UPON ME.
I'M NOT MEANT TO SEE EVERYTHING.

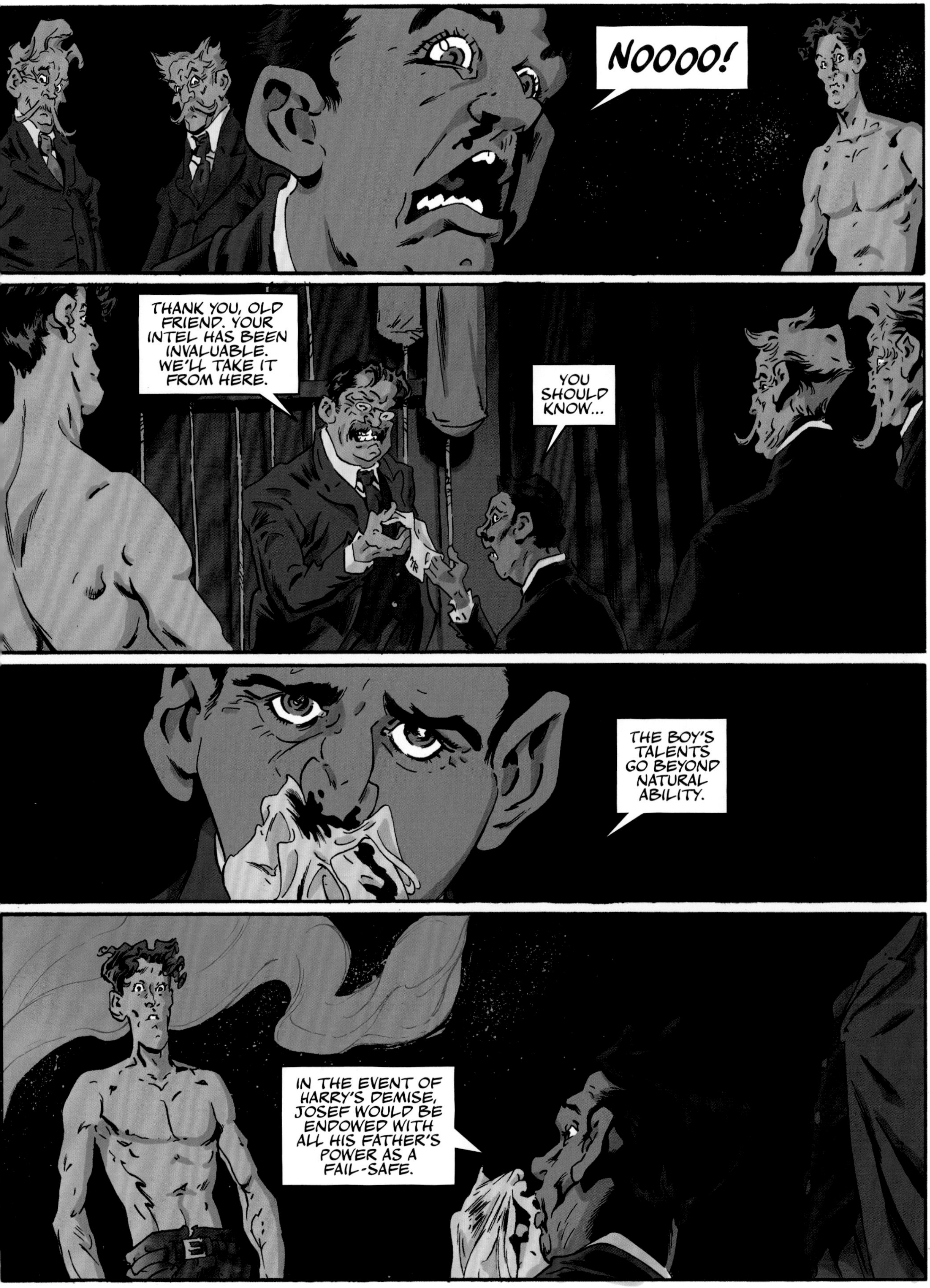
NOOOO!
THANK YOU, OLD FRIEND. YOUR INTEL HAS BEEN INVALUABLE. WE'LL TAKE IT FROM HERE.
YOU SHOULD KNOW...
THE BOY'S TALENTS GO BEYOND NATURAL ABILITY.
IN THE EVENT OF HARRY'S DEMISE, JOSEF WOULD BE ENDOWED WITH ALL HIS FATHER'S POWER AS A FAIL-SAFE.

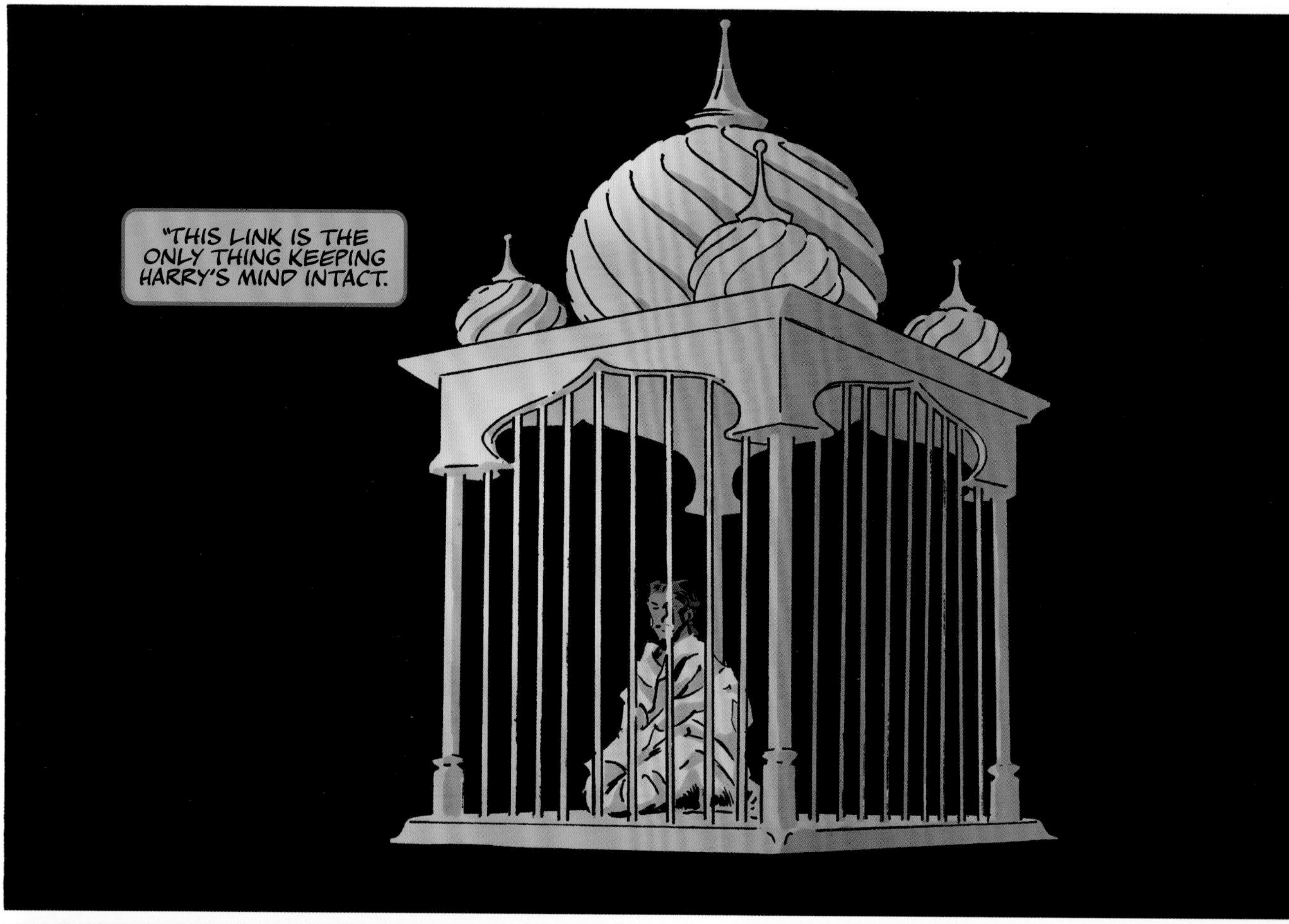
"THIS LINK IS THE ONLY THING KEEPING HARRY'S MIND INTACT.

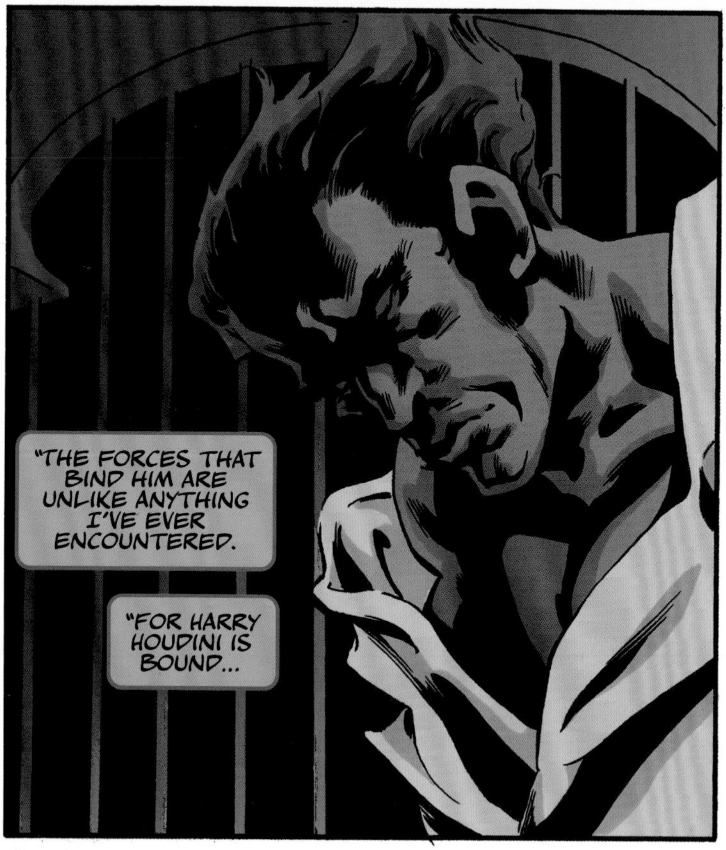
"THE FORCES THAT BIND HIM ARE UNLIKE ANYTHING I'VE EVER ENCOUNTERED.
"FOR HARRY HOUDINI IS BOUND...

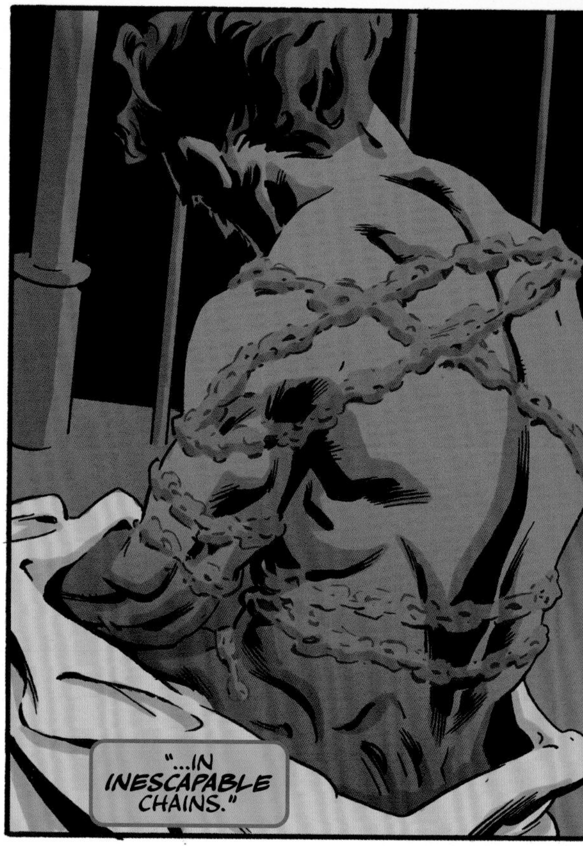
"...IN INESCAPABLE CHAINS."

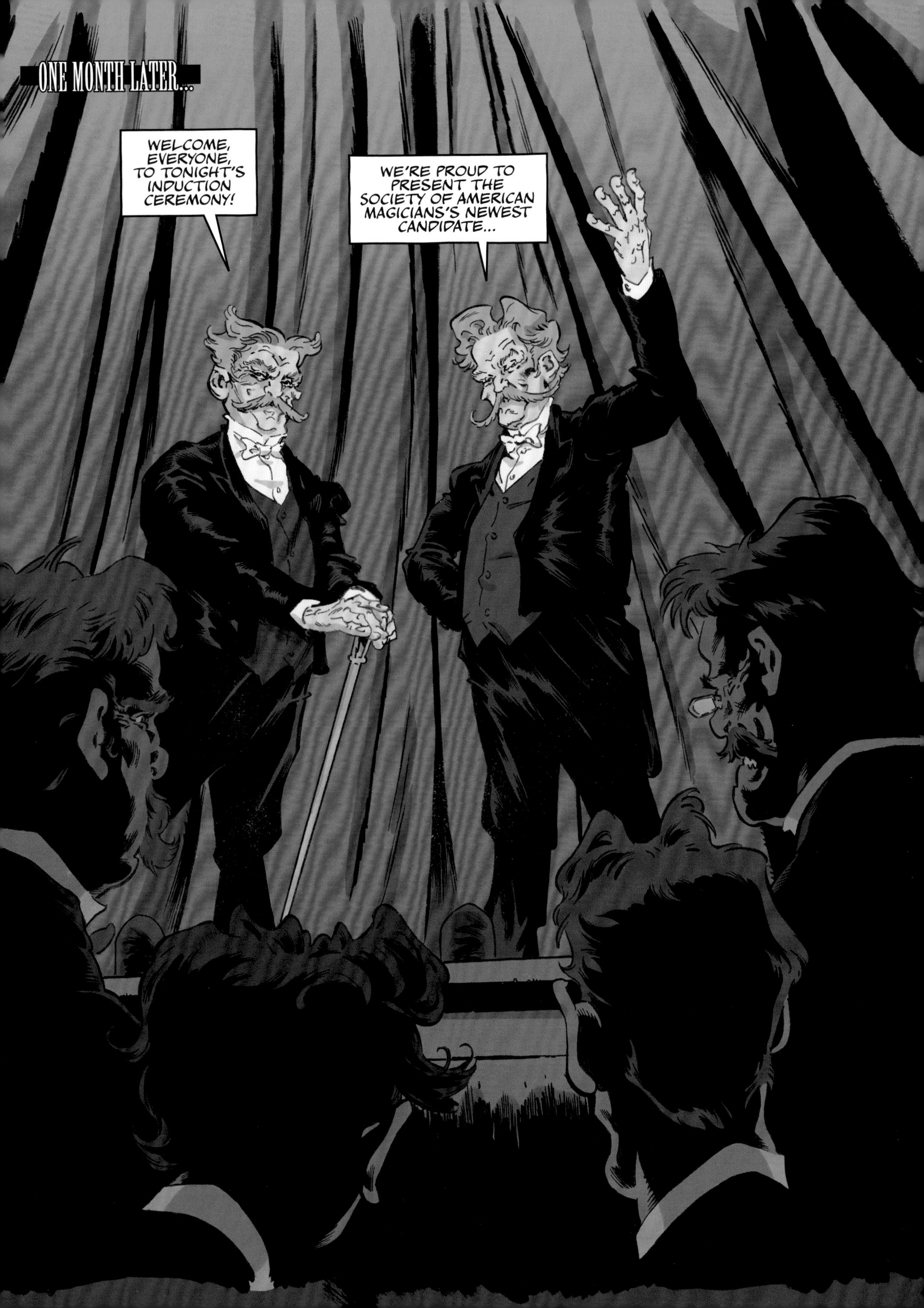
ONE MONTH LATER...
WELCOME, EVERYONE, TO TONIGHT'S INDUCTION CEREMONY!
WE'RE PROUD TO PRESENT THE SOCIETY OF AMERICAN MAGICIANS'S NEWEST CANDIDATE...

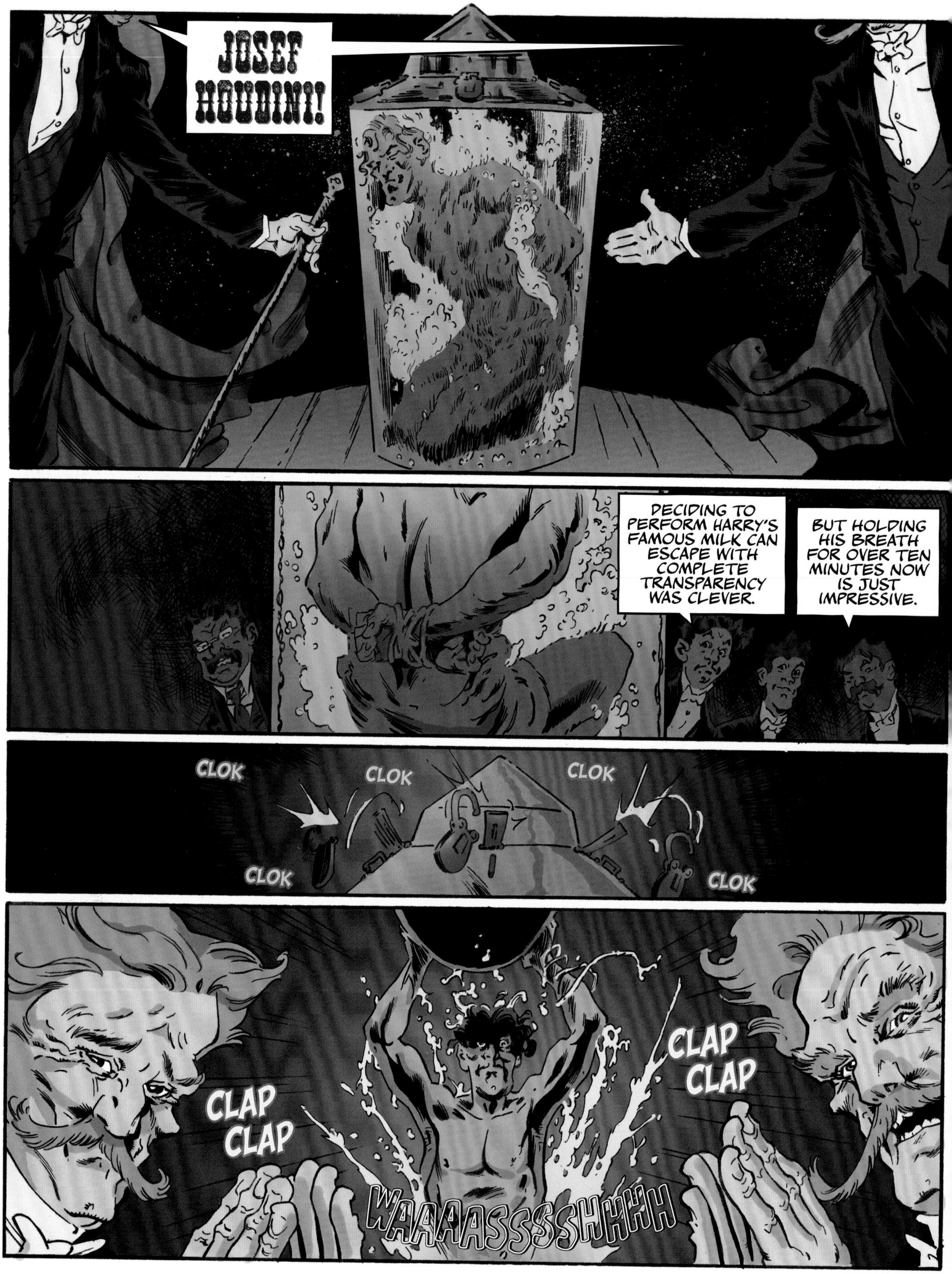
JOSEF HOUDINI!
DECIDING TO PERFORM HARRY'S FAMOUS MILK CAN ESCAPE WITH COMPLETE TRANSPARENCY WAS CLEVER.
BUT HOLDING HIS BREATH FOR OVER TEN MINUTES NOW IS JUST IMPRESSIVE.
CLOK
CLOK
CLOK
CLOK
CLOK
CLAP CLAP
CLAP CLAP
WAAAASSSSSHHHH

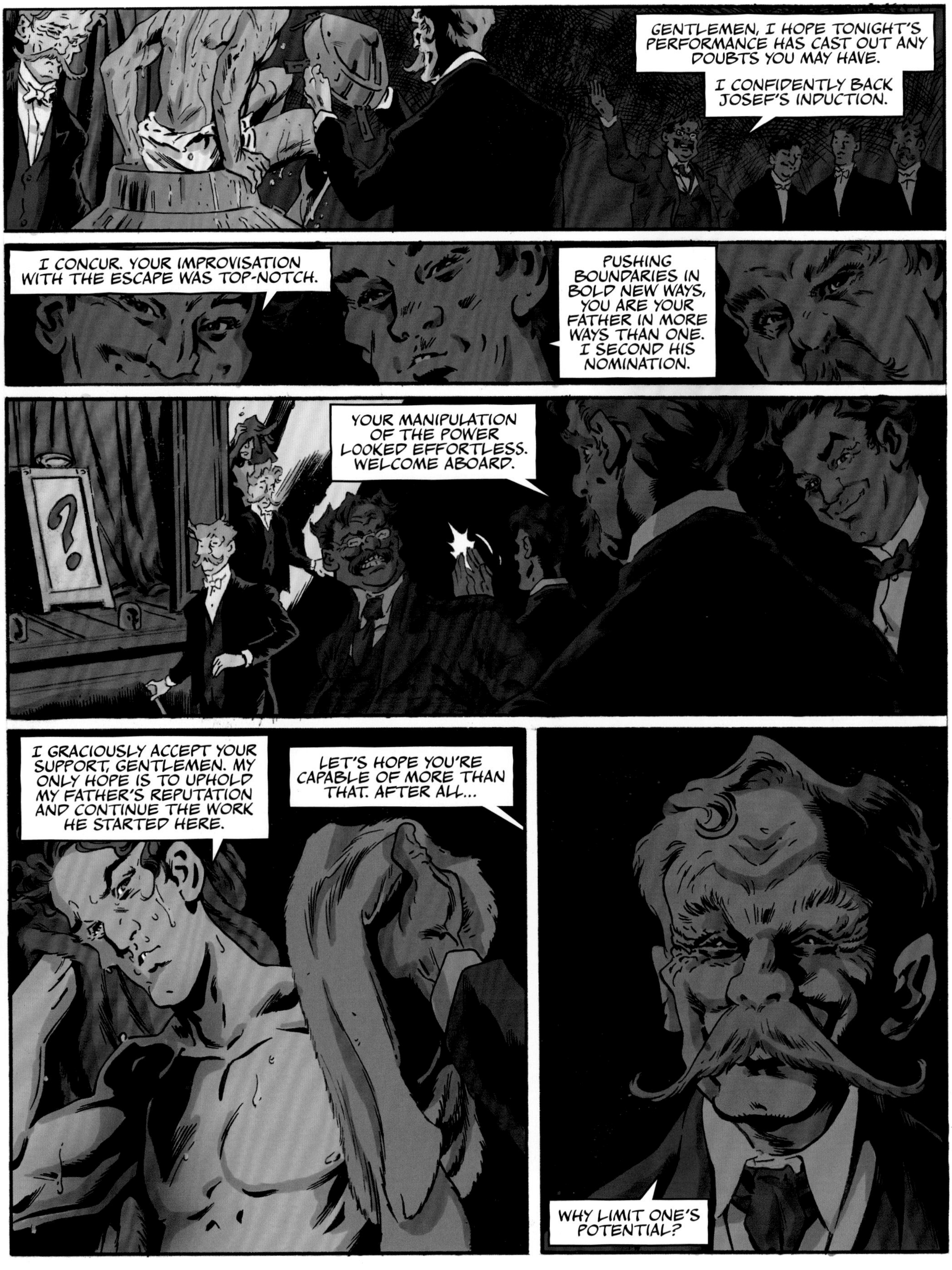
GENTLEMEN, I HOPE TONIGHT'S PERFORMANCE HAS CAST OUT ANY DOUBTS YOU MAY HAVE.
I CONFIDENTLY BACK JOSEF'S INDUCTION.
I CONCUR. YOUR IMPROVISATION WITH THE ESCAPE WAS TOP-NOTCH.
PUSHING BOUNDARIES IN BOLD NEW WAYS, YOU ARE YOUR FATHER IN MORE WAYS THAN ONE. I SECOND HIS NOMINATION.
YOUR MANIPULATION OF THE POWER LOOKED EFFORTLESS. WELCOME ABOARD.
I GRACIOUSLY ACCEPT YOUR SUPPORT, GENTLEMEN. MY ONLY HOPE IS TO UPHOLD MY FATHER'S REPUTATION AND CONTINUE THE WORK HE STARTED HERE.
LET'S HOPE YOU'RE CAPABLE OF MORE THAN THAT. AFTER ALL...
WHY LIMIT ONE'S POTENTIAL?

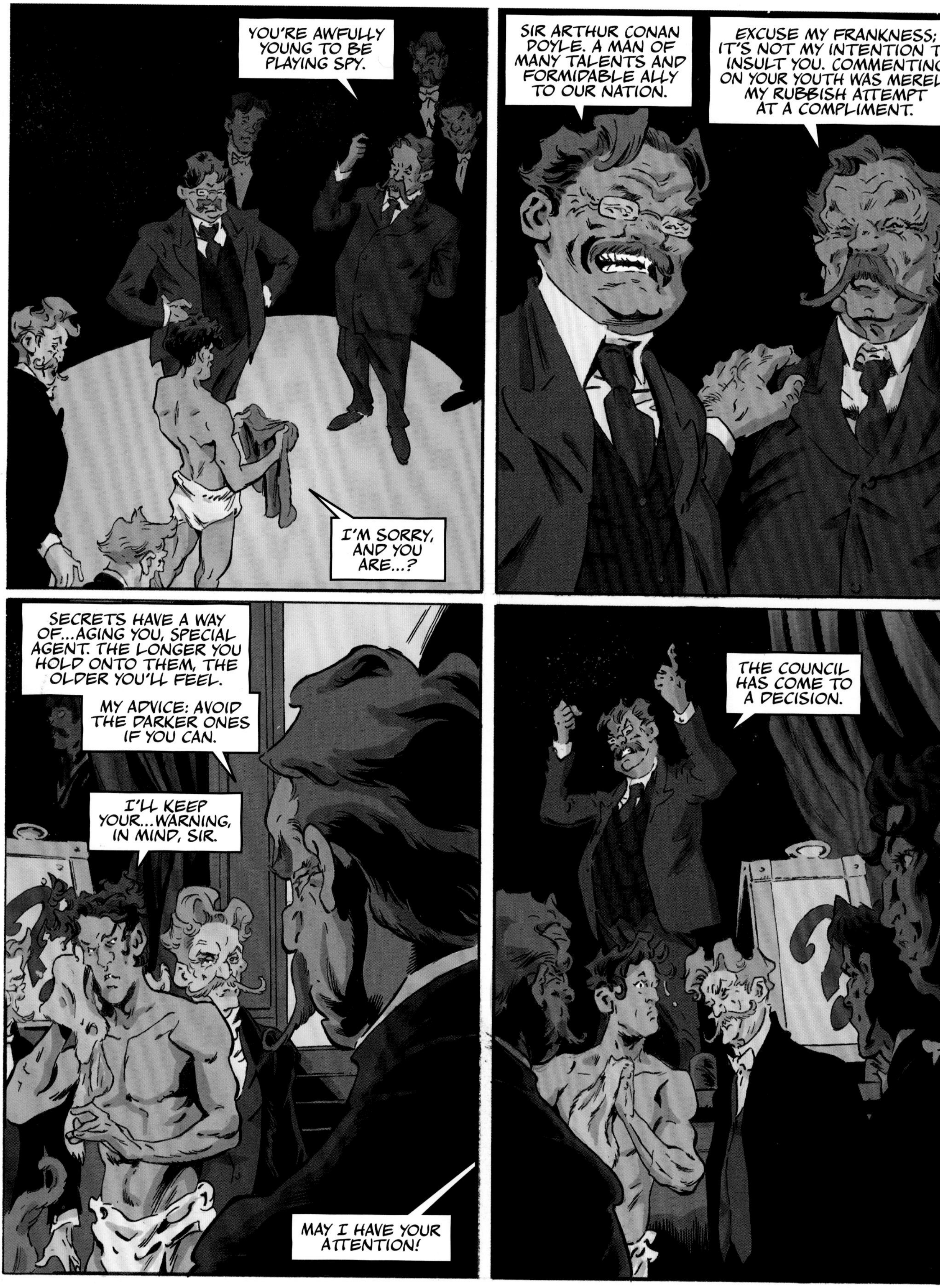
YOU'RE AWFULLY YOUNG TO BE PLAYING SPY.
I'M SORRY, AND YOU ARE...?
SIR ARTHUR CONAN DOYLE. A MAN OF MANY TALENTS AND FORMIDABLE ALLY TO OUR NATION.
EXCUSE MY FRANKNESS; IT'S NOT MY INTENTION TO INSULT YOU. COMMENTING ON YOUR YOUTH WAS MERELY MY RUBBISH ATTEMPT AT A COMPLIMENT.
SECRETS HAVE A WAY OF...AGING YOU, SPECIAL AGENT. THE LONGER YOU HOLD ONTO THEM, THE OLDER YOU'LL FEEL.
MY ADVICE: AVOID THE DARKER ONES IF YOU CAN.
I'LL KEEP YOUR...WARNING, IN MIND, SIR.
MAY I HAVE YOUR ATTENTION!
THE COUNCIL HAS COME TO A DECISION.

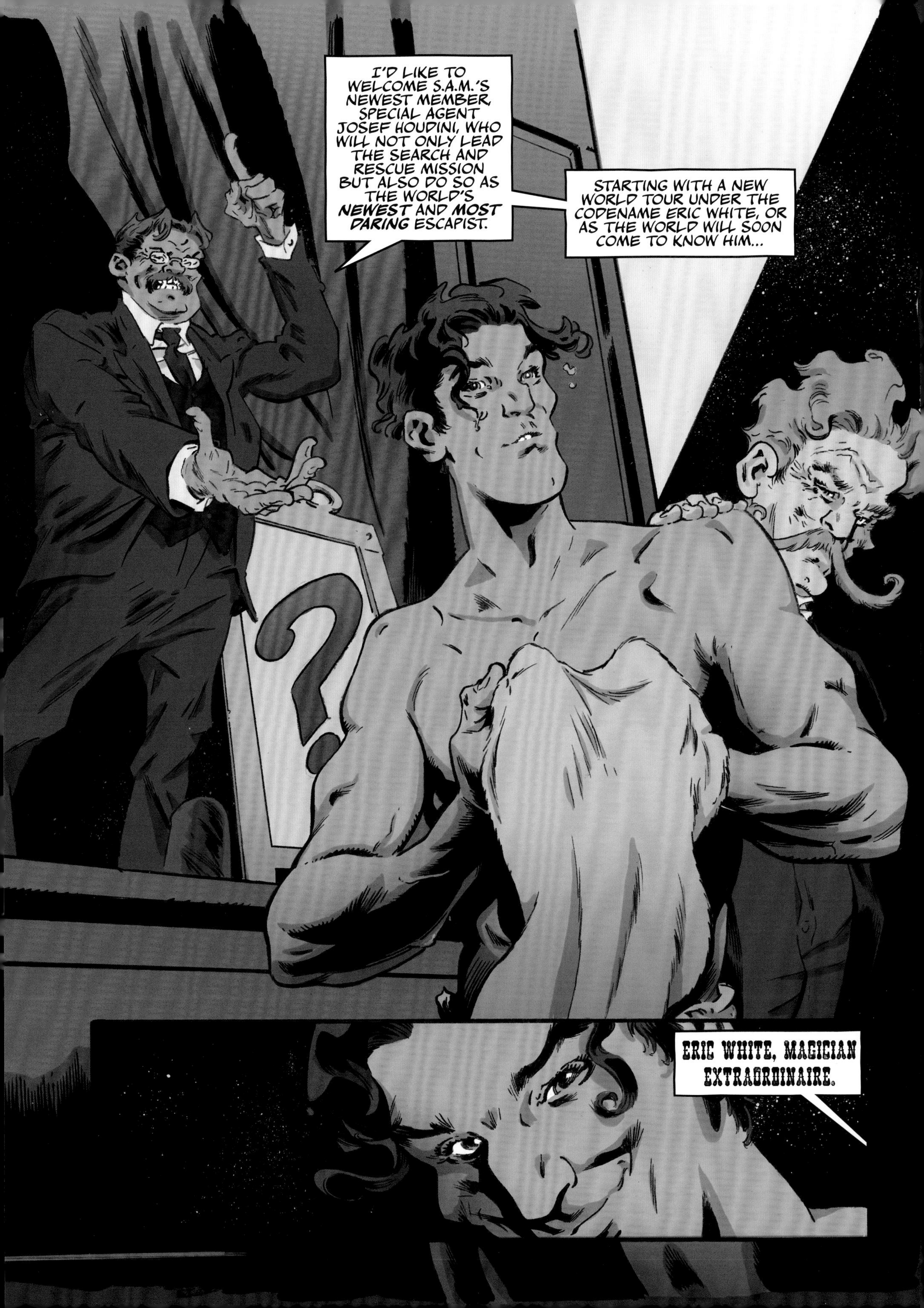
I'D LIKE TO WELCOME S.A.M.'S NEWEST MEMBER, SPECIAL AGENT JOSEF HOUDINI, WHO WILL NOT ONLY LEAD THE SEARCH AND RESCUE MISSION BUT ALSO DO SO AS THE WORLD'S **NEWEST** AND **MOST DARING** ESCAPIST.
STARTING WITH A NEW WORLD TOUR UNDER THE CODENAME ERIC WHITE, OR AS THE WORLD WILL SOON COME TO KNOW HIM...
ERIC WHITE, MAGICIAN EXTRAORDINAIRE.

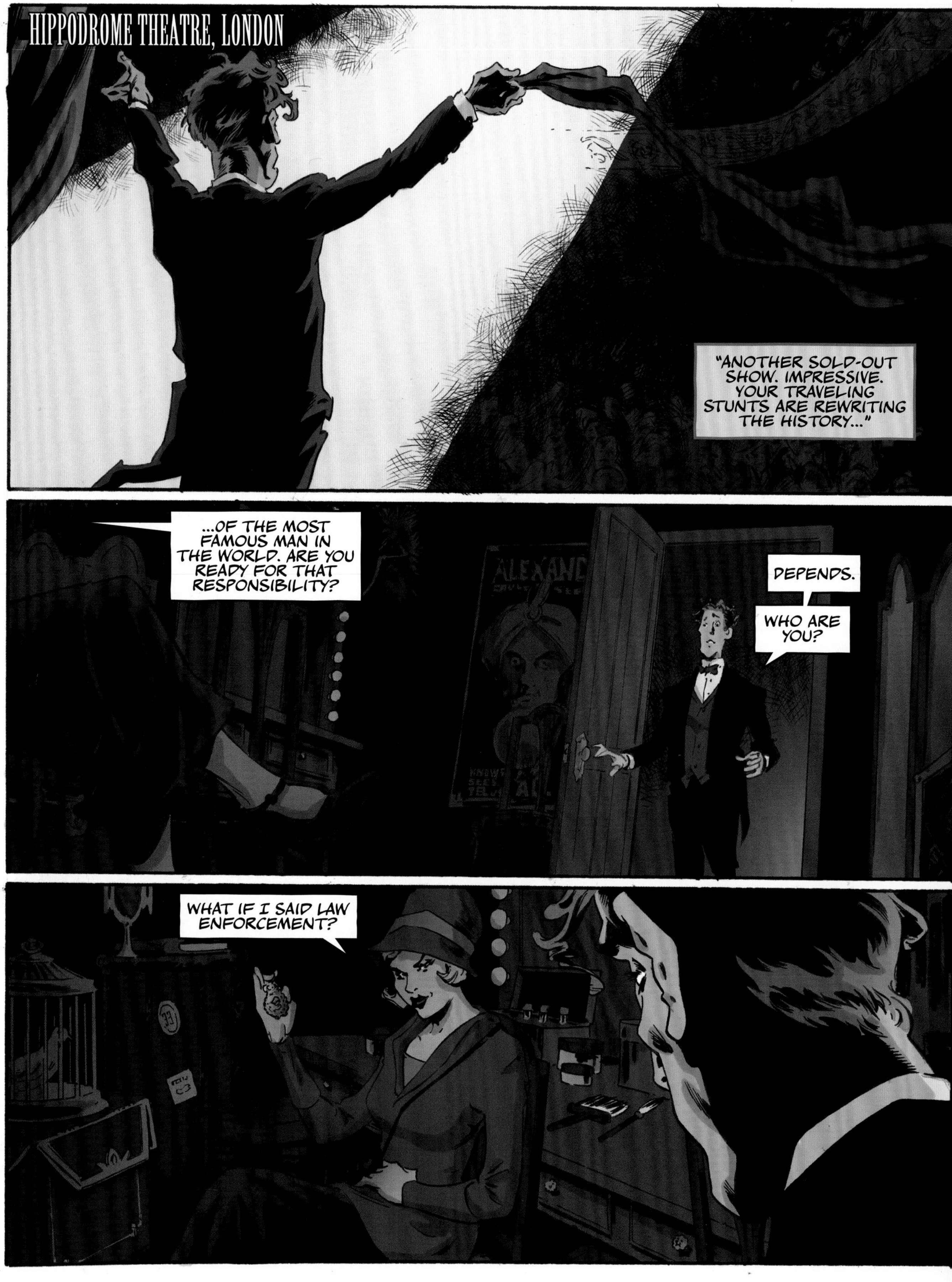
HIPPODROME THEATRE, LONDON
"ANOTHER SOLD-OUT SHOW. IMPRESSIVE. YOUR TRAVELING STUNTS ARE REWRITING THE HISTORY..."
...OF THE MOST FAMOUS MAN IN THE WORLD. ARE YOU READY FOR THAT RESPONSIBILITY?
DEPENDS.
WHO ARE YOU?
WHAT IF I SAID LAW ENFORCEMENT?

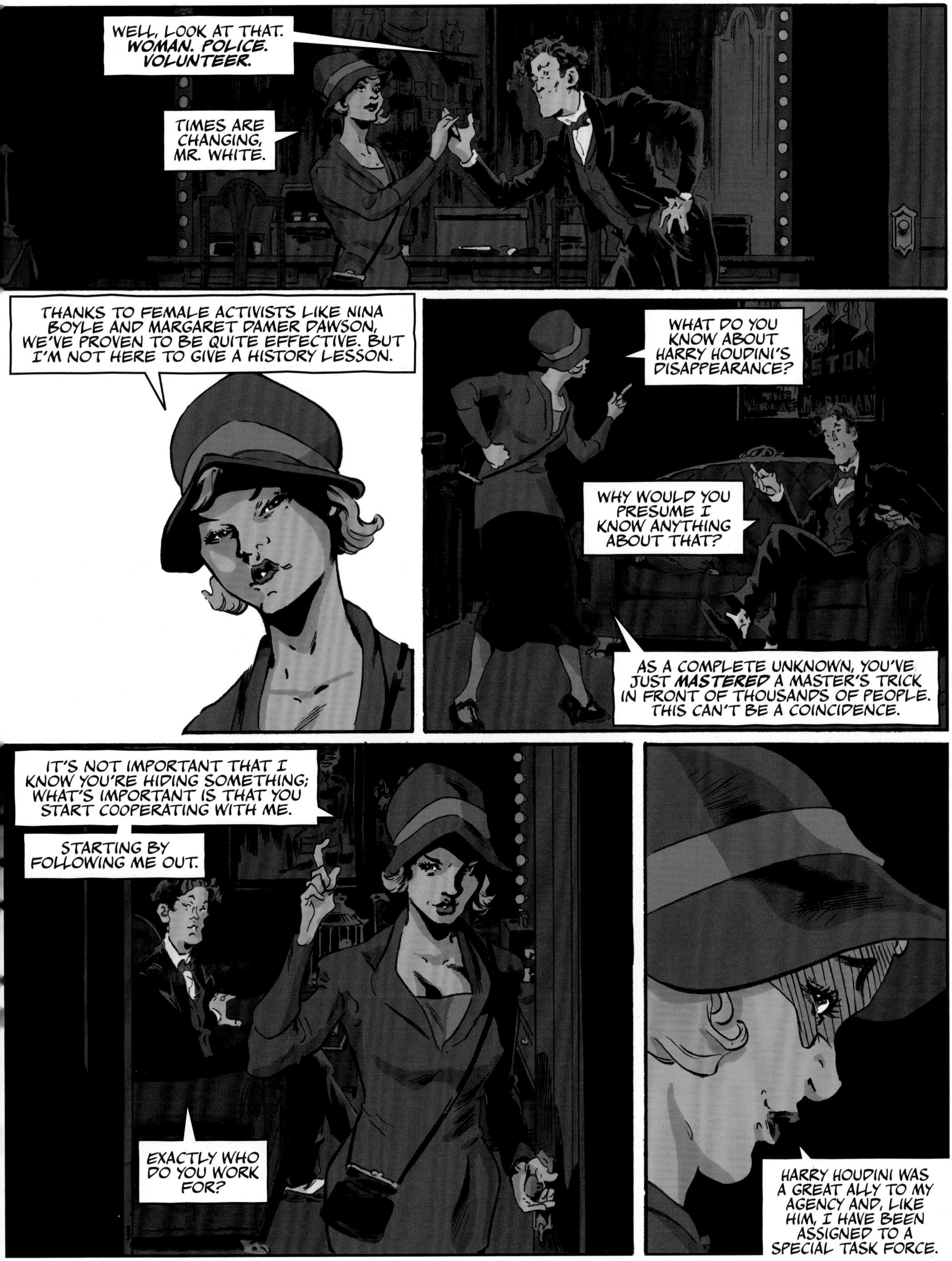
WELL, LOOK AT THAT. WOMAN. POLICE. VOLUNTEER.
TIMES ARE CHANGING, MR. WHITE.
THANKS TO FEMALE ACTIVISTS LIKE NINA BOYLE AND MARGARET DAMER DAWSON, WE'VE PROVEN TO BE QUITE EFFECTIVE. BUT I'M NOT HERE TO GIVE A HISTORY LESSON.
WHAT DO YOU KNOW ABOUT HARRY HOUDINI'S DISAPPEARANCE?
WHY WOULD YOU PRESUME I KNOW ANYTHING ABOUT THAT?
AS A COMPLETE UNKNOWN, YOU'VE JUST MASTERED A MASTER'S TRICK IN FRONT OF THOUSANDS OF PEOPLE. THIS CAN'T BE A COINCIDENCE.
IT'S NOT IMPORTANT THAT I KNOW YOU'RE HIDING SOMETHING; WHAT'S IMPORTANT IS THAT YOU START COOPERATING WITH ME.
STARTING BY FOLLOWING ME OUT.
EXACTLY WHO DO YOU WORK FOR?
HARRY HOUDINI WAS A GREAT ALLY TO MY AGENCY AND, LIKE HIM, I HAVE BEEN ASSIGNED TO A SPECIAL TASK FORCE.

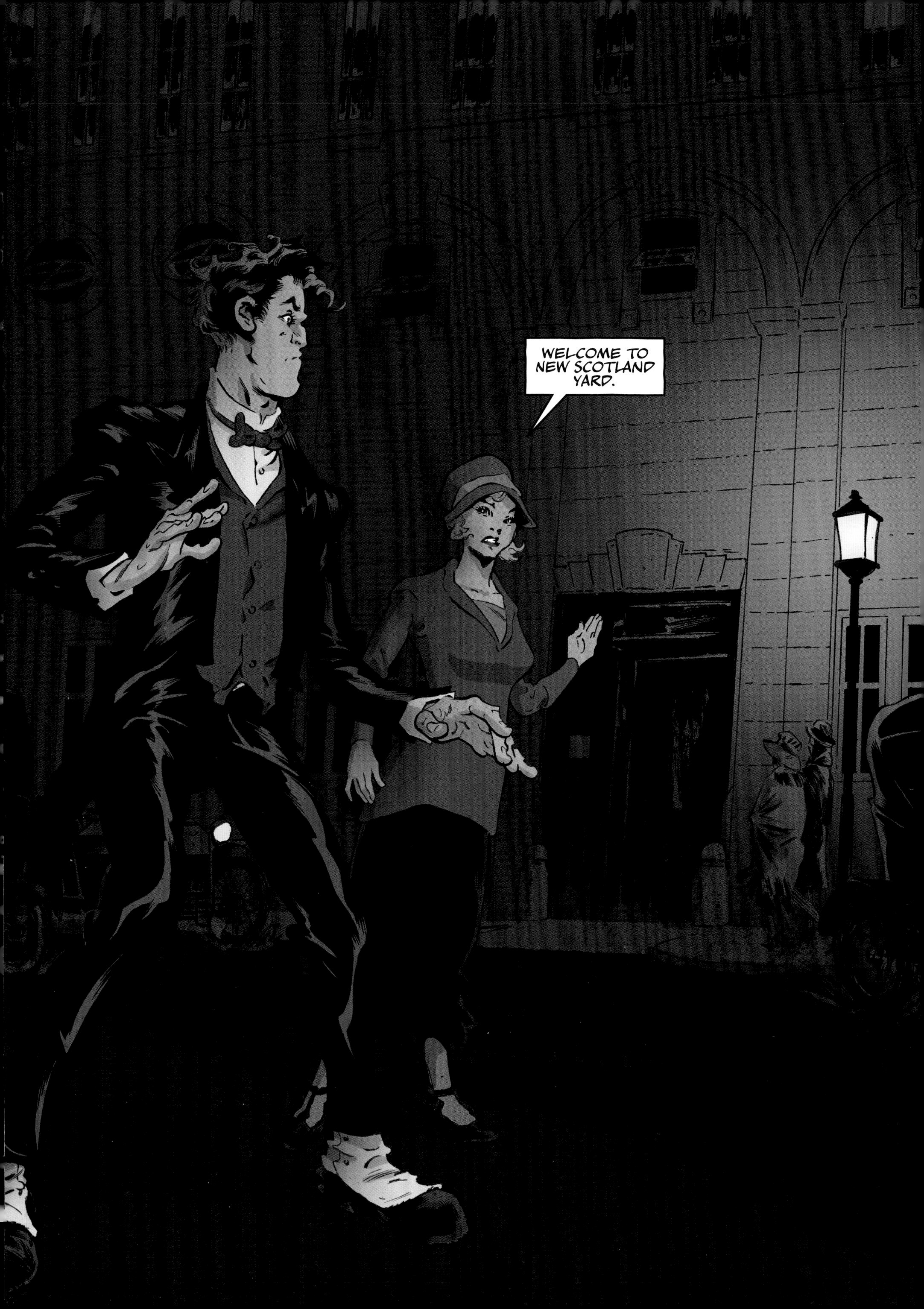
WELCOME TO NEW SCOTLAND YARD.

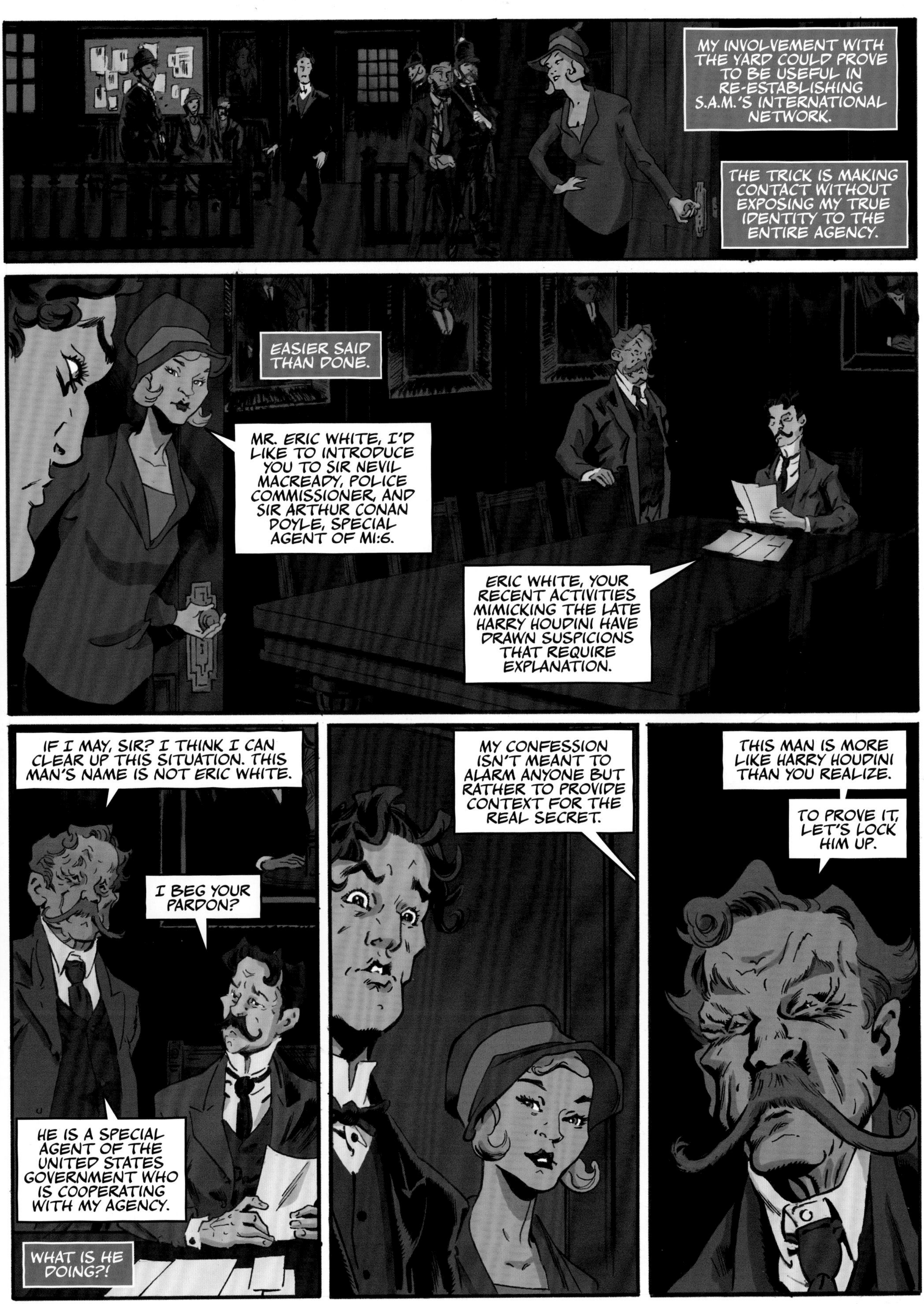
MY INVOLVEMENT WITH THE YARD COULD PROVE TO BE USEFUL IN RE-ESTABLISHING S.A.M.'S INTERNATIONAL NETWORK.
THE TRICK IS MAKING CONTACT WITHOUT EXPOSING MY TRUE IDENTITY TO THE ENTIRE AGENCY.
EASIER SAID THAN DONE.
MR. ERIC WHITE, I'D LIKE TO INTRODUCE YOU TO SIR NEVIL MACREADY, POLICE COMMISSIONER, AND SIR ARTHUR CONAN DOYLE, SPECIAL AGENT OF MI:6.
ERIC WHITE, YOUR RECENT ACTIVITIES MIMICKING THE LATE HARRY HOUDINI HAVE DRAWN SUSPICIONS THAT REQUIRE EXPLANATION.
IF I MAY, SIR? I THINK I CAN CLEAR UP THIS SITUATION. THIS MAN'S NAME IS NOT ERIC WHITE.
I BEG YOUR PARDON?
HE IS A SPECIAL AGENT OF THE UNITED STATES GOVERNMENT WHO IS COOPERATING WITH MY AGENCY.
WHAT IS HE DOING?!
MY CONFESSION ISN'T MEANT TO ALARM ANYONE BUT RATHER TO PROVIDE CONTEXT FOR THE REAL SECRET.
THIS MAN IS MORE LIKE HARRY HOUDINI THAN YOU REALIZE.
TO PROVE IT, LET'S LOCK HIM UP.

MY FATHER'S FAMOUS ESCAPE FROM THIS PLACE MADE IT INEVITABLE THAT I WOULD END UP HERE.

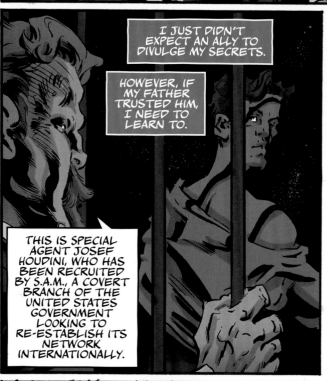

I JUST DIDN'T EXPECT AN ALLY TO DIVULGE MY SECRETS.

HOWEVER, IF MY FATHER TRUSTED HIM, I NEED TO LEARN TO.

THIS IS SPECIAL AGENT JOSEF HOUDINI, WHO HAS BEEN RECRUITED BY S.A.M., A COVERT BRANCH OF THE UNITED STATES GOVERNMENT LOOKING TO RE-ESTABLISH ITS NETWORK INTERNATIONALLY.

WHAT YOU'RE ABOUT TO WITNESS IS A DEMONSTRATION OF THEIR DEFENSE.

DEFENSE? AGAINST WHAT?

A WAR IS COMING, AND IT INVOLVES AN ENEMY THAT DEFIES ALL EARTHLY LAWS.

WITH YOUR COOPERATION, S.A.M. WOULD LIKE TO EMBED YOUR AGENCY WITH QUALIFIED AGENTS.

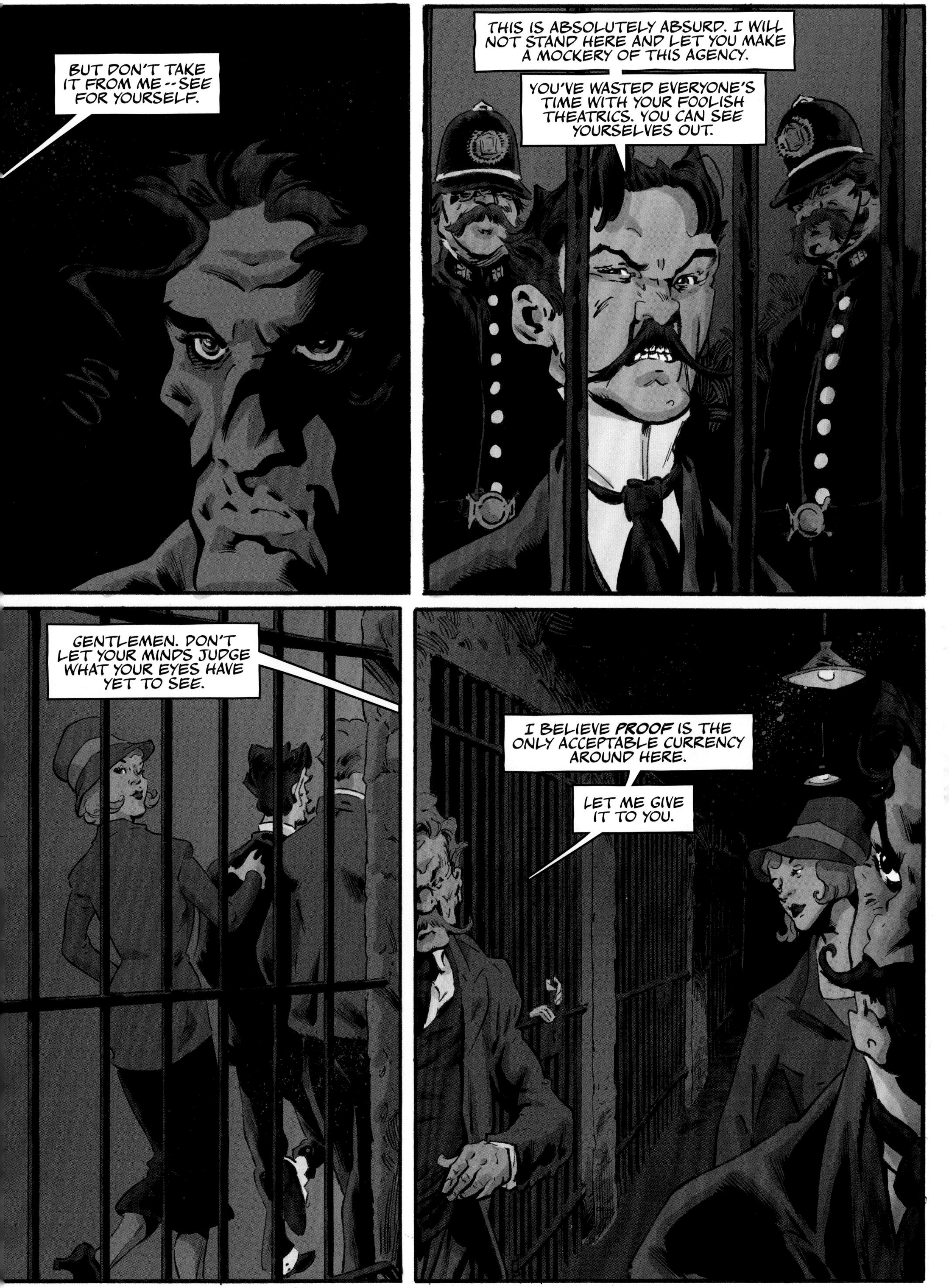
BUT DON'T TAKE IT FROM ME--SEE FOR YOURSELF.
THIS IS ABSOLUTELY ABSURD. I WILL NOT STAND HERE AND LET YOU MAKE A MOCKERY OF THIS AGENCY.
YOU'VE WASTED EVERYONE'S TIME WITH YOUR FOOLISH THEATRICS. YOU CAN SEE YOURSELVES OUT.
GENTLEMEN. DON'T LET YOUR MINDS JUDGE WHAT YOUR EYES HAVE YET TO SEE.
I BELIEVE *PROOF* IS THE ONLY ACCEPTABLE CURRENCY AROUND HERE.
LET ME GIVE IT TO YOU.

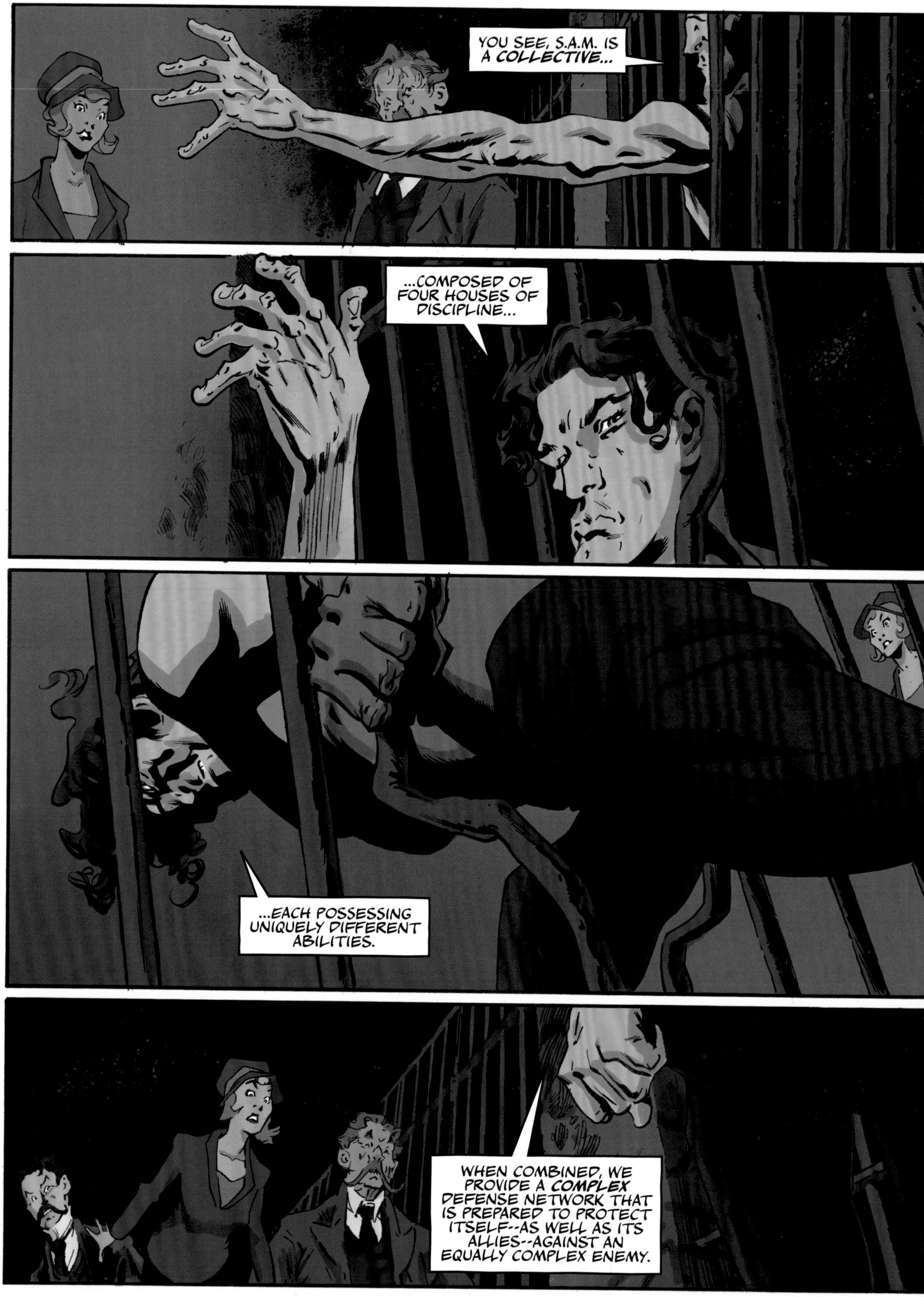
YOU SEE, S.A.M. IS A *COLLECTIVE*...
...COMPOSED OF FOUR HOUSES OF DISCIPLINE...
...EACH POSSESSING UNIQUELY DIFFERENT ABILITIES.
WHEN COMBINED, WE PROVIDE A **COMPLEX** DEFENSE NETWORK THAT IS PREPARED TO PROTECT ITSELF--AS WELL AS ITS ALLIES--AGAINST AN EQUALLY COMPLEX ENEMY.

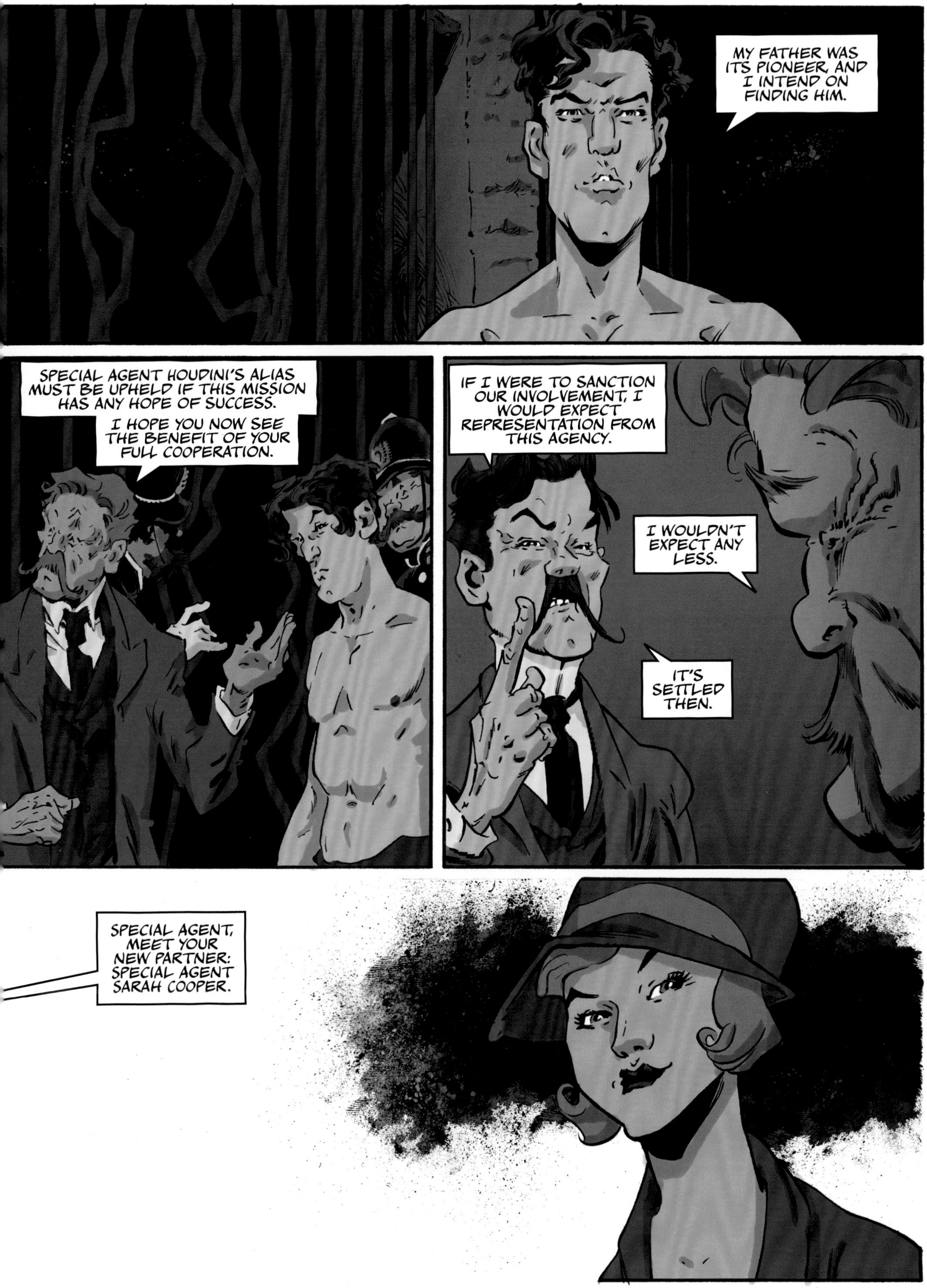
MY FATHER WAS ITS PIONEER, AND I INTEND ON FINDING HIM.
SPECIAL AGENT HOUDINI'S ALIAS MUST BE UPHELD IF THIS MISSION HAS ANY HOPE OF SUCCESS.
I HOPE YOU NOW SEE THE BENEFIT OF YOUR FULL COOPERATION.
IF I WERE TO SANCTION OUR INVOLVEMENT, I WOULD EXPECT REPRESENTATION FROM THIS AGENCY.
I WOULDN'T EXPECT ANY LESS.
IT'S SETTLED THEN.
SPECIAL AGENT, MEET YOUR NEW PARTNER: SPECIAL AGENT SARAH COOPER.

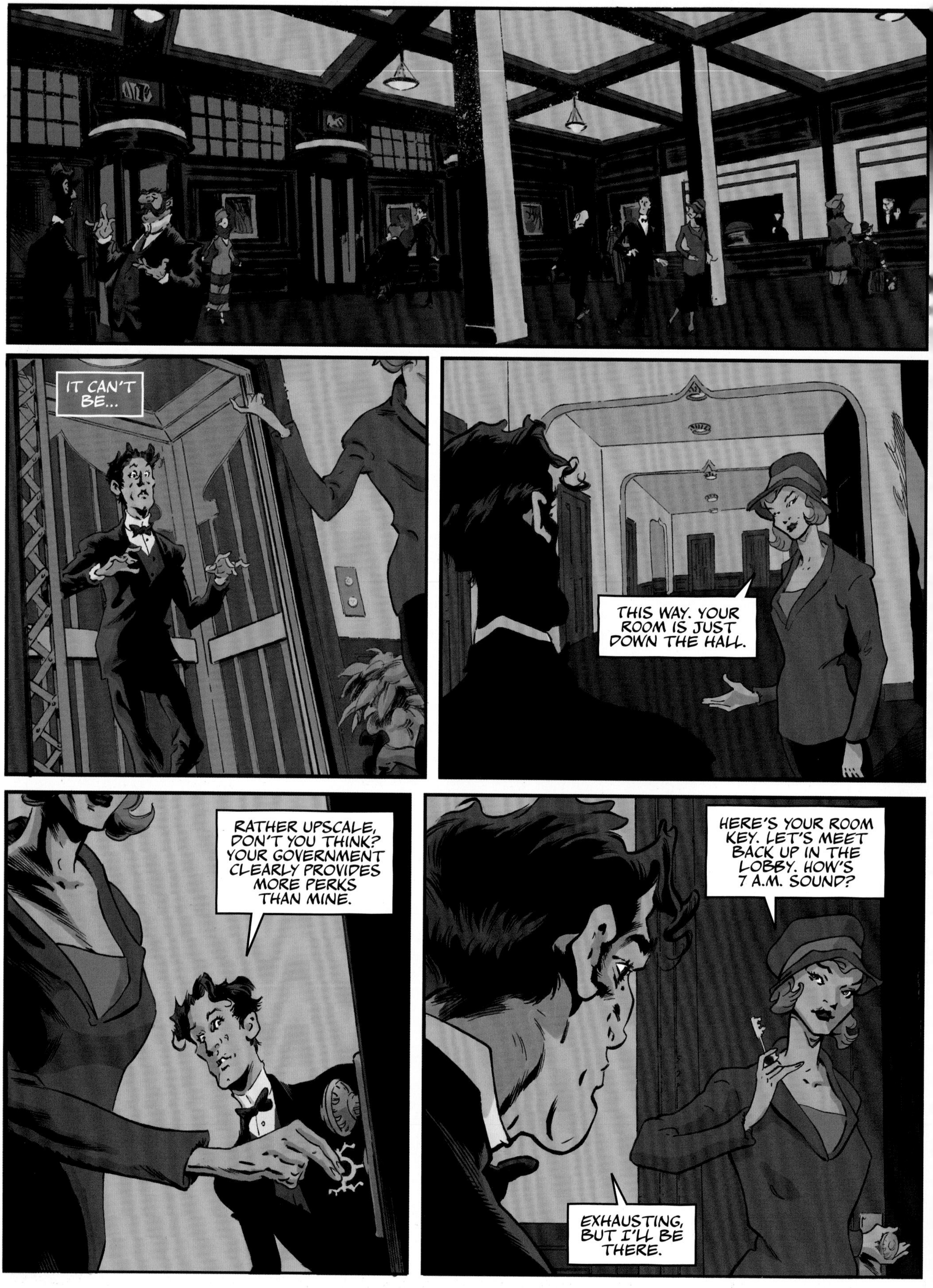
IT CAN'T BE...
THIS WAY. YOUR ROOM IS JUST DOWN THE HALL.
RATHER UPSCALE, DON'T YOU THINK? YOUR GOVERNMENT CLEARLY PROVIDES MORE PERKS THAN MINE.
HERE'S YOUR ROOM KEY. LET'S MEET BACK UP IN THE LOBBY. HOW'S 7 A.M. SOUND?
EXHAUSTING, BUT I'LL BE THERE.

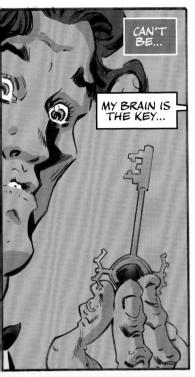

CAN'T BE...

MY BRAIN IS THE KEY...

...THAT SETS ME FREE.

WHAT DID YOU SAY?

MY BRAIN IS THE *KEY* THAT SETS ME FREE.

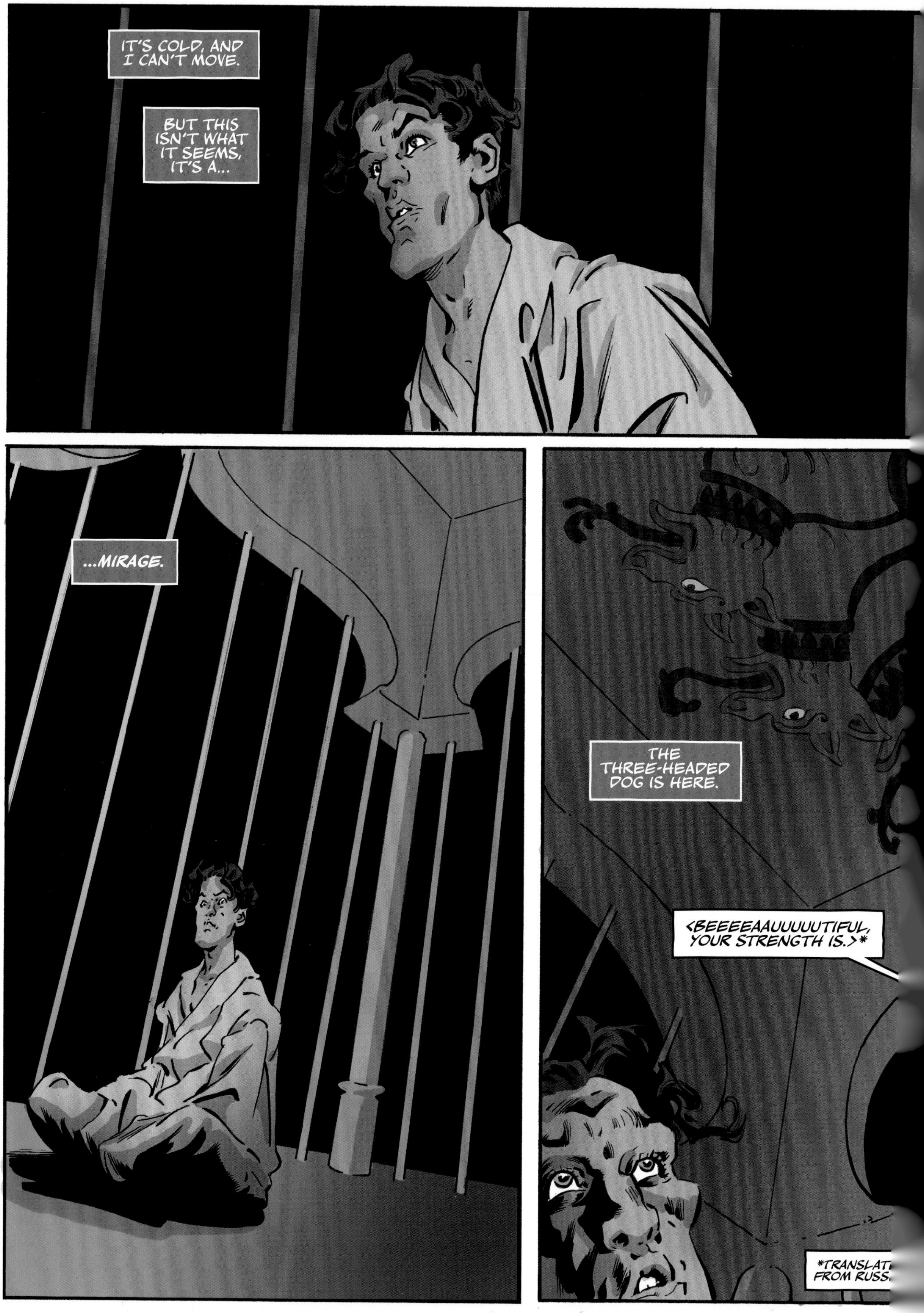
IT'S COLD, AND I CAN'T MOVE.
BUT THIS ISN'T WHAT IT SEEMS, IT'S A...
...MIRAGE.
THE THREE-HEADED DOG IS HERE.
<BEEEEAAUUUUUTIFUL, YOUR STRENGTH IS.>*
*TRANSLAT
FROM RUSS

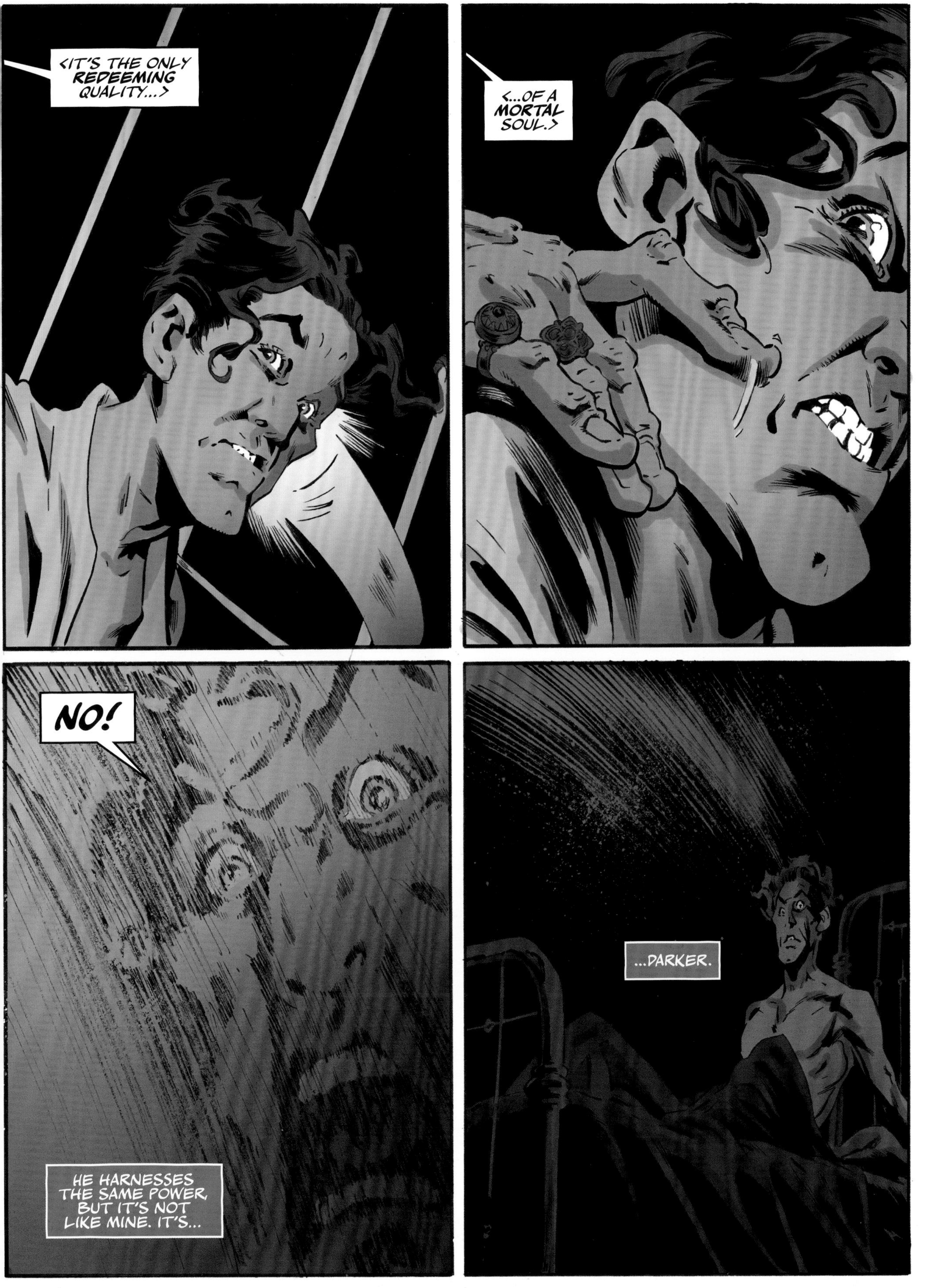

<IT'S THE ONLY REDEEMING QUALITY...>
<...OF A MORTAL SOUL.>
NO!
HE HARNESSES THE SAME POWER, BUT IT'S NOT LIKE MINE. IT'S...
...DARKER.

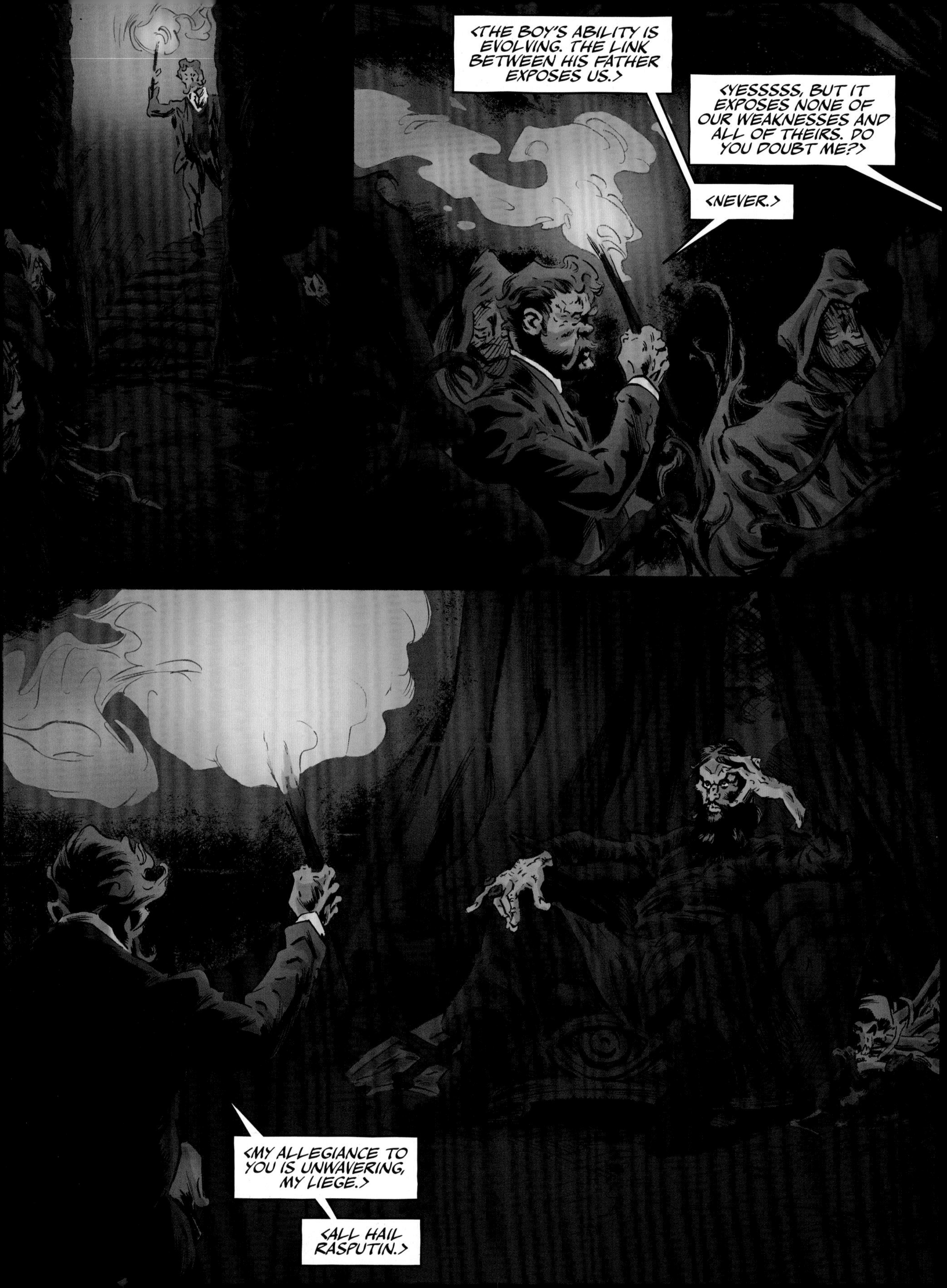

<THE BOY'S ABILITY IS EVOLVING. THE LINK BETWEEN HIS FATHER EXPOSES US.>
<YESSSSS, BUT IT EXPOSES NONE OF OUR WEAKNESSES AND ALL OF THEIRS. DO YOU DOUBT ME?>
<NEVER.>
<MY ALLEGIANCE TO YOU IS UNWAVERING, MY LIEGE.>
<ALL HAIL RASPUTIN.>

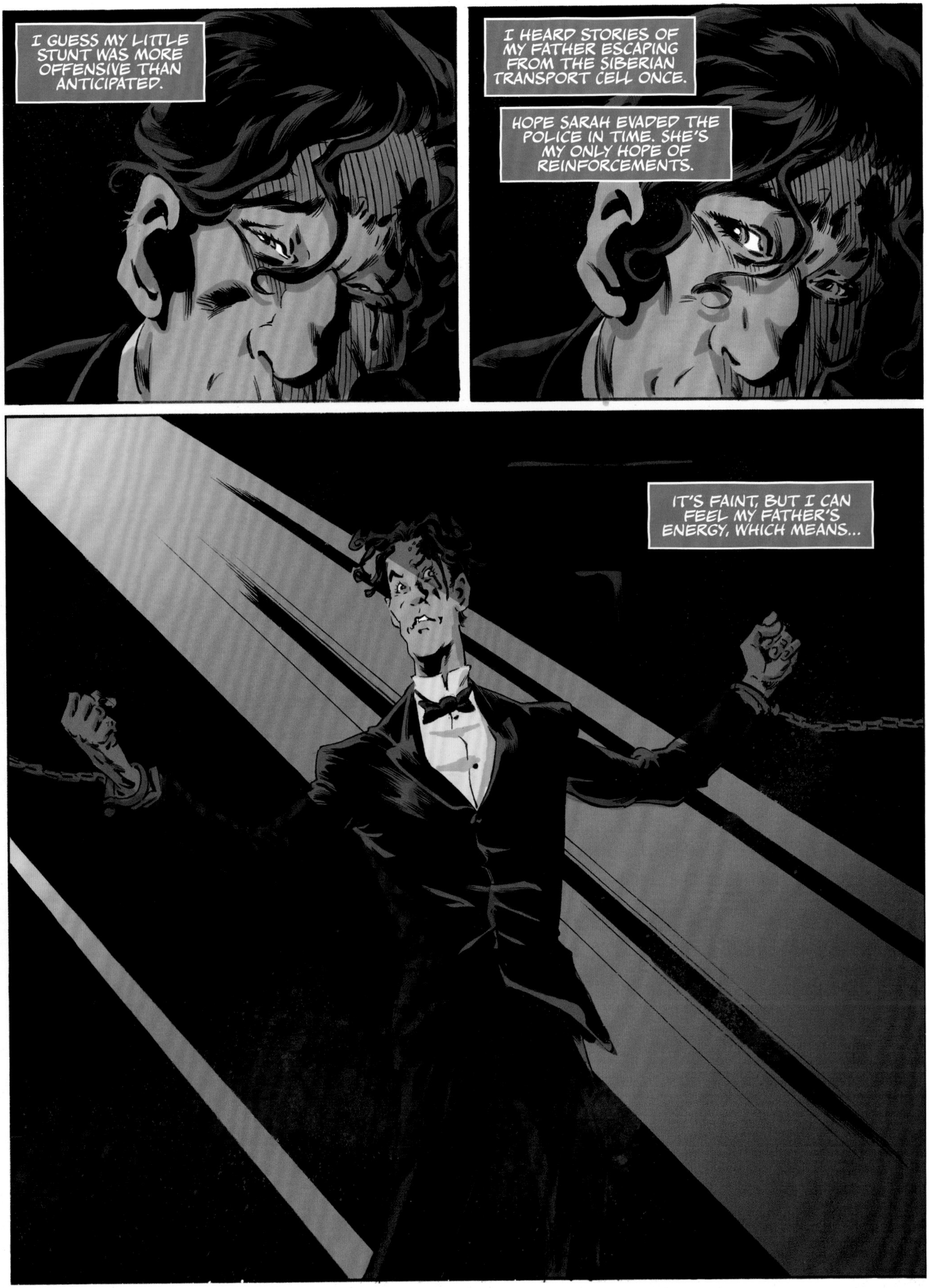
I GUESS MY LITTLE STUNT WAS MORE OFFENSIVE THAN ANTICIPATED.
I HEARD STORIES OF MY FATHER ESCAPING FROM THE SIBERIAN TRANSPORT CELL ONCE.
HOPE SARAH EVADED THE POLICE IN TIME. SHE'S MY ONLY HOPE OF REINFORCEMENTS.
IT'S FAINT, BUT I CAN FEEL MY FATHER'S ENERGY, WHICH MEANS...

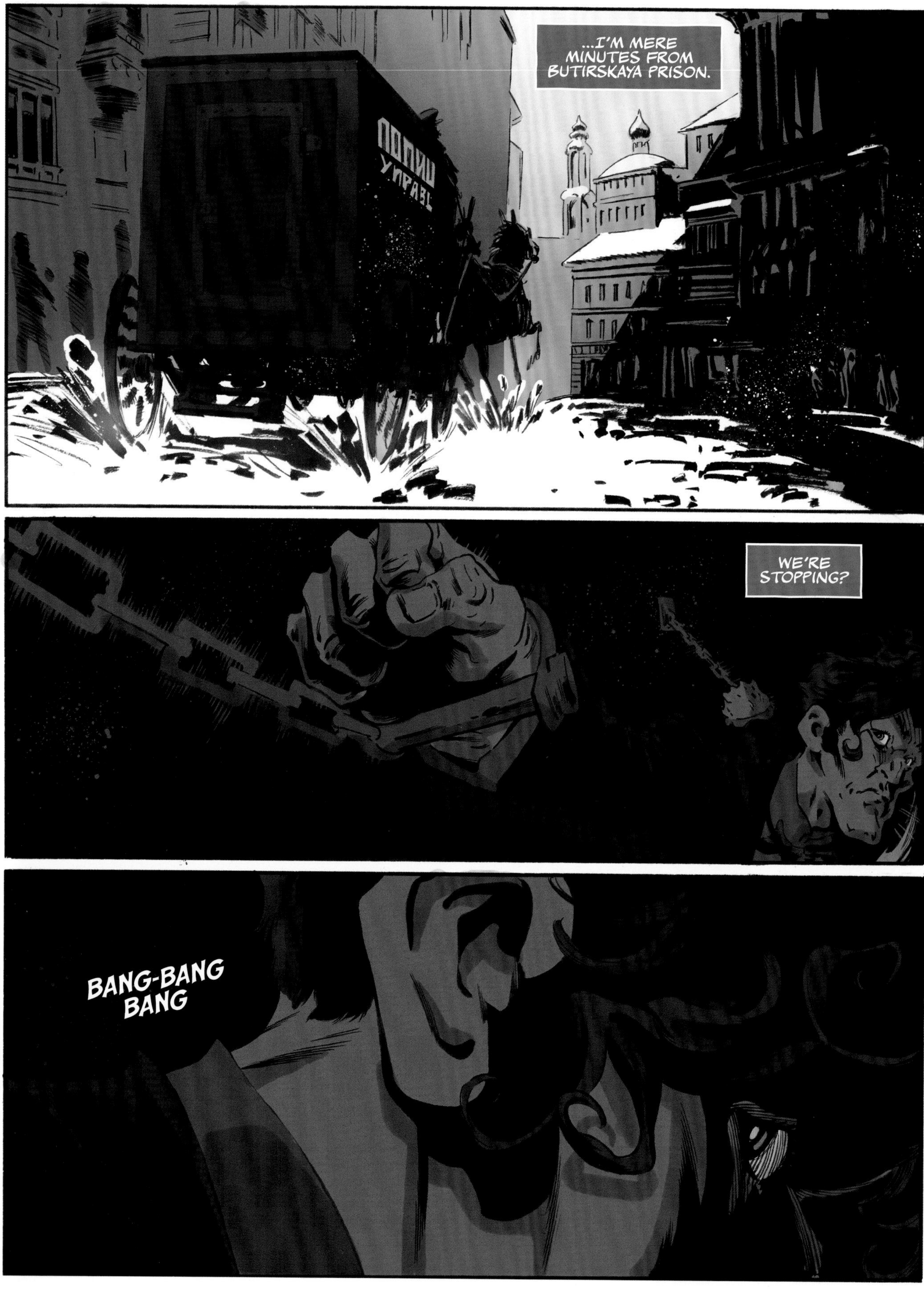
...I'M MERE MINUTES FROM BUTIRSKAYA PRISON.
WE'RE STOPPING?
BANG-BANG BANG

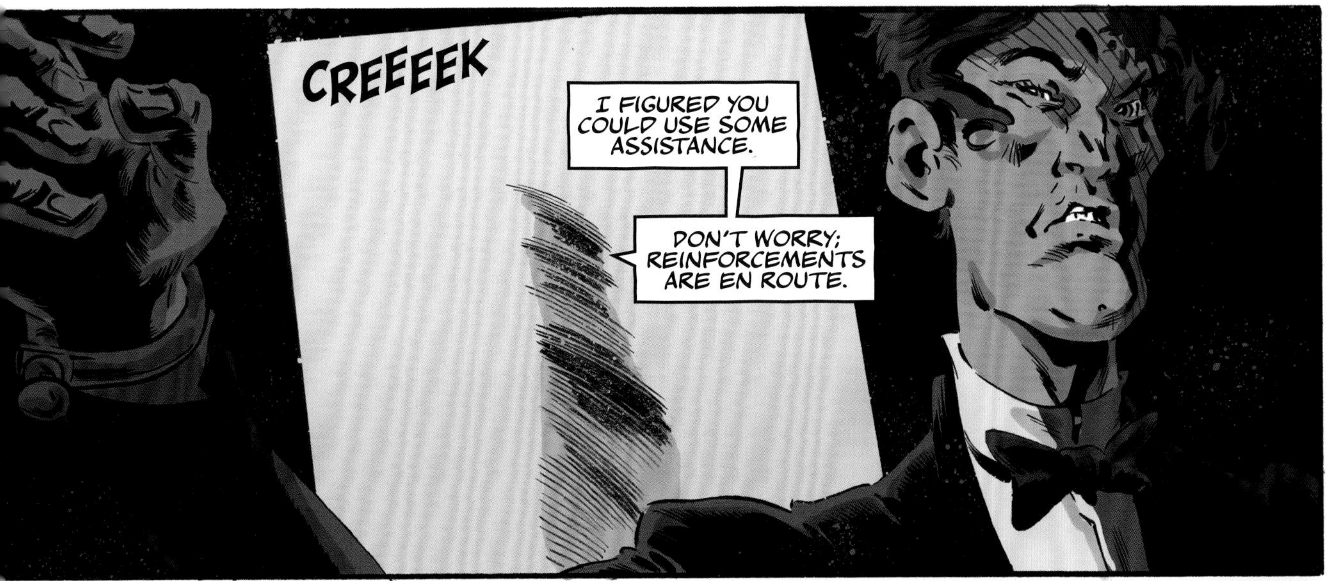
CREEEEK
I FIGURED YOU COULD USE SOME ASSISTANCE.
DON'T WORRY; REINFORCEMENTS ARE EN ROUTE.

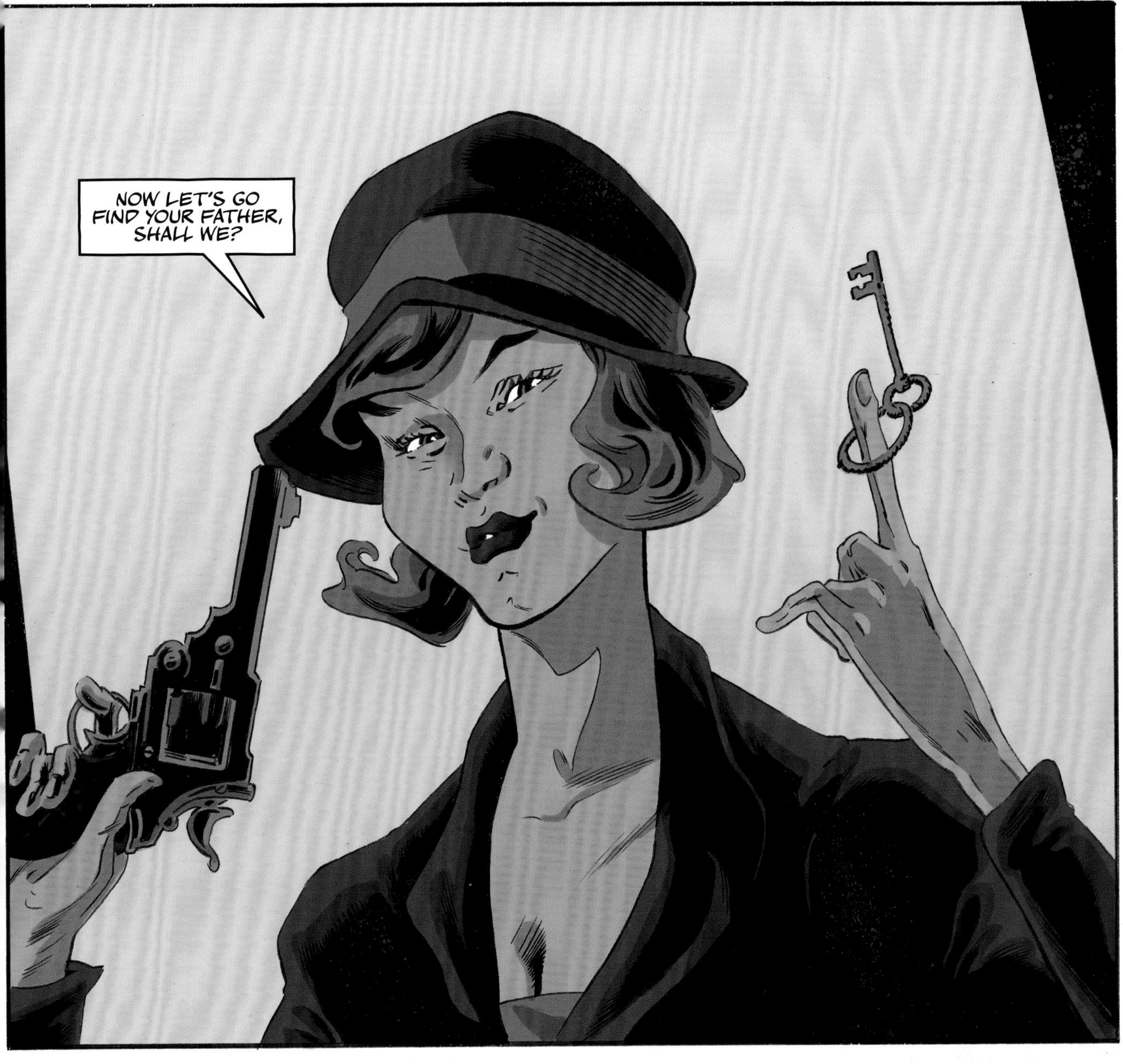
NOW LET'S GO FIND YOUR FATHER, SHALL WE?

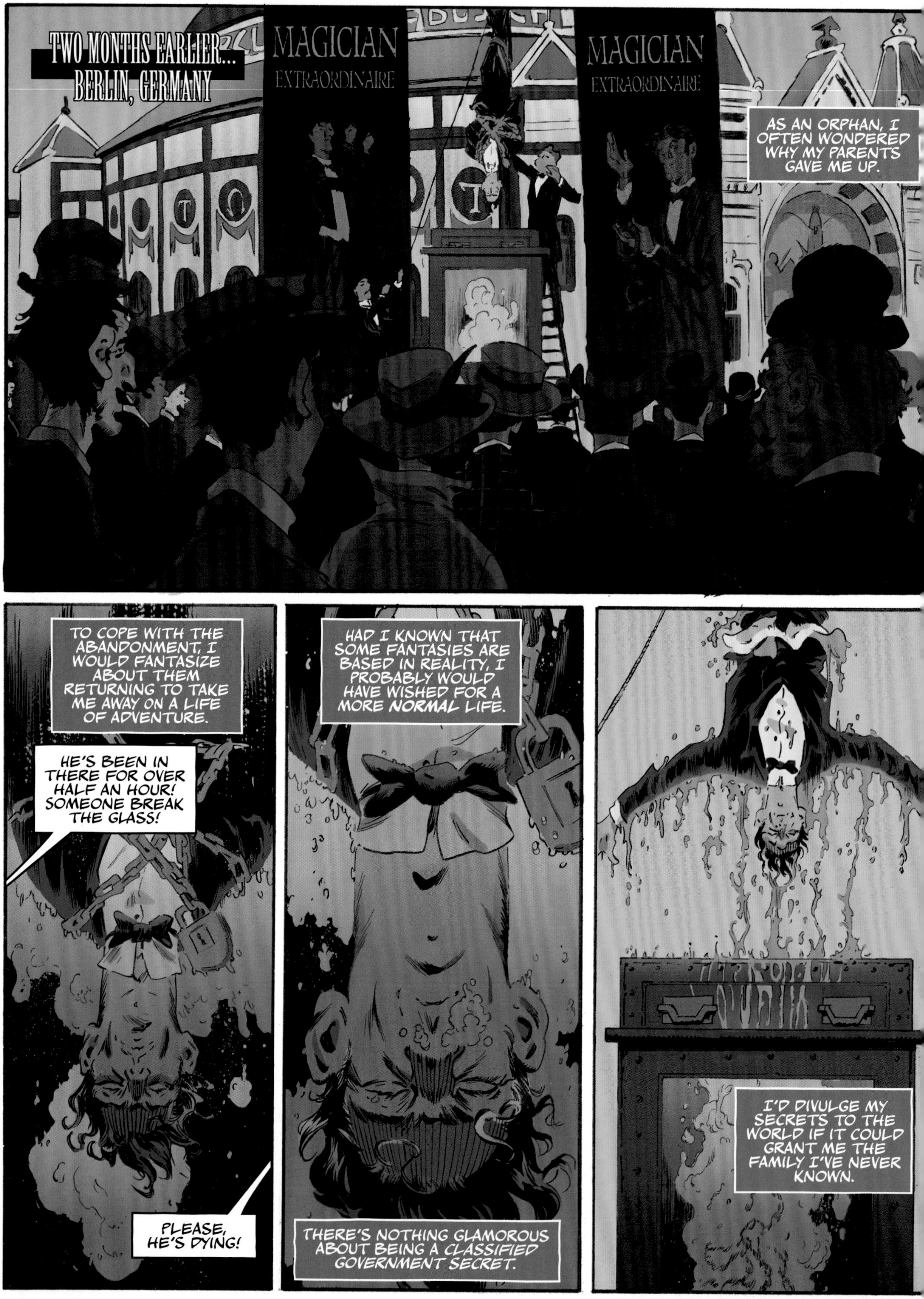
TWO MONTHS EARLIER...
BERLIN, GERMANY
MAGICIAN EXTRAORDINAIRE
MAGICIAN EXTRAORDINAIRE
AS AN ORPHAN, I OFTEN WONDERED WHY MY PARENTS GAVE ME UP.
TO COPE WITH THE ABANDONMENT, I WOULD FANTASIZE ABOUT THEM RETURNING TO TAKE ME AWAY ON A LIFE OF ADVENTURE.
HE'S BEEN IN THERE FOR OVER HALF AN HOUR! SOMEONE BREAK THE GLASS!
PLEASE, HE'S DYING!
HAD I KNOWN THAT SOME FANTASIES ARE BASED IN REALITY, I PROBABLY WOULD HAVE WISHED FOR A MORE NORMAL LIFE.
THERE'S NOTHING GLAMOROUS ABOUT BEING A CLASSIFIED GOVERNMENT SECRET.
I'D DIVULGE MY SECRETS TO THE WORLD IF IT COULD GRANT ME THE FAMILY I'VE NEVER KNOWN.

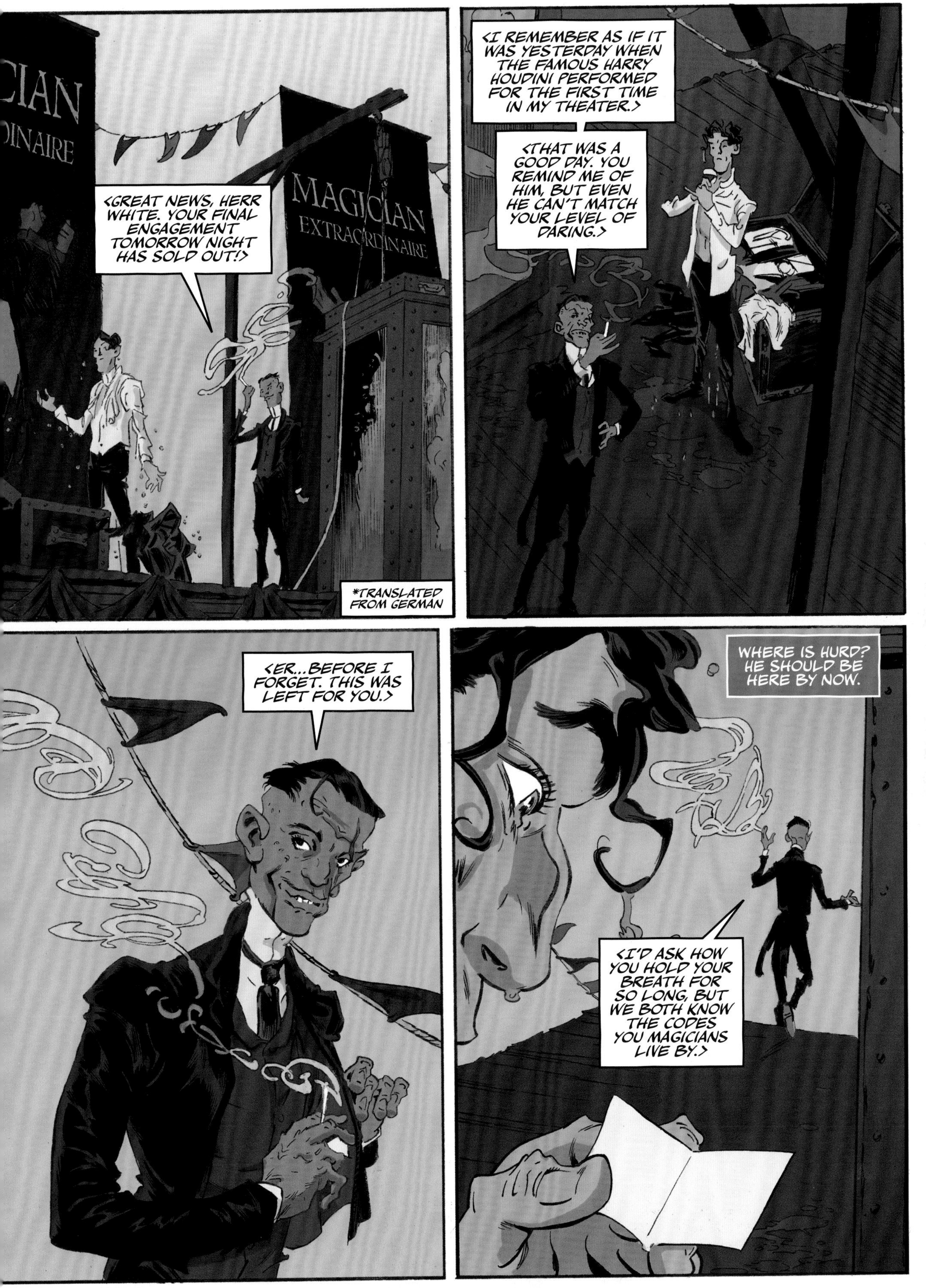
CIAN
DINAIRE
MAGICIAN
EXTRAORDINAIRE
<GREAT NEWS, HERR WHITE. YOUR FINAL ENGAGEMENT TOMORROW NIGHT HAS SOLD OUT!>
*TRANSLATED FROM GERMAN
<I REMEMBER AS IF IT WAS YESTERDAY WHEN THE FAMOUS HARRY HOUDINI PERFORMED FOR THE FIRST TIME IN MY THEATER.>
<THAT WAS A GOOD DAY. YOU REMIND ME OF HIM, BUT EVEN HE CAN'T MATCH YOUR LEVEL OF DARING.>
<ER...BEFORE I FORGET. THIS WAS LEFT FOR YOU.>
WHERE IS HURD? HE SHOULD BE HERE BY NOW.
<I'D ASK HOW YOU HOLD YOUR BREATH FOR SO LONG, BUT WE BOTH KNOW THE CODES YOU MAGICIANS LIVE BY.>

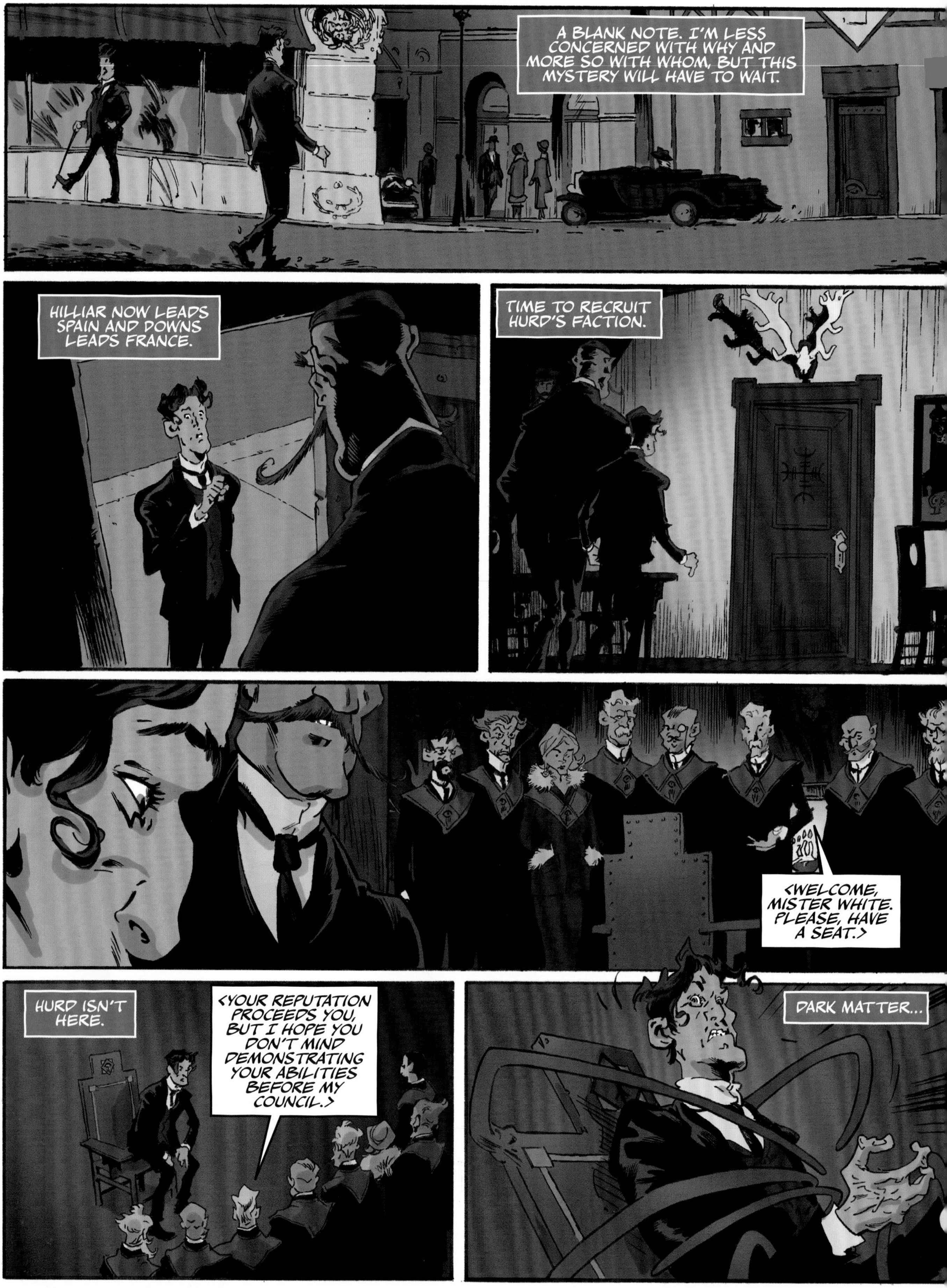
A BLANK NOTE. I'M LESS CONCERNED WITH WHY AND MORE SO WITH WHOM, BUT THIS MYSTERY WILL HAVE TO WAIT.
HILLIAR NOW LEADS SPAIN AND DOWNS LEADS FRANCE.
TIME TO RECRUIT HURD'S FACTION.
<WELCOME, MISTER WHITE. PLEASE, HAVE A SEAT.>
HURD ISN'T HERE.
<YOUR REPUTATION PROCEEDS YOU, BUT I HOPE YOU DON'T MIND DEMONSTRATING YOUR ABILITIES BEFORE MY COUNCIL.>
DARK MATTER...

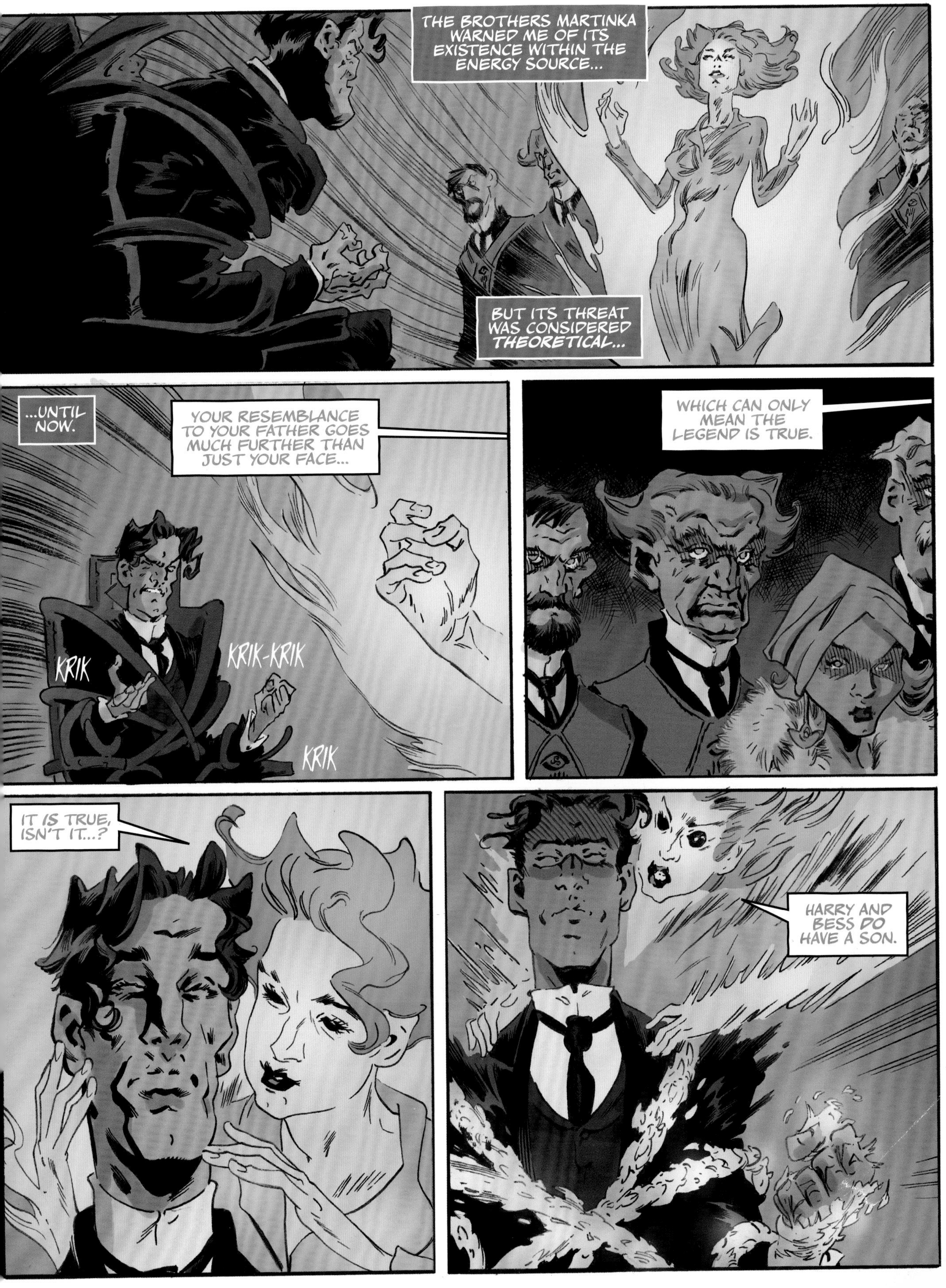
THE BROTHERS MARTINKA WARNED ME OF ITS EXISTENCE WITHIN THE ENERGY SOURCE...
BUT ITS THREAT WAS CONSIDERED *THEORETICAL*...
...UNTIL NOW.
YOUR RESEMBLANCE TO YOUR FATHER GOES MUCH FURTHER THAN JUST YOUR FACE...
KRIK
KRIK-KRIK
KRIK
WHICH CAN ONLY MEAN THE LEGEND IS TRUE.
IT *IS* TRUE, ISN'T IT...?
HARRY AND BESS *DO* HAVE A SON.

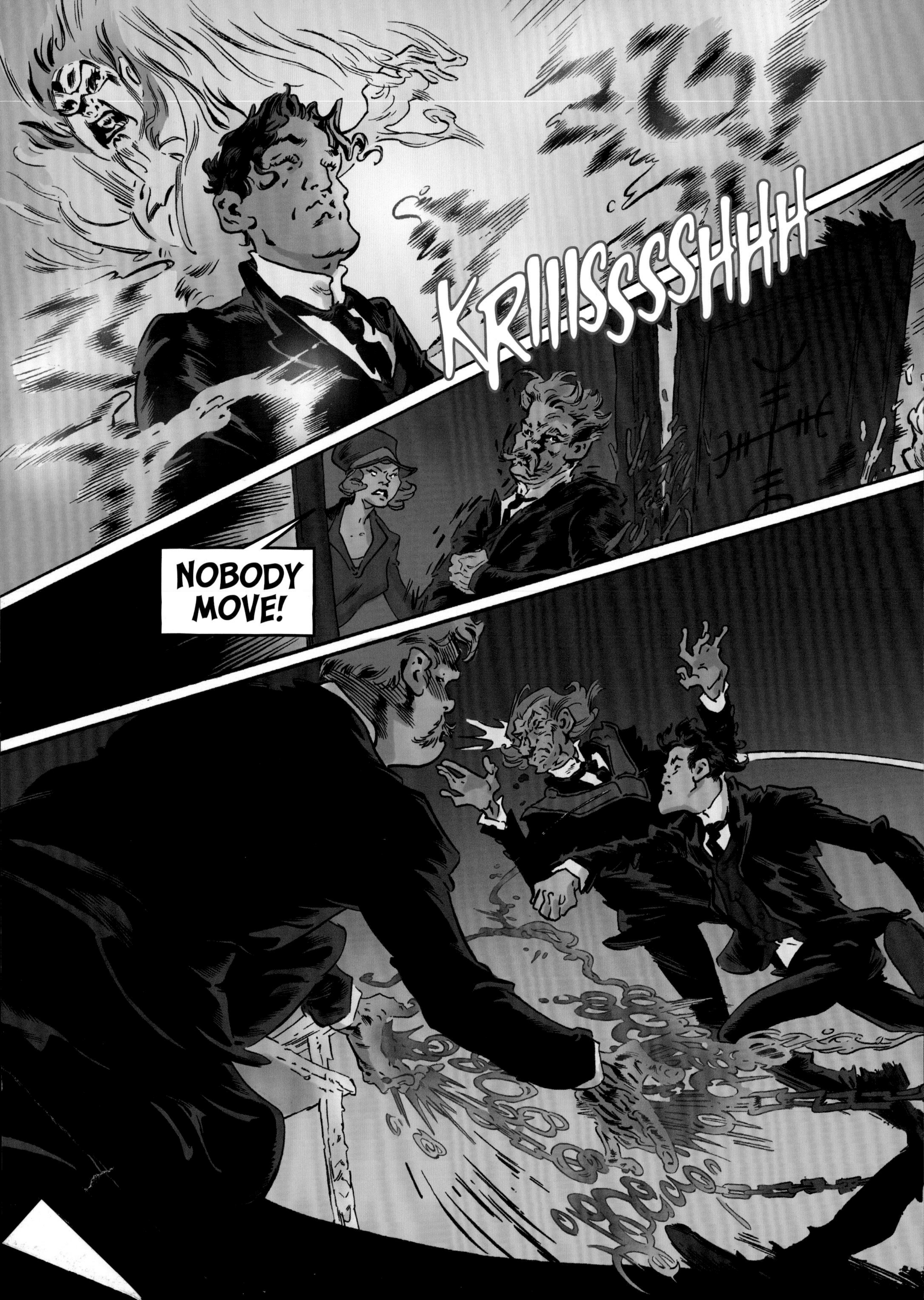
KRIIISSSSHHH
NOBODY MOVE!

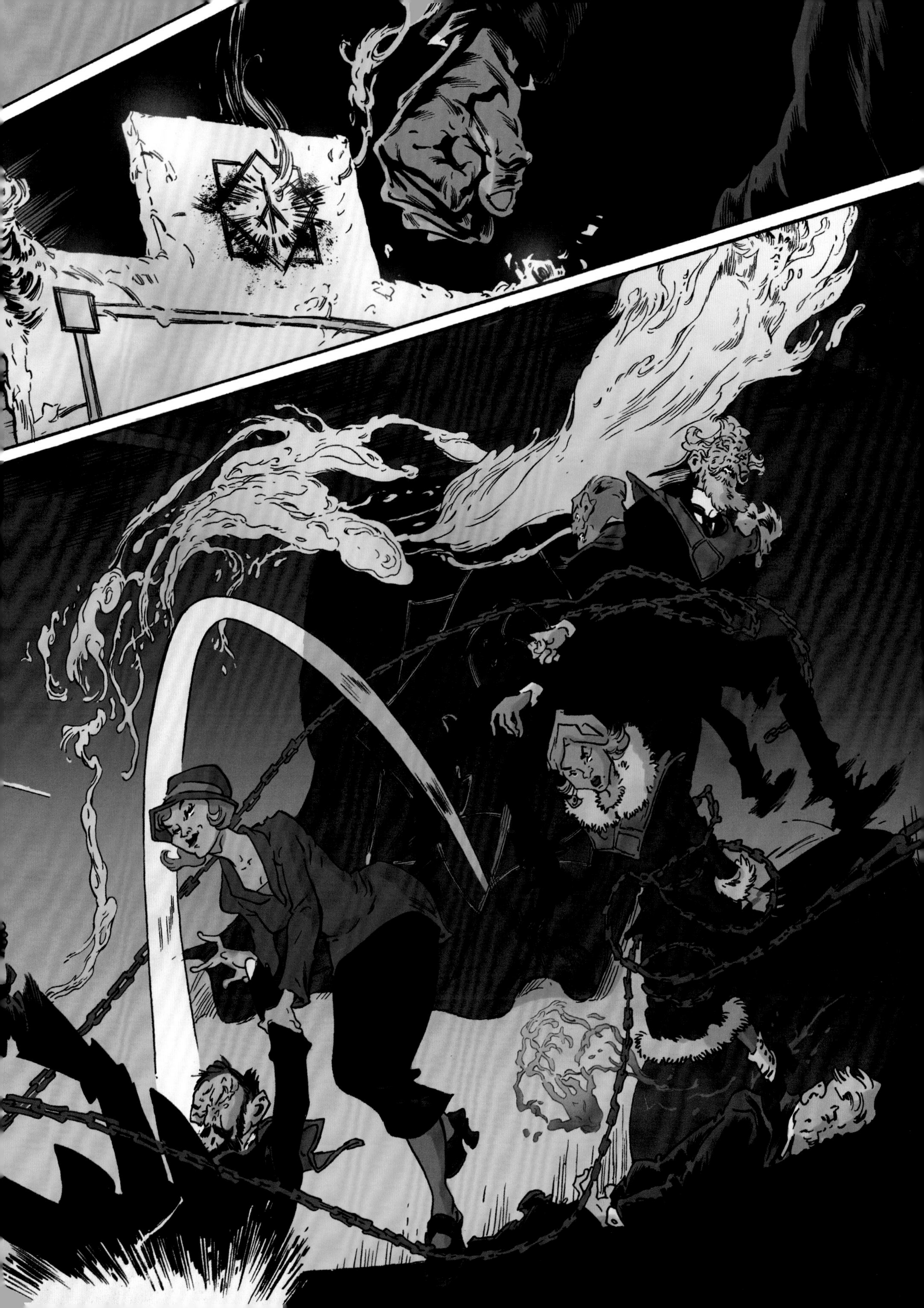

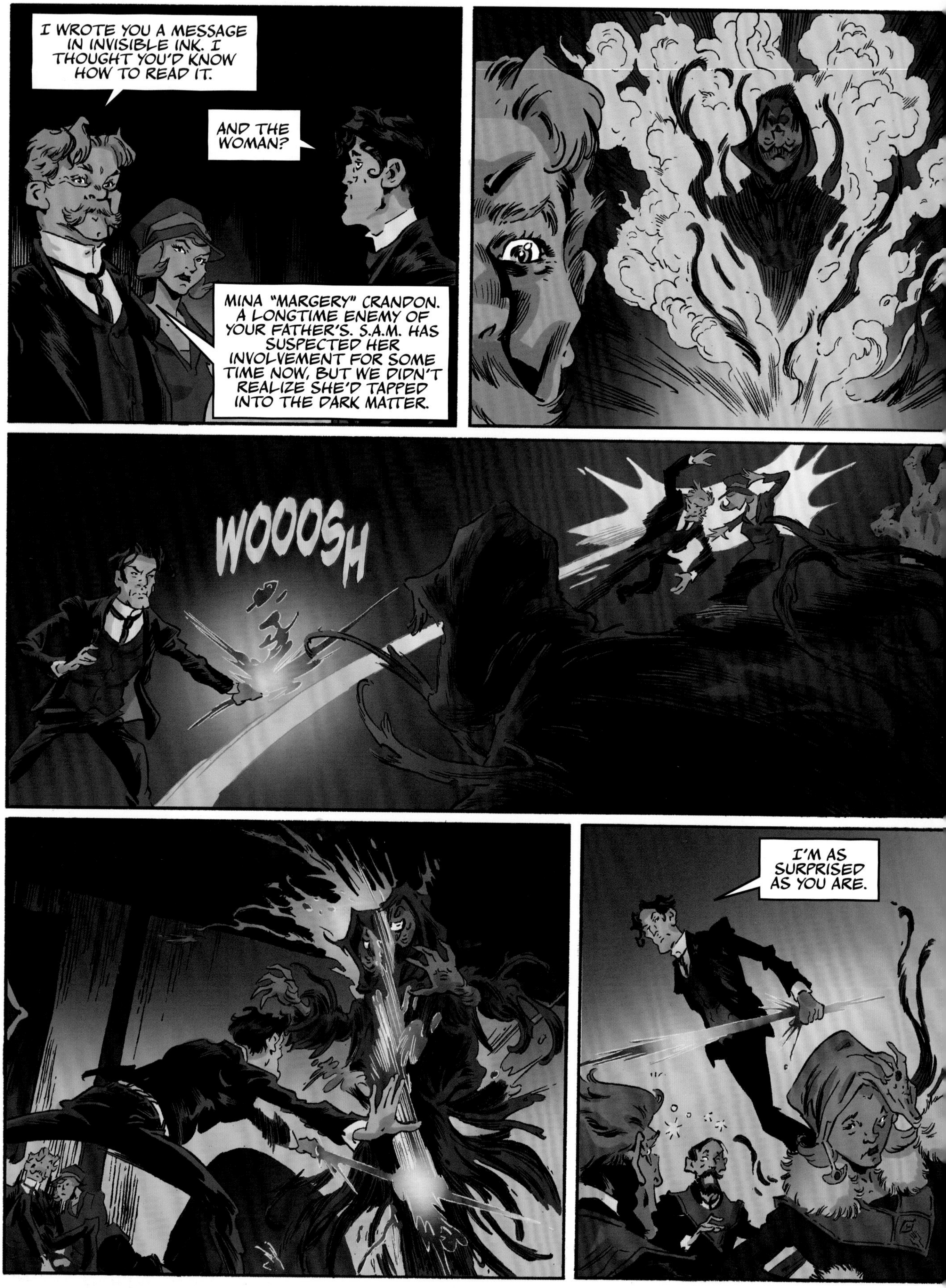
I WROTE YOU A MESSAGE IN INVISIBLE INK. I THOUGHT YOU'D KNOW HOW TO READ IT.
AND THE WOMAN?
MINA "MARGERY" CRANDON. A LONGTIME ENEMY OF YOUR FATHER'S. S.A.M. HAS SUSPECTED HER INVOLVEMENT FOR SOME TIME NOW, BUT WE DIDN'T REALIZE SHE'D TAPPED INTO THE DARK MATTER.
WOOOSH
I'M AS SURPRISED AS YOU ARE.

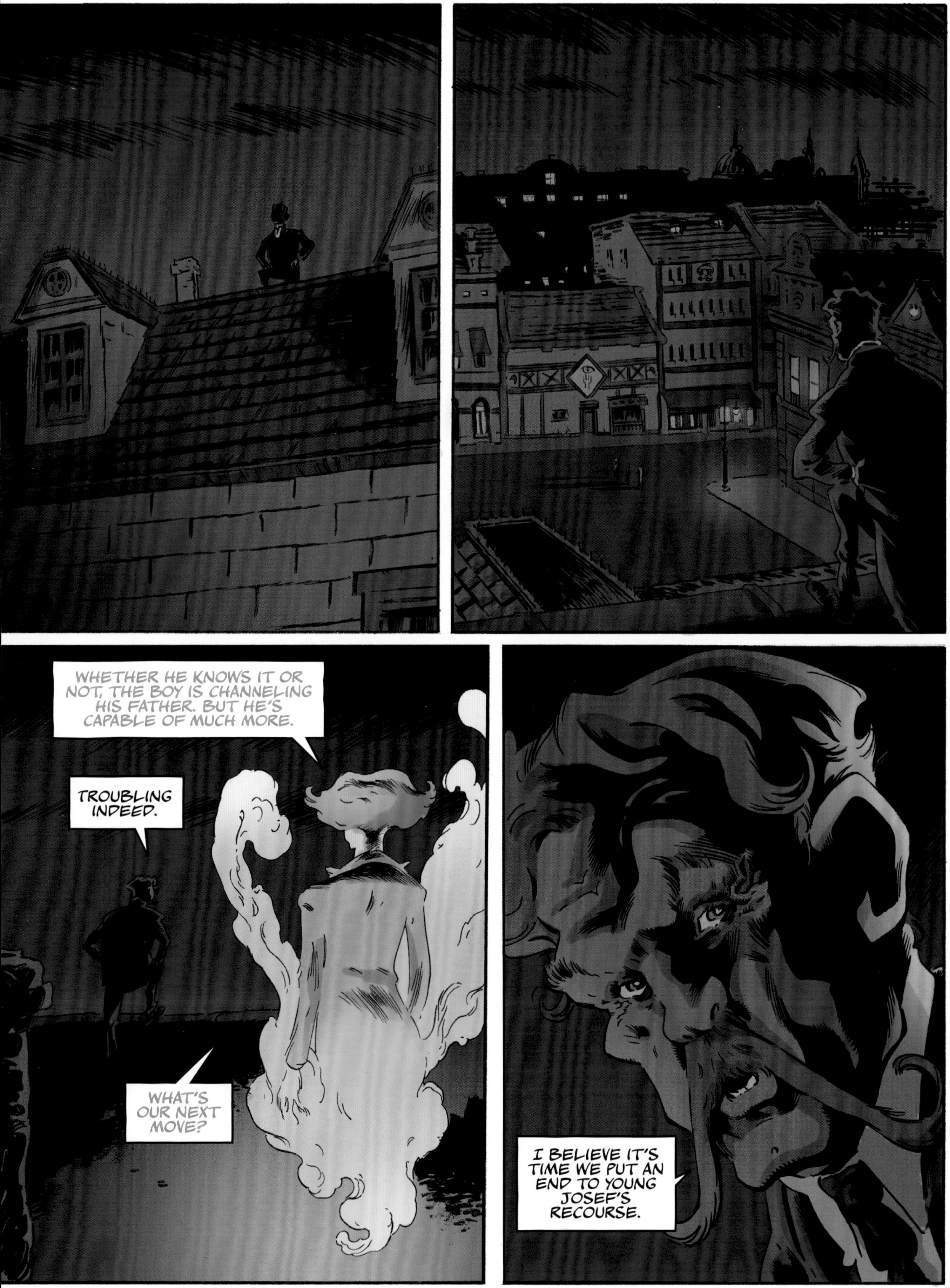
WHETHER HE KNOWS IT OR NOT, THE BOY IS CHANNELING HIS FATHER. BUT HE'S CAPABLE OF MUCH MORE.
TROUBLING INDEED.
WHAT'S OUR NEXT MOVE?
I BELIEVE IT'S TIME WE PUT AN END TO YOUNG JOSEF'S RECOURSE.

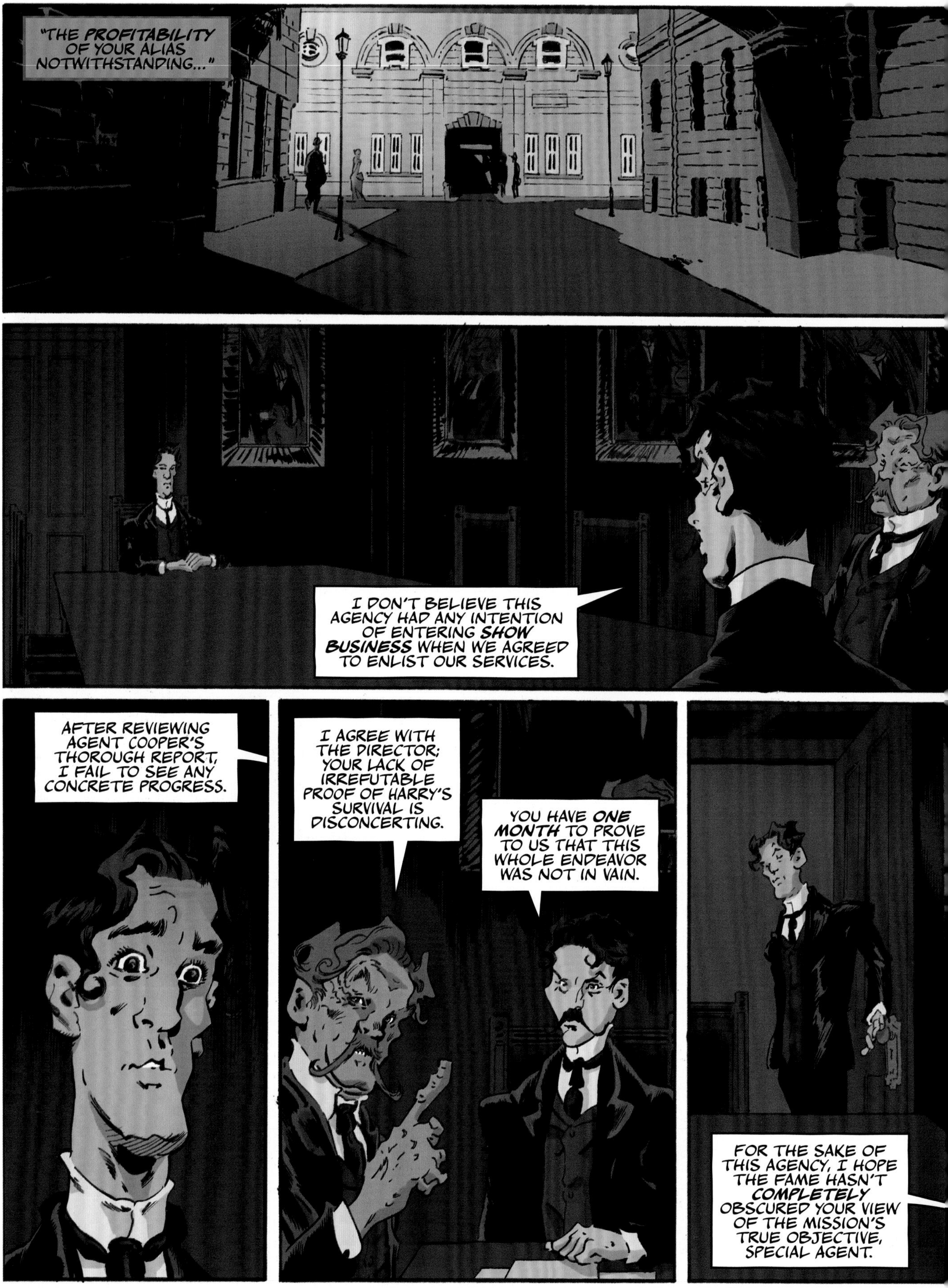
"THE PROFITABILITY OF YOUR ALIAS NOTWITHSTANDING..."
I DON'T BELIEVE THIS AGENCY HAD ANY INTENTION OF ENTERING SHOW BUSINESS WHEN WE AGREED TO ENLIST OUR SERVICES.
AFTER REVIEWING AGENT COOPER'S THOROUGH REPORT, I FAIL TO SEE ANY CONCRETE PROGRESS.
I AGREE WITH THE DIRECTOR; YOUR LACK OF IRREFUTABLE PROOF OF HARRY'S SURVIVAL IS DISCONCERTING.
YOU HAVE ONE MONTH TO PROVE TO US THAT THIS WHOLE ENDEAVOR WAS NOT IN VAIN.
FOR THE SAKE OF THIS AGENCY, I HOPE THE FAME HASN'T COMPLETELY OBSCURED YOUR VIEW OF THE MISSION'S TRUE OBJECTIVE, SPECIAL AGENT.

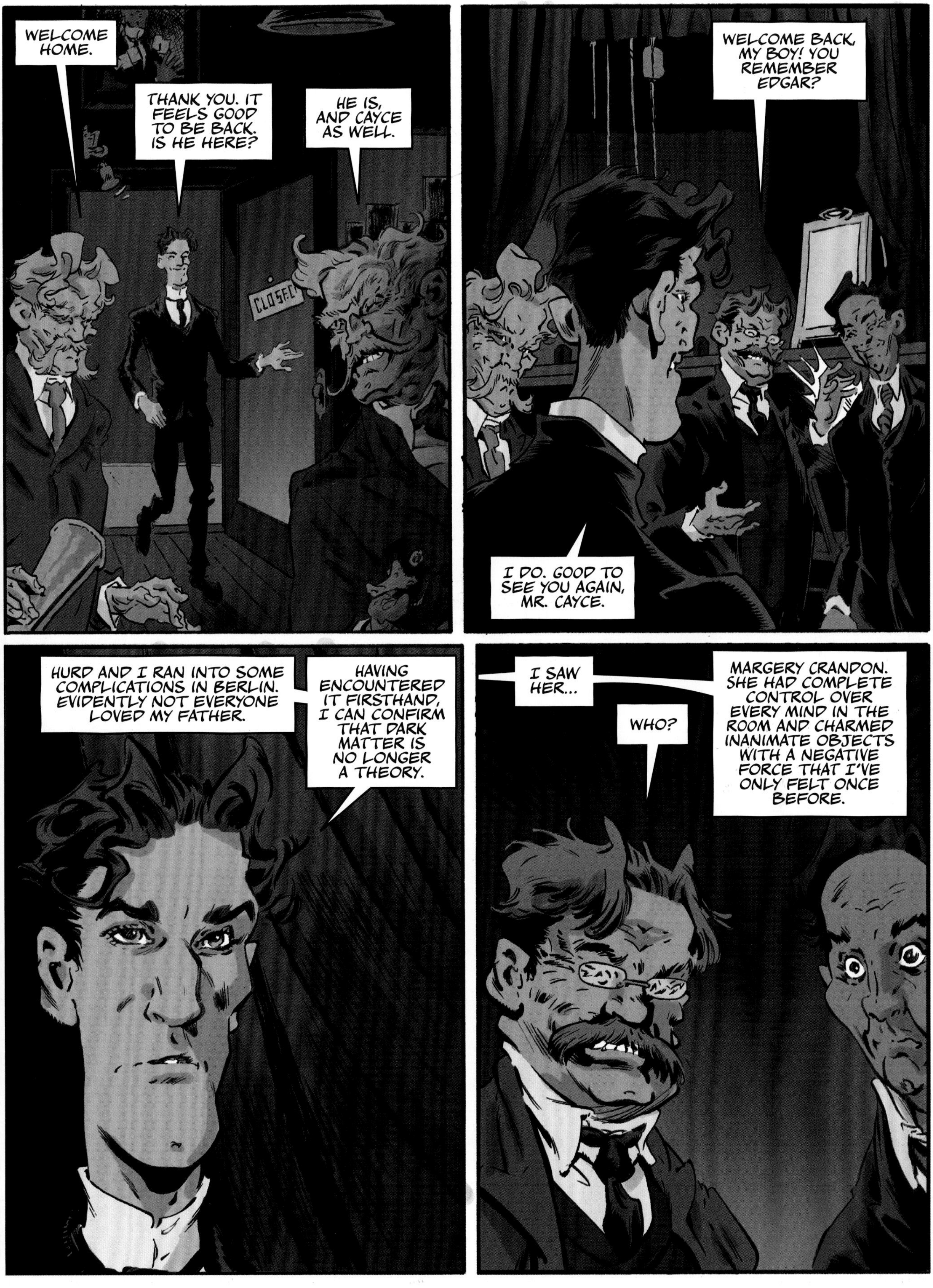
WELCOME HOME.
THANK YOU. IT FEELS GOOD TO BE BACK. IS HE HERE?
HE IS, AND CAYCE AS WELL.
CLOSED
WELCOME BACK, MY BOY! YOU REMEMBER EDGAR?
I DO. GOOD TO SEE YOU AGAIN, MR. CAYCE.
HURD AND I RAN INTO SOME COMPLICATIONS IN BERLIN. EVIDENTLY NOT EVERYONE LOVED MY FATHER.
HAVING ENCOUNTERED IT FIRSTHAND, I CAN CONFIRM THAT DARK MATTER IS NO LONGER A THEORY.
I SAW HER...
WHO?
MARGERY CRANDON. SHE HAD COMPLETE CONTROL OVER EVERY MIND IN THE ROOM AND CHARMED INANIMATE OBJECTS WITH A NEGATIVE FORCE THAT I'VE ONLY FELT ONCE BEFORE.

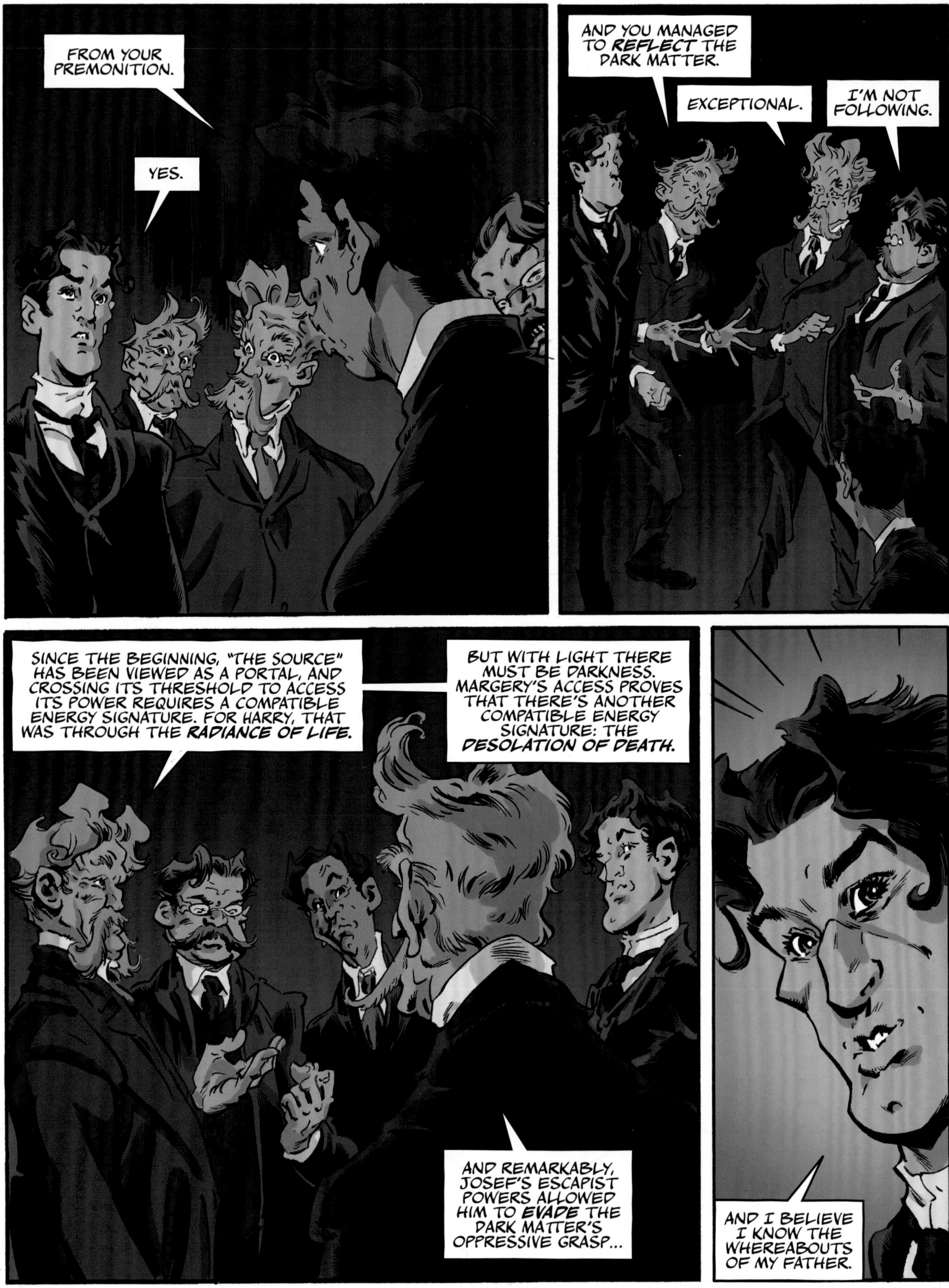
FROM YOUR PREMONITION.
YES.
AND YOU MANAGED TO *REFLECT* THE DARK MATTER.
EXCEPTIONAL.
I'M NOT FOLLOWING.
SINCE THE BEGINNING, "THE SOURCE" HAS BEEN VIEWED AS A PORTAL, AND CROSSING ITS THRESHOLD TO ACCESS ITS POWER REQUIRES A COMPATIBLE ENERGY SIGNATURE. FOR HARRY, THAT WAS THROUGH THE *RADIANCE OF LIFE*.
BUT WITH LIGHT THERE MUST BE DARKNESS. MARGERY'S ACCESS PROVES THAT THERE'S ANOTHER COMPATIBLE ENERGY SIGNATURE: THE *DESOLATION OF DEATH*.
AND REMARKABLY, JOSEF'S ESCAPIST POWERS ALLOWED HIM TO *EVADE* THE DARK MATTER'S OPPRESSIVE GRASP...
AND I BELIEVE I KNOW THE WHEREABOUTS OF MY FATHER.

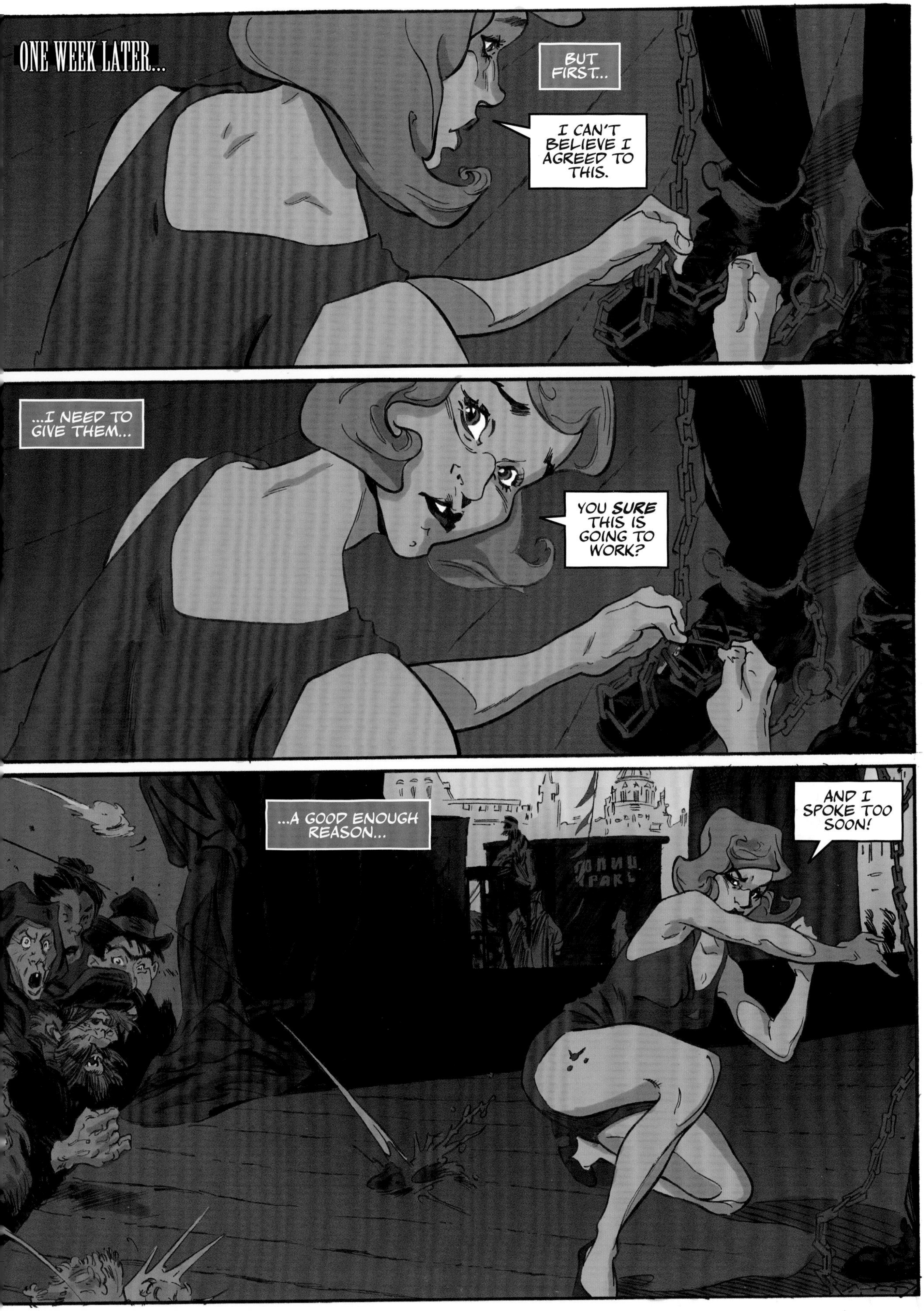
ONE WEEK LATER...
BUT FIRST...
I CAN'T BELIEVE I AGREED TO THIS.
...I NEED TO GIVE THEM...
YOU SURE THIS IS GOING TO WORK?
...A GOOD ENOUGH REASON...
AND I SPOKE TOO SOON!

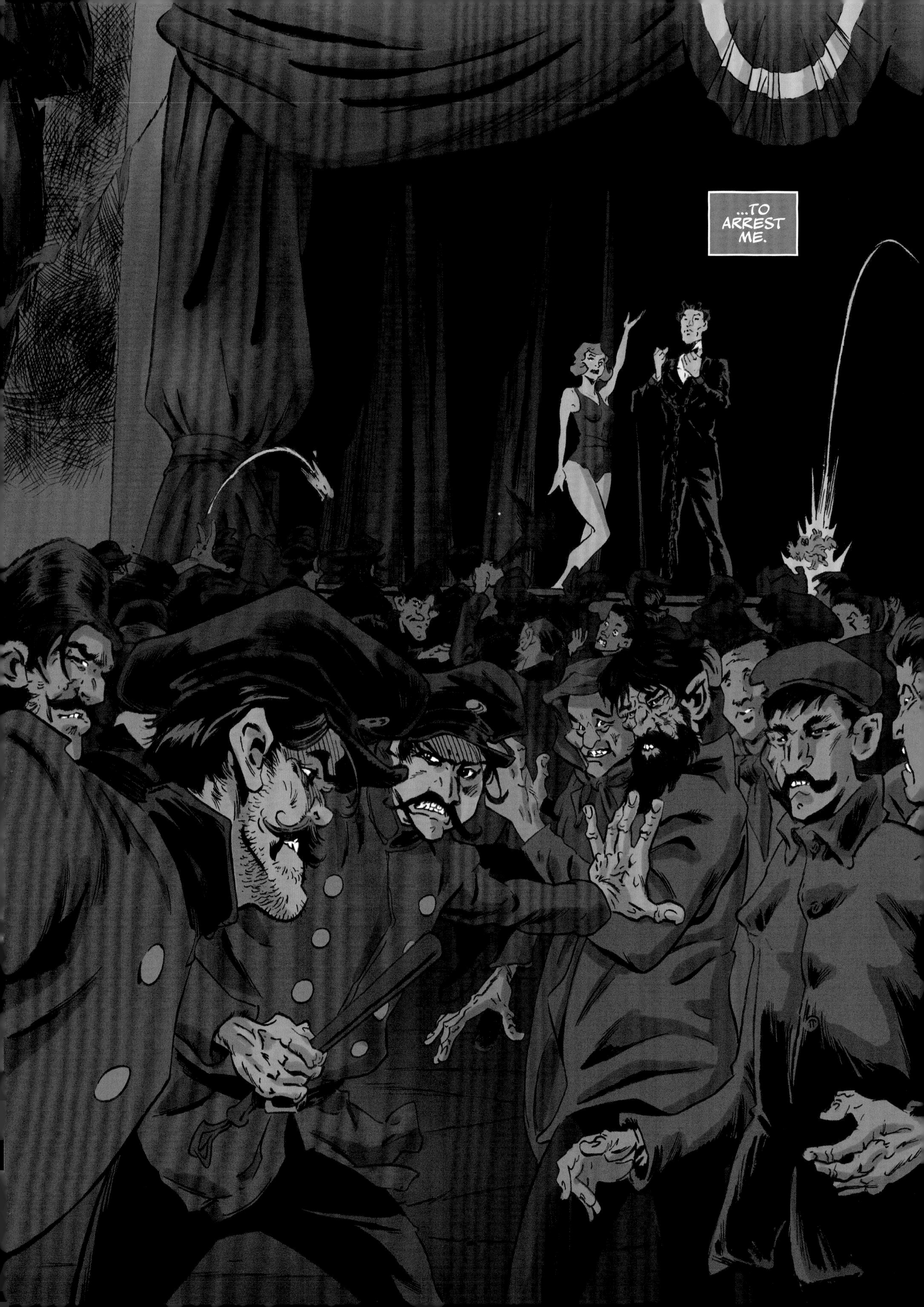
...TO
ARREST
ME.

"WHERE ARE WE ON THE VOLSTEAD ACT?"

"MR. PRESIDENT. IT APPEARS THAT THE HOUSE HAS OVERRIDDEN YOUR VETO."

"HOW DID WE LET THIS HAPPEN?"

"WAYNE WHEELER, SIR. HIS INFLUENCE IN CONGRESS RUNS DEEPER THAN WE INITIALLY THOUGHT."

"OUR LAST HOPE IS FOR A MAJORITY OF THE STATES TO REJECT THE BILL."

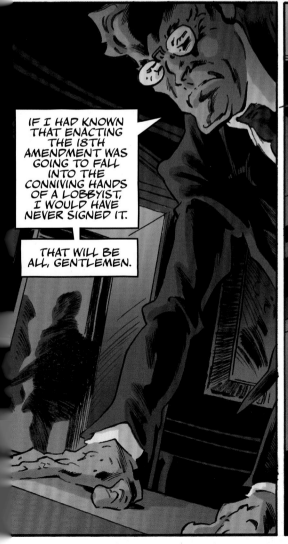

IF I HAD KNOWN THAT ENACTING THE 18TH AMENDMENT WAS GOING TO FALL INTO THE CONNIVING HANDS OF A LOBBYIST, I WOULD HAVE NEVER SIGNED IT.

THAT WILL BE ALL, GENTLEMEN.

YOU MUSTN'T BE DISCOURAGED, MR. PRESIDENT.

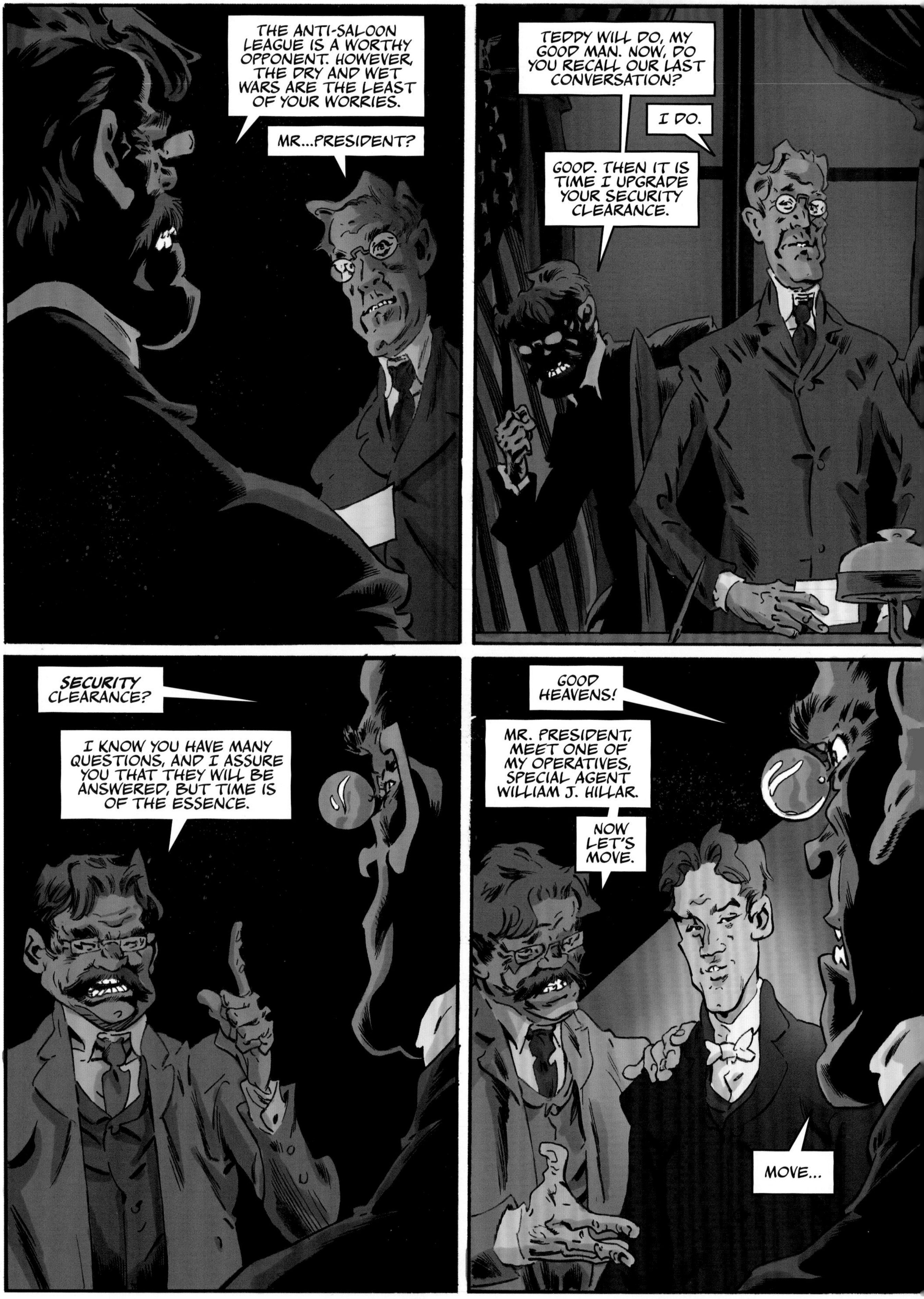
THE ANTI-SALOON LEAGUE IS A WORTHY OPPONENT. HOWEVER, THE DRY AND WET WARS ARE THE LEAST OF YOUR WORRIES.
MR...PRESIDENT?
TEDDY WILL DO, MY GOOD MAN. NOW, DO YOU RECALL OUR LAST CONVERSATION?
I DO.
GOOD. THEN IT IS TIME I UPGRADE YOUR SECURITY CLEARANCE.
SECURITY CLEARANCE?
I KNOW YOU HAVE MANY QUESTIONS, AND I ASSURE YOU THAT THEY WILL BE ANSWERED, BUT TIME IS OF THE ESSENCE.
GOOD HEAVENS!
MR. PRESIDENT, MEET ONE OF MY OPERATIVES, SPECIAL AGENT WILLIAM J. HILLAR.
NOW LET'S MOVE.
MOVE...

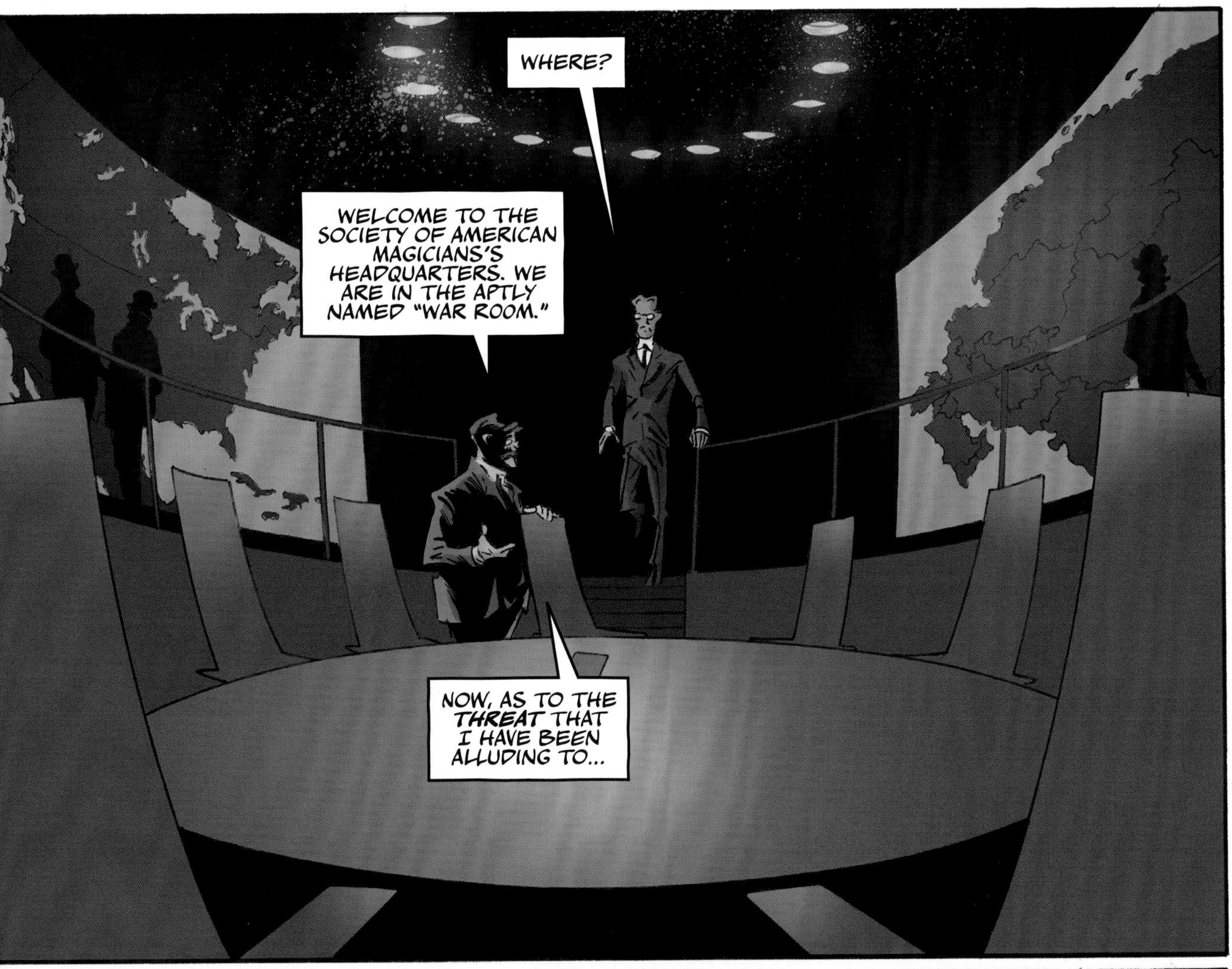
WHERE?
WELCOME TO THE SOCIETY OF AMERICAN MAGICIANS'S HEADQUARTERS. WE ARE IN THE APTLY NAMED "WAR ROOM."
NOW, AS TO THE *THREAT* THAT I HAVE BEEN ALLUDING TO...

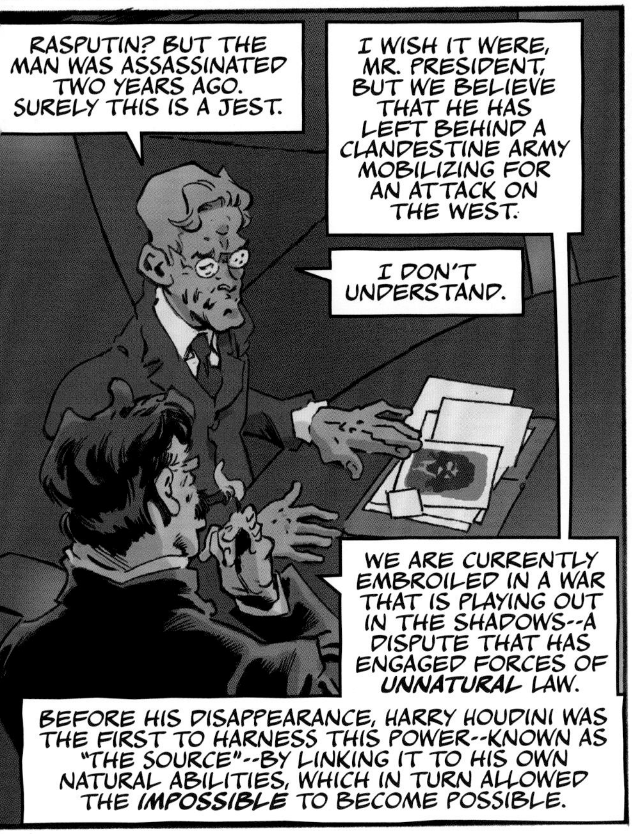
RASPUTIN? BUT THE MAN WAS ASSASSINATED TWO YEARS AGO. SURELY THIS IS A JEST.
I WISH IT WERE, MR. PRESIDENT, BUT WE BELIEVE THAT HE HAS LEFT BEHIND A CLANDESTINE ARMY MOBILIZING FOR AN ATTACK ON THE WEST.
I DON'T UNDERSTAND.
WE ARE CURRENTLY EMBROILED IN A WAR THAT IS PLAYING OUT IN THE SHADOWS--A DISPUTE THAT HAS ENGAGED FORCES OF *UNNATURAL* LAW.
BEFORE HIS DISAPPEARANCE, HARRY HOUDINI WAS THE FIRST TO HARNESS THIS POWER--KNOWN AS "THE SOURCE"--BY LINKING IT TO HIS OWN NATURAL ABILITIES, WHICH IN TURN ALLOWED THE *IMPOSSIBLE* TO BECOME POSSIBLE.

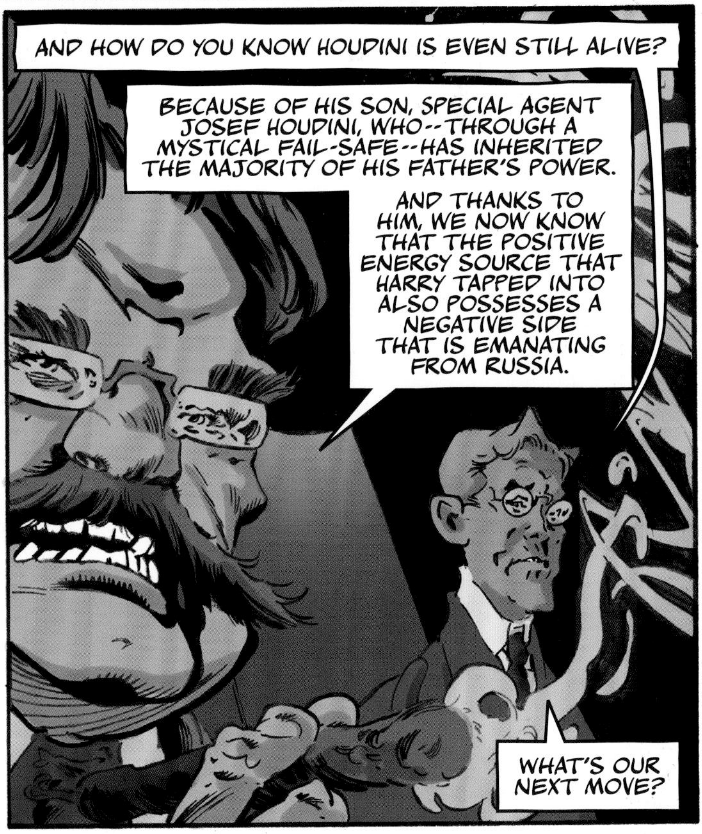
AND HOW DO YOU KNOW HOUDINI IS EVEN STILL ALIVE?
BECAUSE OF HIS SON, SPECIAL AGENT JOSEF HOUDINI, WHO--THROUGH A MYSTICAL FAIL-SAFE--HAS INHERITED THE MAJORITY OF HIS FATHER'S POWER.
AND THANKS TO HIM, WE NOW KNOW THAT THE POSITIVE ENERGY SOURCE THAT HARRY TAPPED INTO ALSO POSSESSES A NEGATIVE SIDE THAT IS EMANATING FROM RUSSIA.
WHAT'S OUR NEXT MOVE?

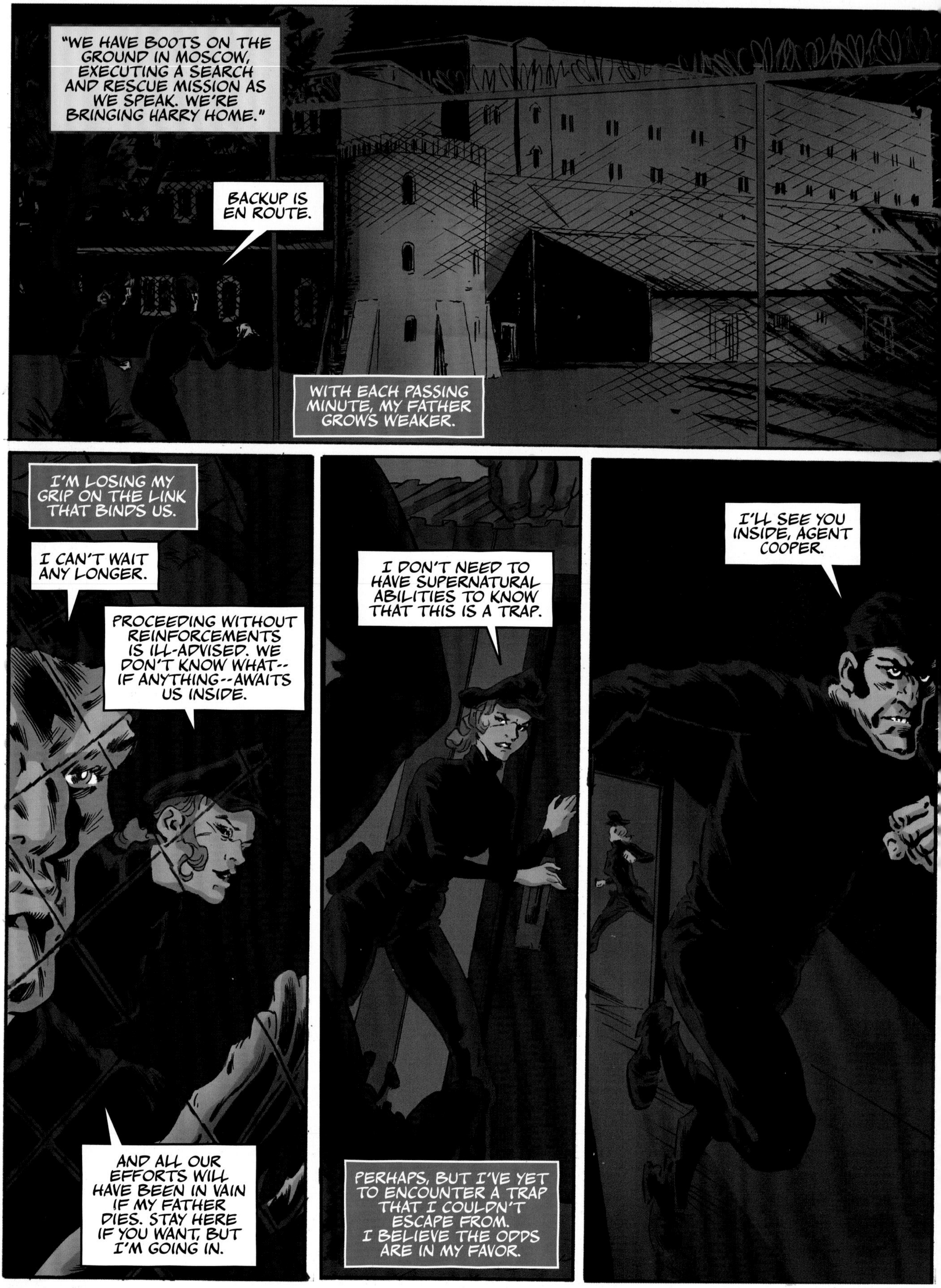
"WE HAVE BOOTS ON THE GROUND IN MOSCOW, EXECUTING A SEARCH AND RESCUE MISSION AS WE SPEAK. WE'RE BRINGING HARRY HOME."
BACKUP IS EN ROUTE.
WITH EACH PASSING MINUTE, MY FATHER GROWS WEAKER.
I'M LOSING MY GRIP ON THE LINK THAT BINDS US.
I CAN'T WAIT ANY LONGER.
PROCEEDING WITHOUT REINFORCEMENTS IS ILL-ADVISED. WE DON'T KNOW WHAT--IF ANYTHING--AWAITS US INSIDE.
AND ALL OUR EFFORTS WILL HAVE BEEN IN VAIN IF MY FATHER DIES. STAY HERE IF YOU WANT, BUT I'M GOING IN.
I DON'T NEED TO HAVE SUPERNATURAL ABILITIES TO KNOW THAT THIS IS A TRAP.
PERHAPS, BUT I'VE YET TO ENCOUNTER A TRAP THAT I COULDN'T ESCAPE FROM. I BELIEVE THE ODDS ARE IN MY FAVOR.
I'LL SEE YOU INSIDE, AGENT COOPER.

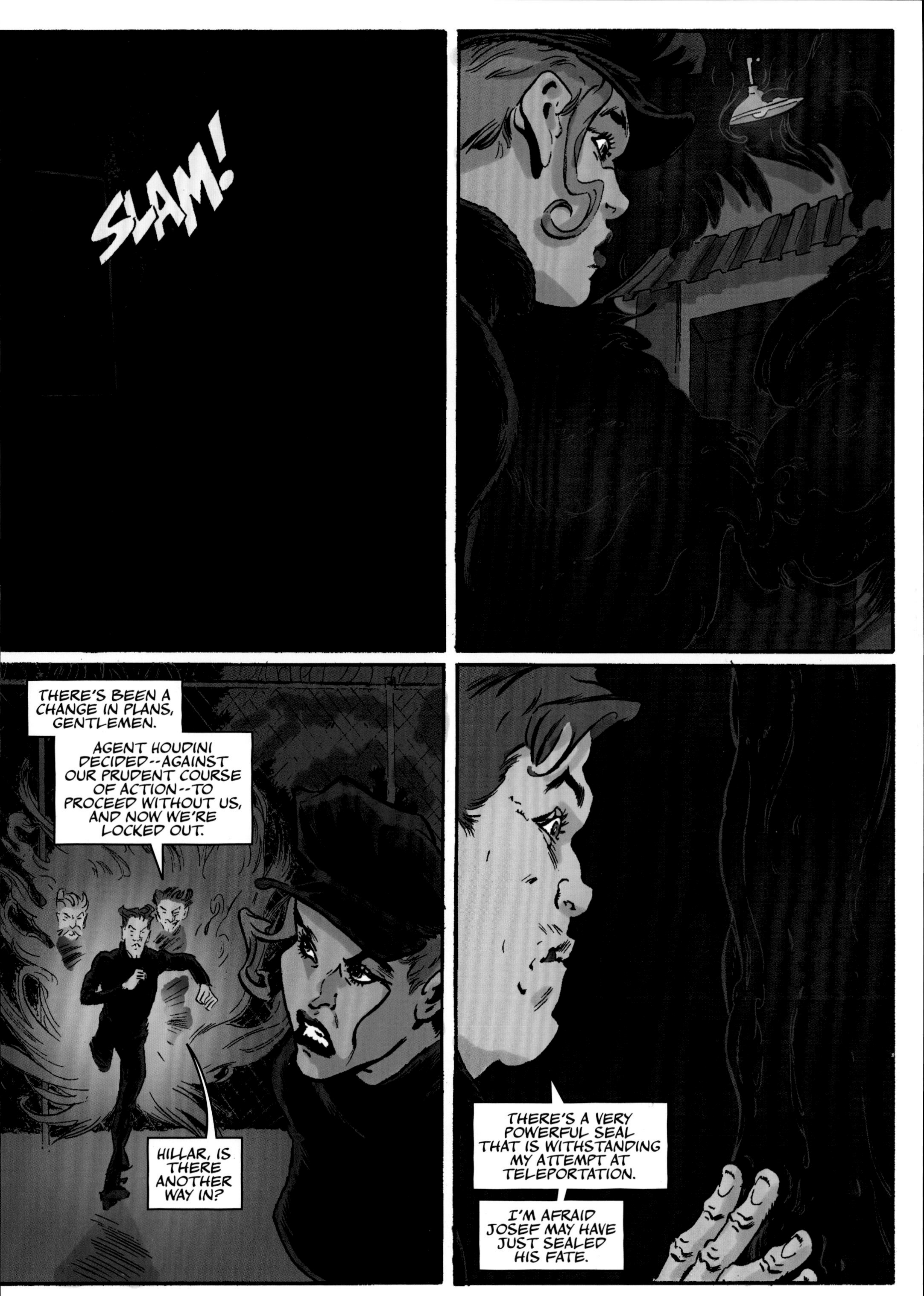
SLAM!
THERE'S BEEN A CHANGE IN PLANS, GENTLEMEN.
AGENT HOUDINI DECIDED--AGAINST OUR PRUDENT COURSE OF ACTION--TO PROCEED WITHOUT US, AND NOW WE'RE LOCKED OUT.
HILLAR, IS THERE ANOTHER WAY IN?
THERE'S A VERY POWERFUL SEAL THAT IS WITHSTANDING MY ATTEMPT AT TELEPORTATION.
I'M AFRAID JOSEF MAY HAVE JUST SEALED HIS FATE.

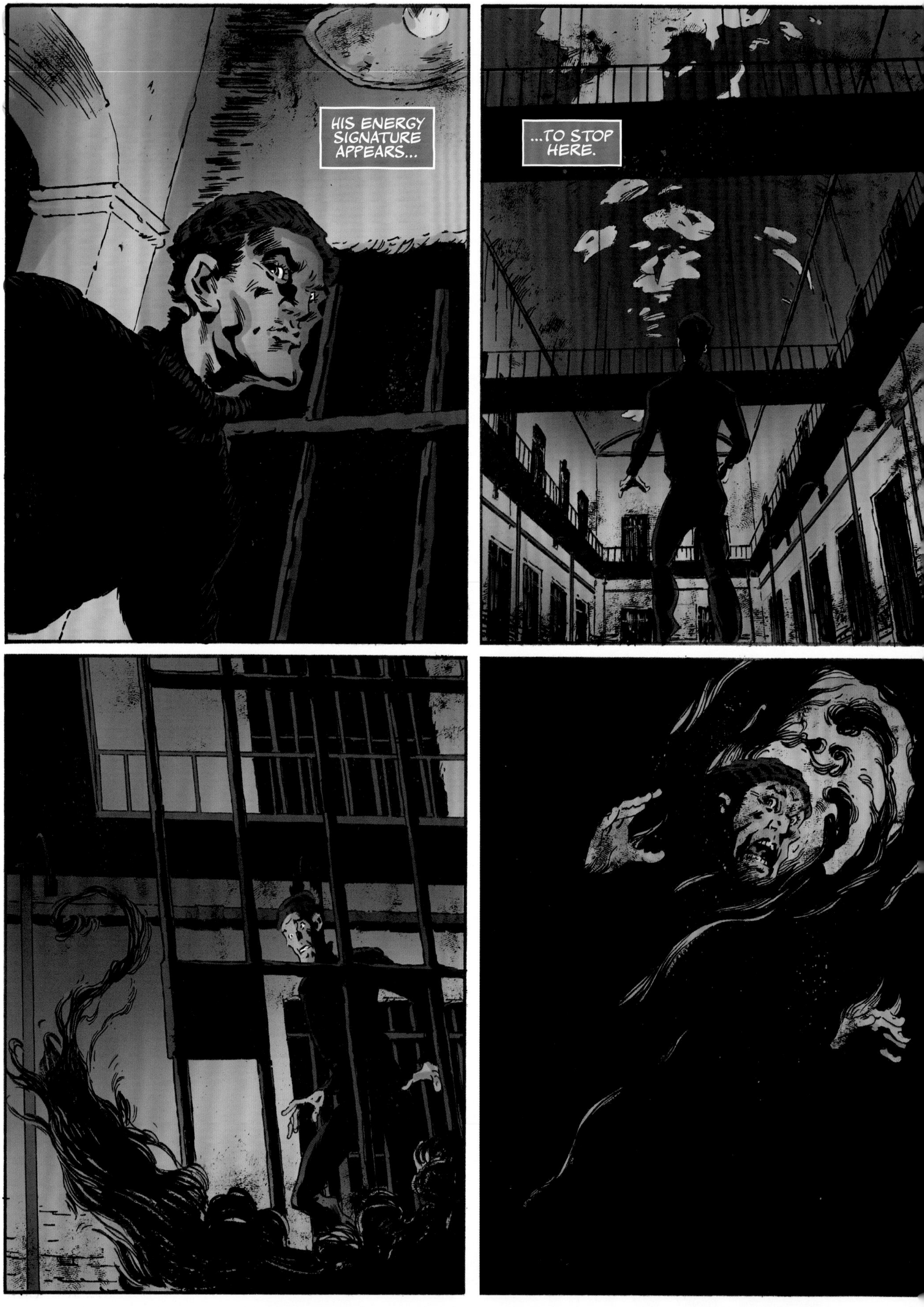
HIS ENERGY SIGNATURE APPEARS...
...TO STOP HERE.

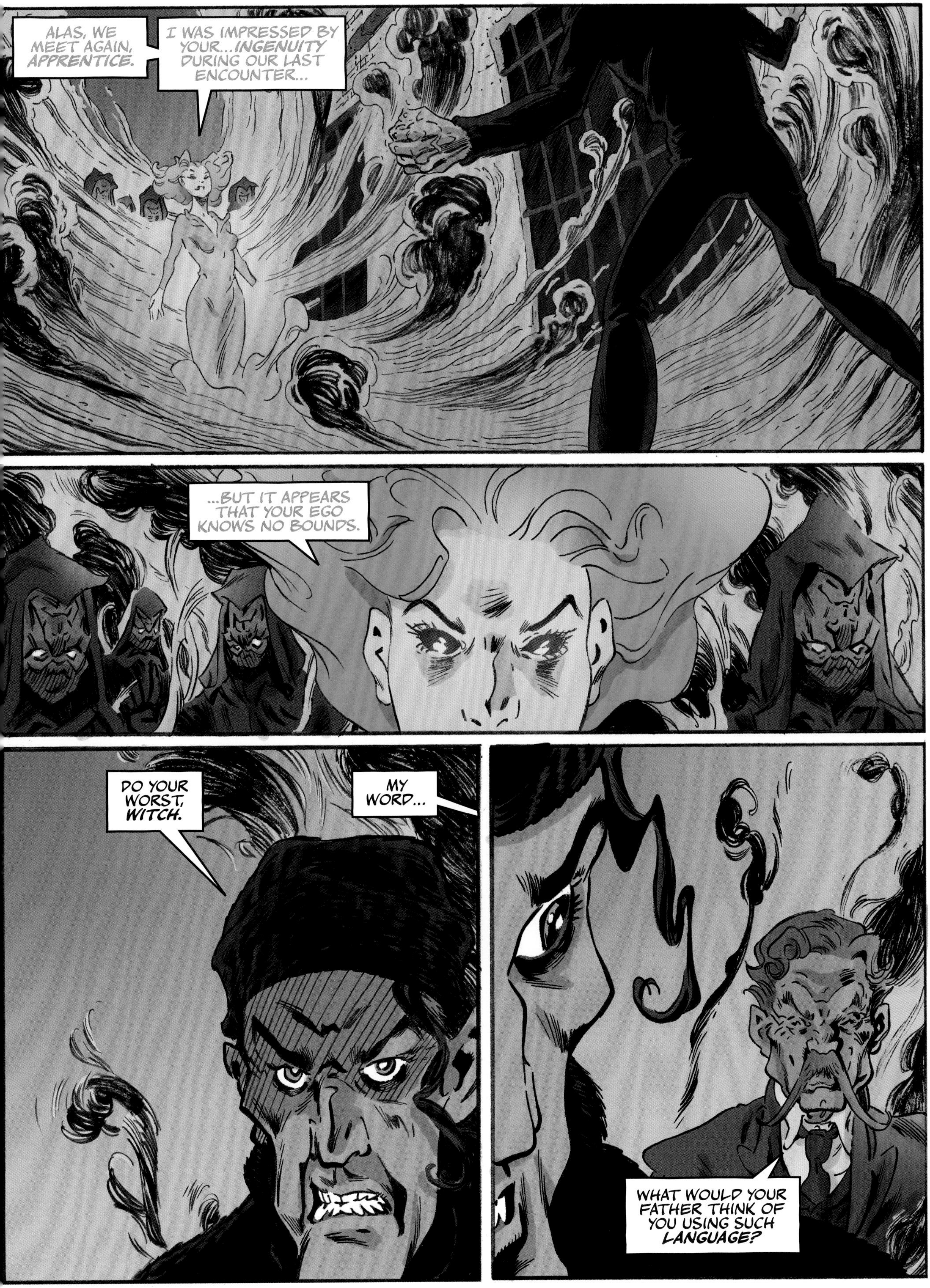
ALAS, WE MEET AGAIN, APPRENTICE.
I WAS IMPRESSED BY YOUR...INGENUITY DURING OUR LAST ENCOUNTER...
...BUT IT APPEARS THAT YOUR EGO KNOWS NO BOUNDS.
DO YOUR WORST, WITCH.
MY WORD...
WHAT WOULD YOUR FATHER THINK OF YOU USING SUCH LANGUAGE?

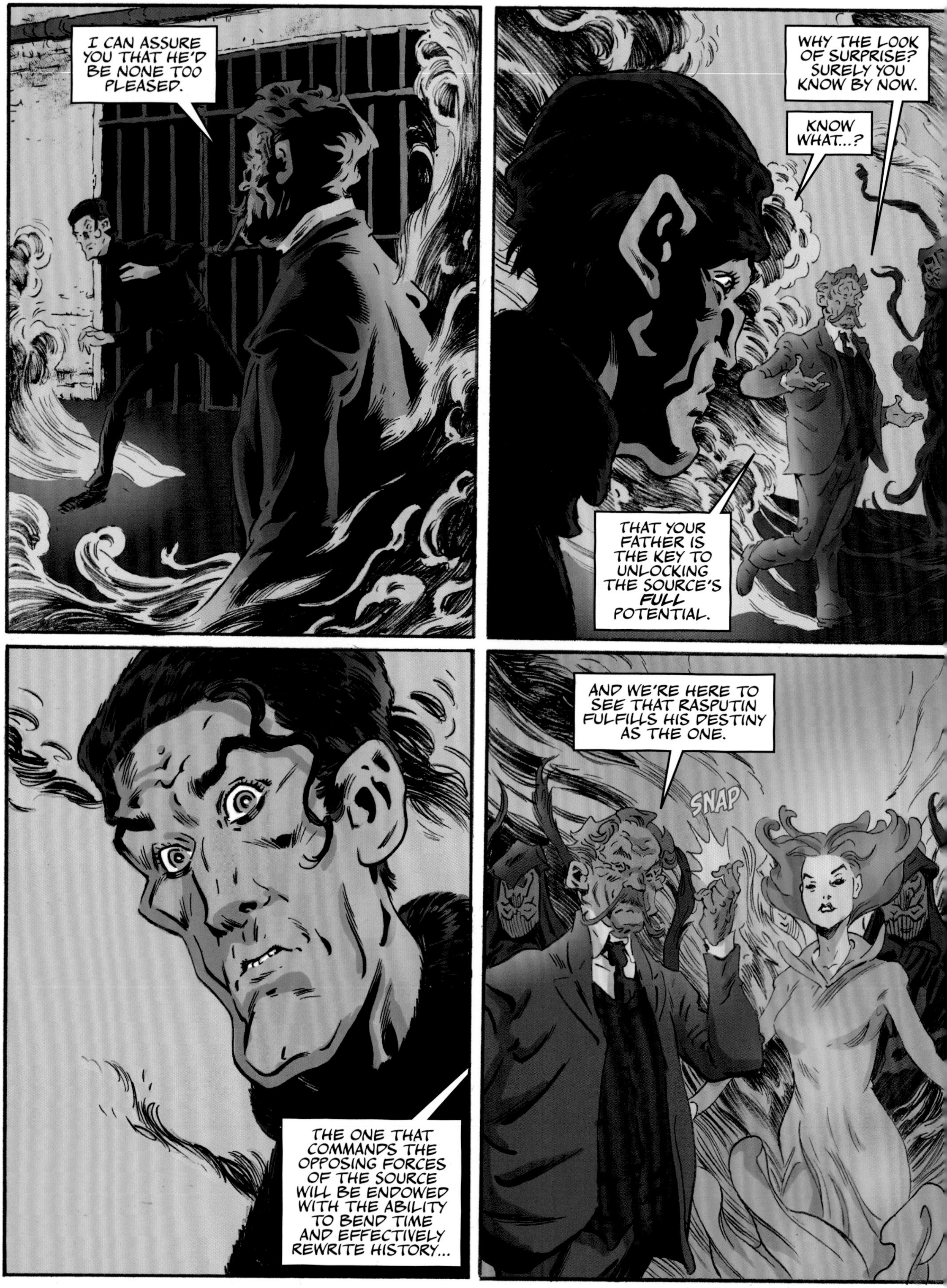
I CAN ASSURE YOU THAT HE'D BE NONE TOO PLEASED.
WHY THE LOOK OF SURPRISE? SURELY YOU KNOW BY NOW.
KNOW WHAT...?
THAT YOUR FATHER IS THE KEY TO UNLOCKING THE SOURCE'S FULL POTENTIAL.
THE ONE THAT COMMANDS THE OPPOSING FORCES OF THE SOURCE WILL BE ENDOWED WITH THE ABILITY TO BEND TIME AND EFFECTIVELY REWRITE HISTORY...
AND WE'RE HERE TO SEE THAT RASPUTIN FULFILLS HIS DESTINY AS THE ONE.
SNAP

REMEMBER WHAT THE MARTINKA BROTHERS TAUGHT YOU...

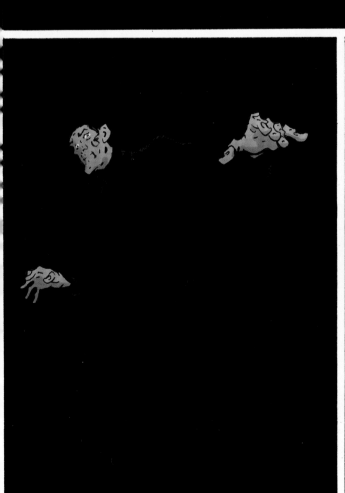

RIGHT NOW YOU'RE SIMPLY SCRATCHING AT A DRY *SHALLOW* SURFACE.

IT'S TIME TO DIG *DEEPER* FOR THE RICHER SOIL, AND WHEN I'M READY...

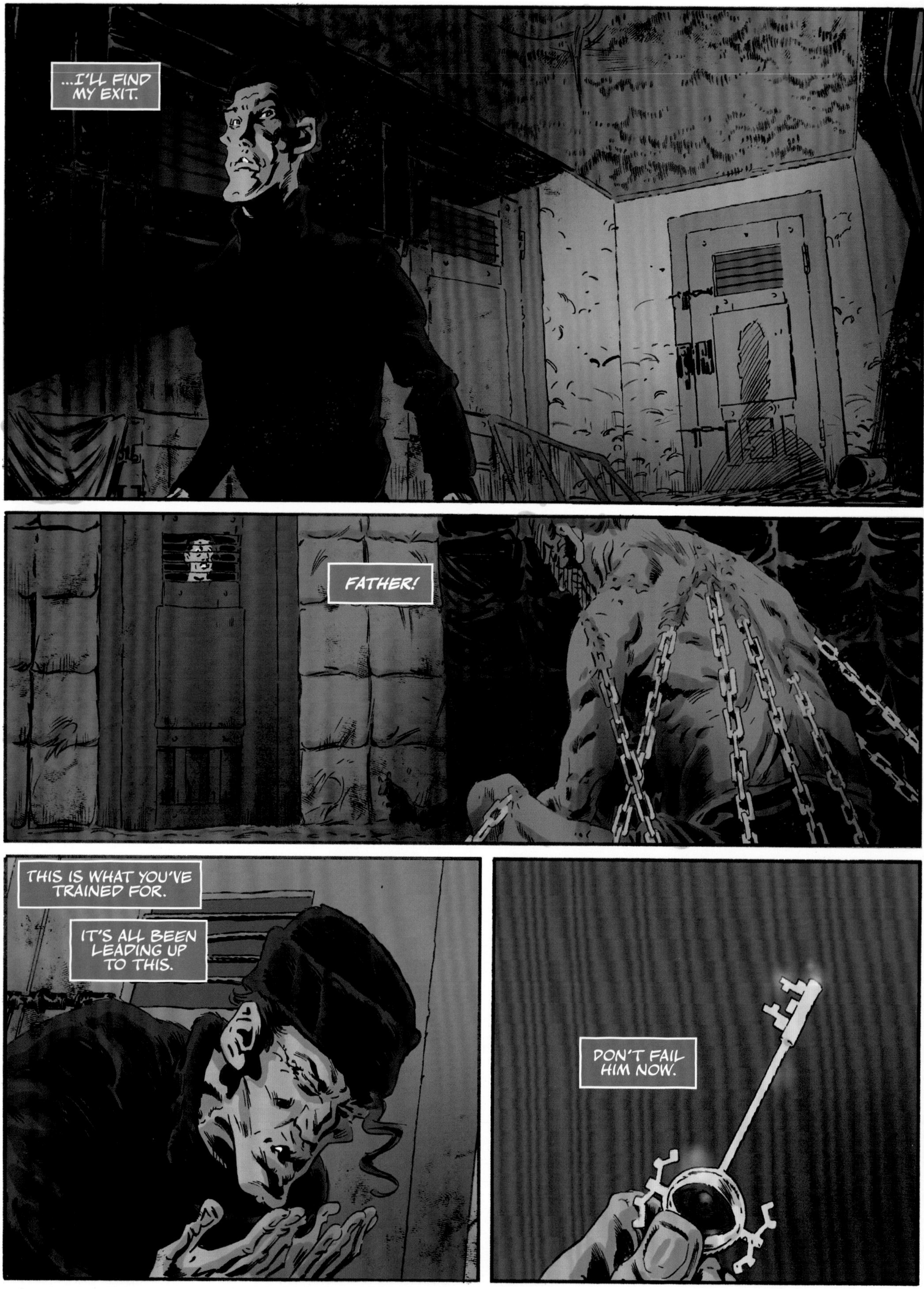
...I'LL FIND MY EXIT.
FATHER!
THIS IS WHAT YOU'VE TRAINED FOR.
IT'S ALL BEEN LEADING UP TO THIS.
DON'T FAIL HIM NOW.

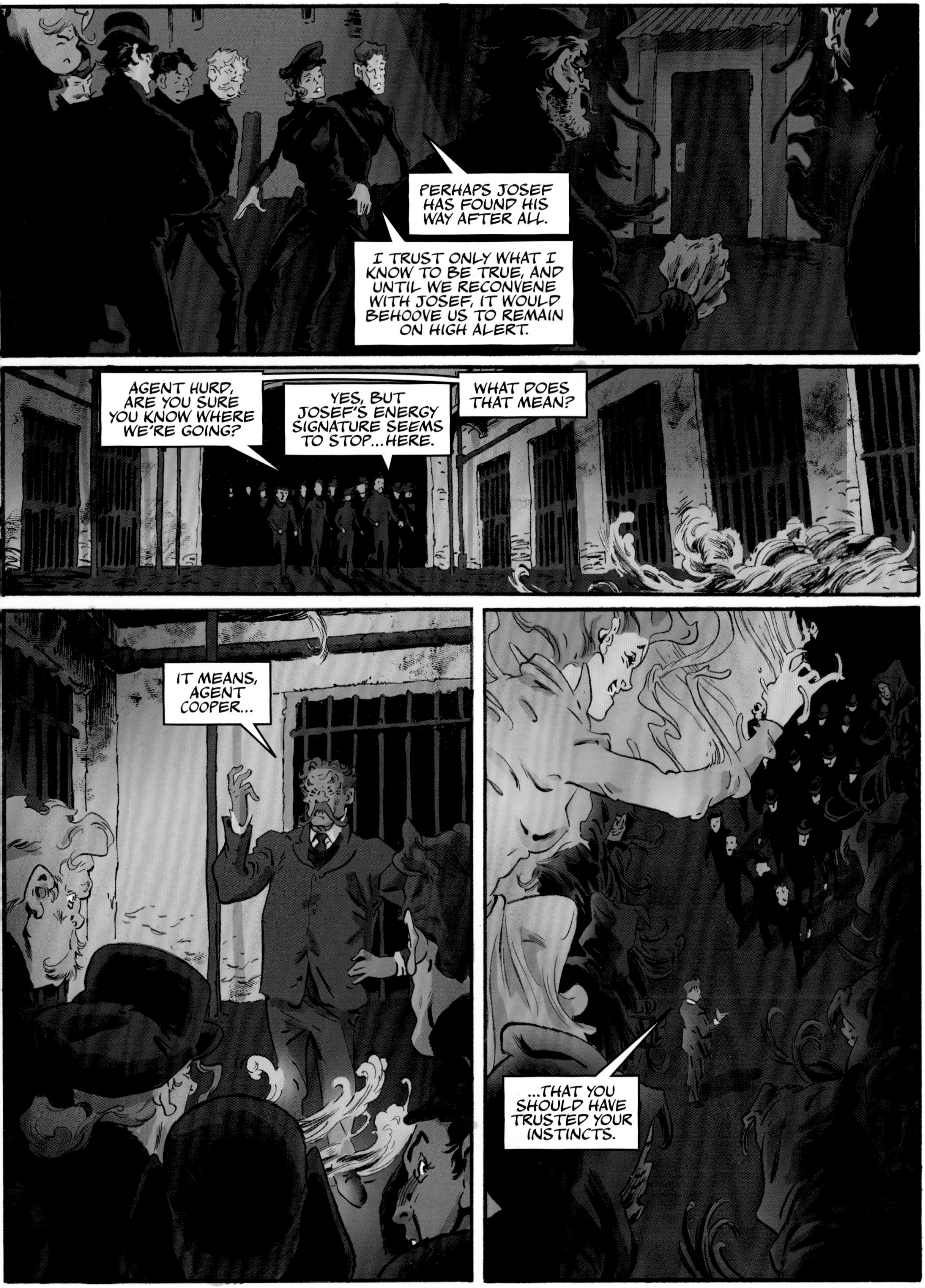
PERHAPS JOSEF HAS FOUND HIS WAY AFTER ALL.
I TRUST ONLY WHAT I KNOW TO BE TRUE, AND UNTIL WE RECONVENE WITH JOSEF, IT WOULD BEHOOVE US TO REMAIN ON HIGH ALERT.
AGENT HURD, ARE YOU SURE YOU KNOW WHERE WE'RE GOING?
YES, BUT JOSEF'S ENERGY SIGNATURE SEEMS TO STOP...HERE.
WHAT DOES THAT MEAN?
IT MEANS, AGENT COOPER...
...THAT YOU SHOULD HAVE TRUSTED YOUR INSTINCTS.

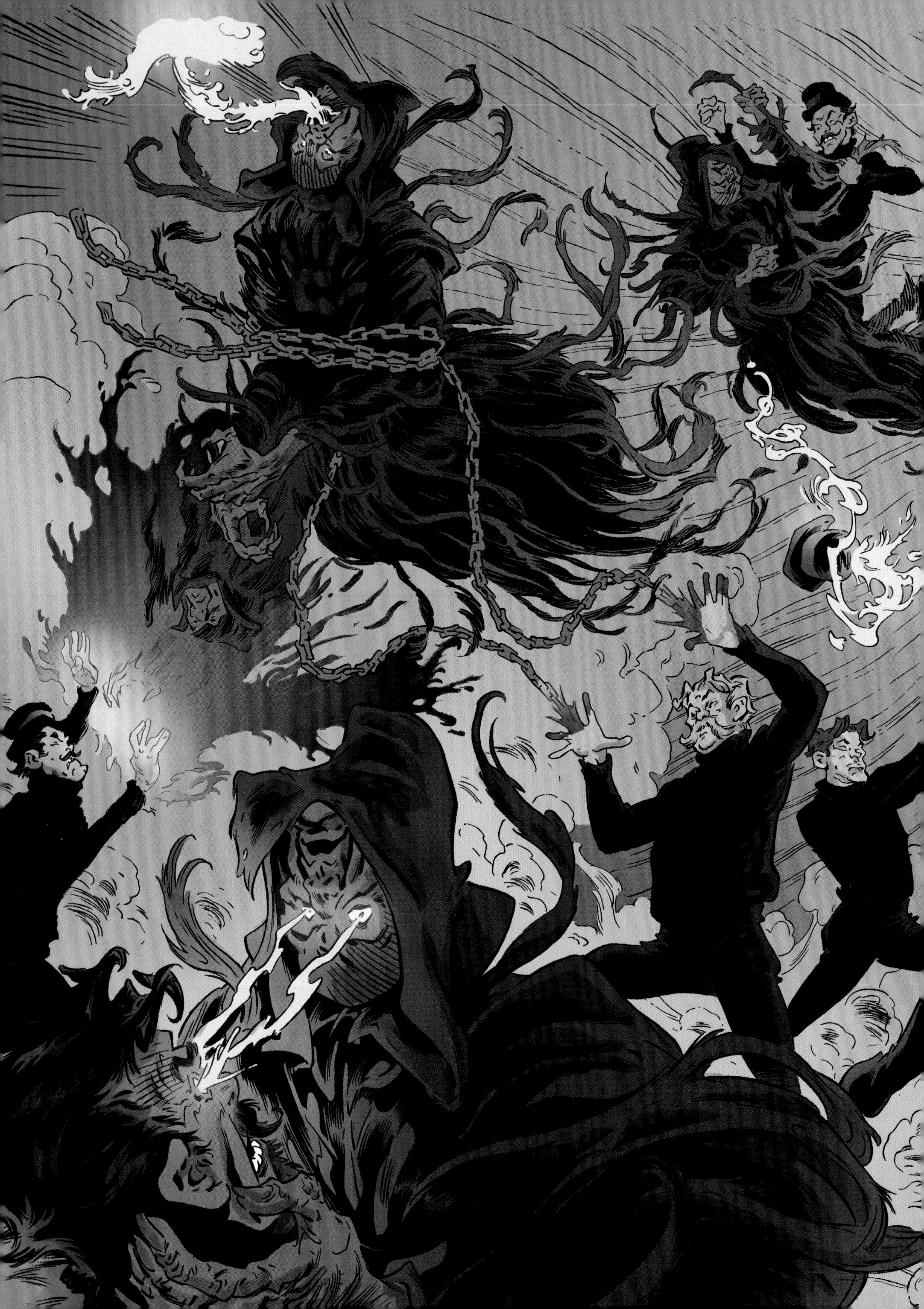

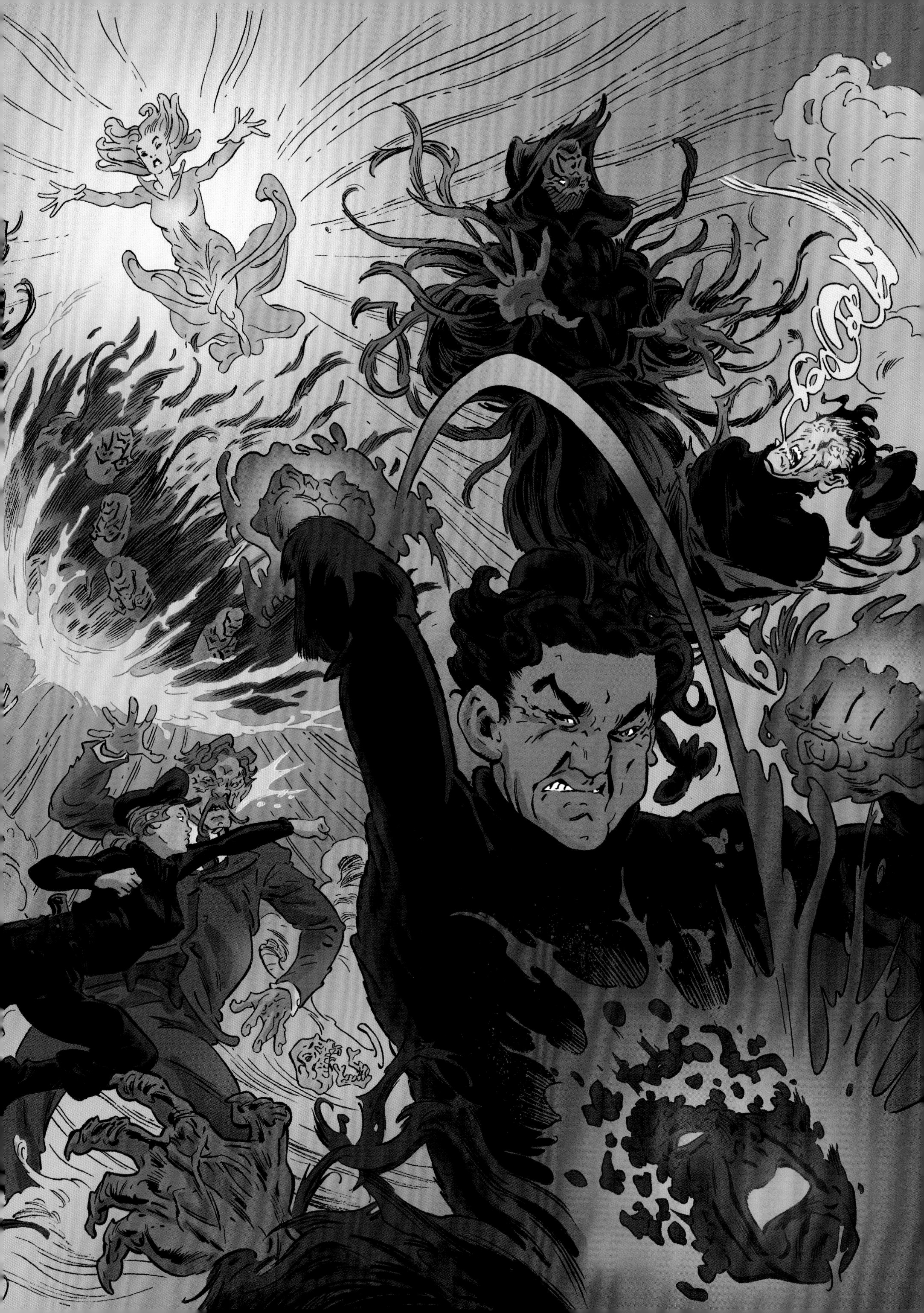

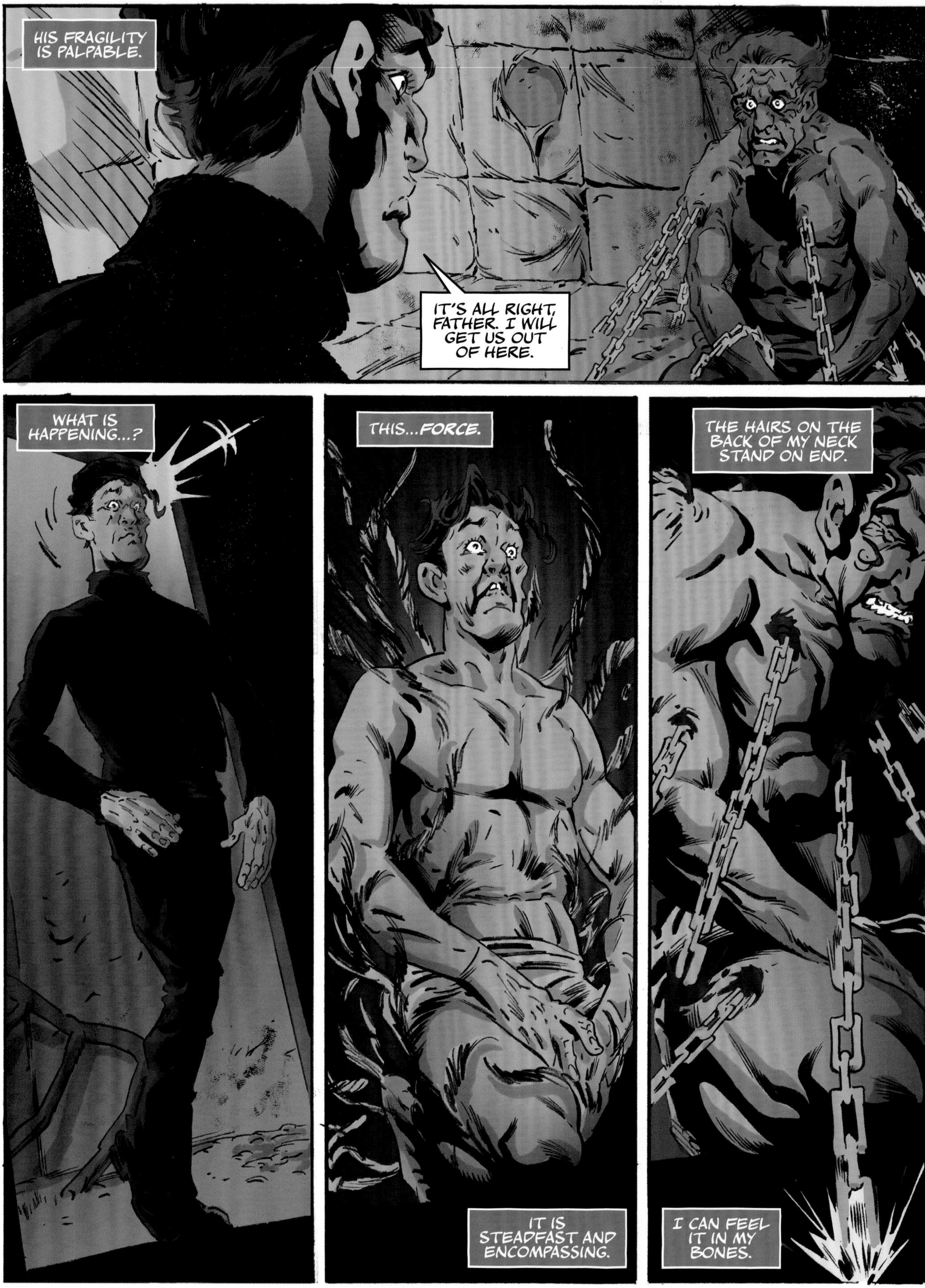
HIS FRAGILITY IS PALPABLE.
IT'S ALL RIGHT, FATHER. I WILL GET US OUT OF HERE.
WHAT IS HAPPENING...?
THIS...FORCE.
IT IS STEADFAST AND ENCOMPASSING.
THE HAIRS ON THE BACK OF MY NECK STAND ON END.
I CAN FEEL IT IN MY BONES.

DEATH AND DECAY...

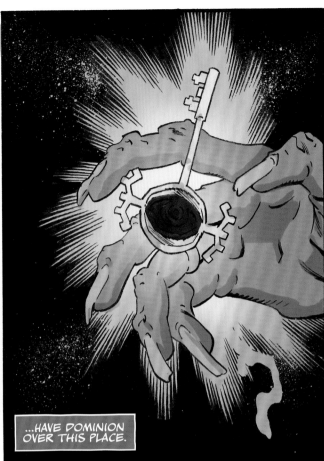

...HAVE DOMINION OVER THIS PLACE.

FOR I AM NO MATCH AGAINST...

...THE DARK MATTER'S SENTINEL.

SALT, GATHERED FROM THE TEARS OF A THOUSAND ANGELS...

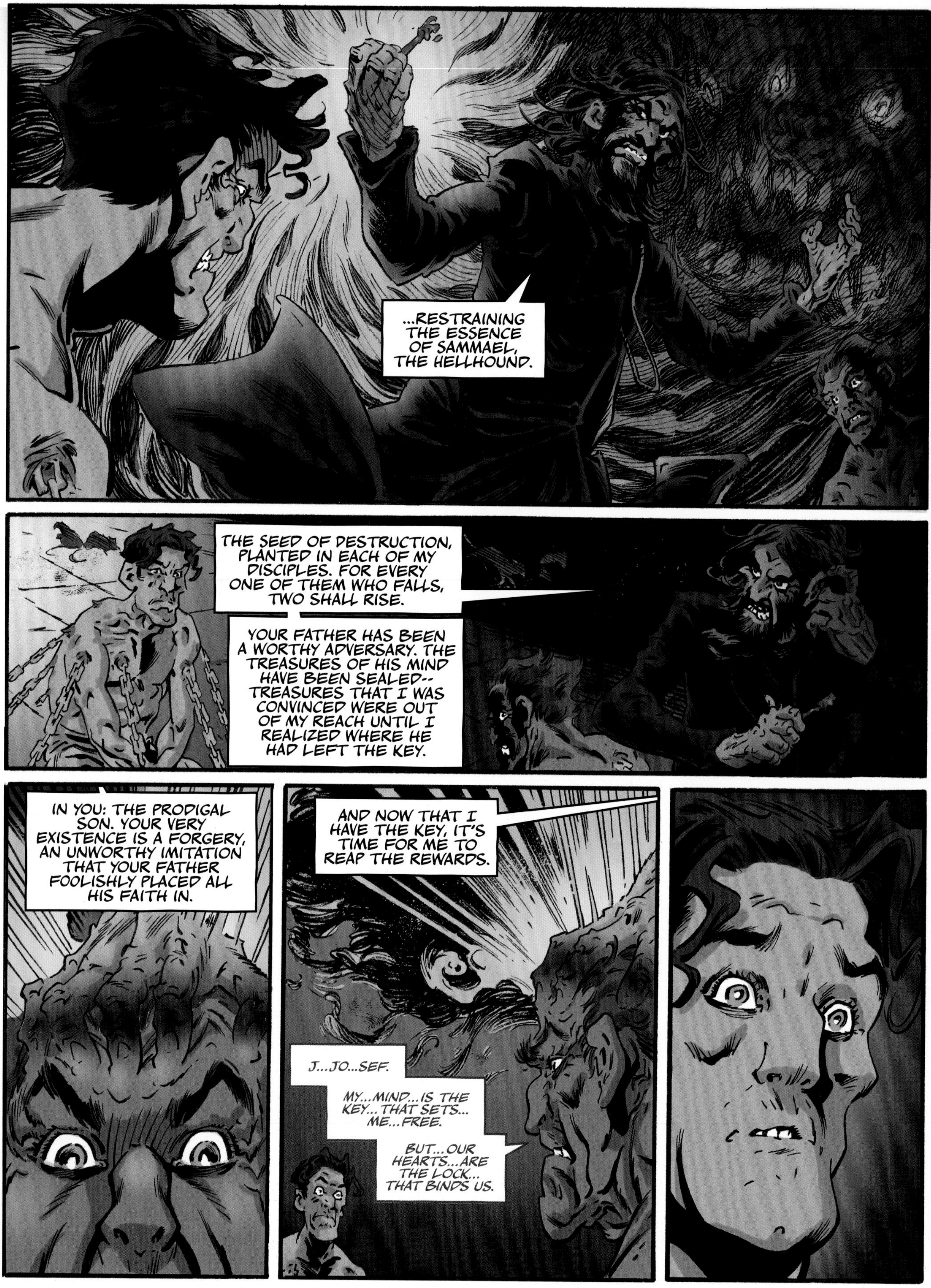
...RESTRAINING THE ESSENCE OF SAMMAEL, THE HELLHOUND.
THE SEED OF DESTRUCTION, PLANTED IN EACH OF MY DISCIPLES. FOR EVERY ONE OF THEM WHO FALLS, TWO SHALL RISE.
YOUR FATHER HAS BEEN A WORTHY ADVERSARY. THE TREASURES OF HIS MIND HAVE BEEN SEALED-- TREASURES THAT I WAS CONVINCED WERE OUT OF MY REACH UNTIL I REALIZED WHERE HE HAD LEFT THE KEY.
IN YOU: THE PRODIGAL SON. YOUR VERY EXISTENCE IS A FORGERY, AN UNWORTHY IMITATION THAT YOUR FATHER FOOLISHLY PLACED ALL HIS FAITH IN.
AND NOW THAT I HAVE THE KEY, IT'S TIME FOR ME TO REAP THE REWARDS.
J...JO...SEF.
MY...MIND...IS THE KEY...THAT SETS... ME...FREE.
BUT...OUR HEARTS...ARE THE LOCK... THAT BINDS US.

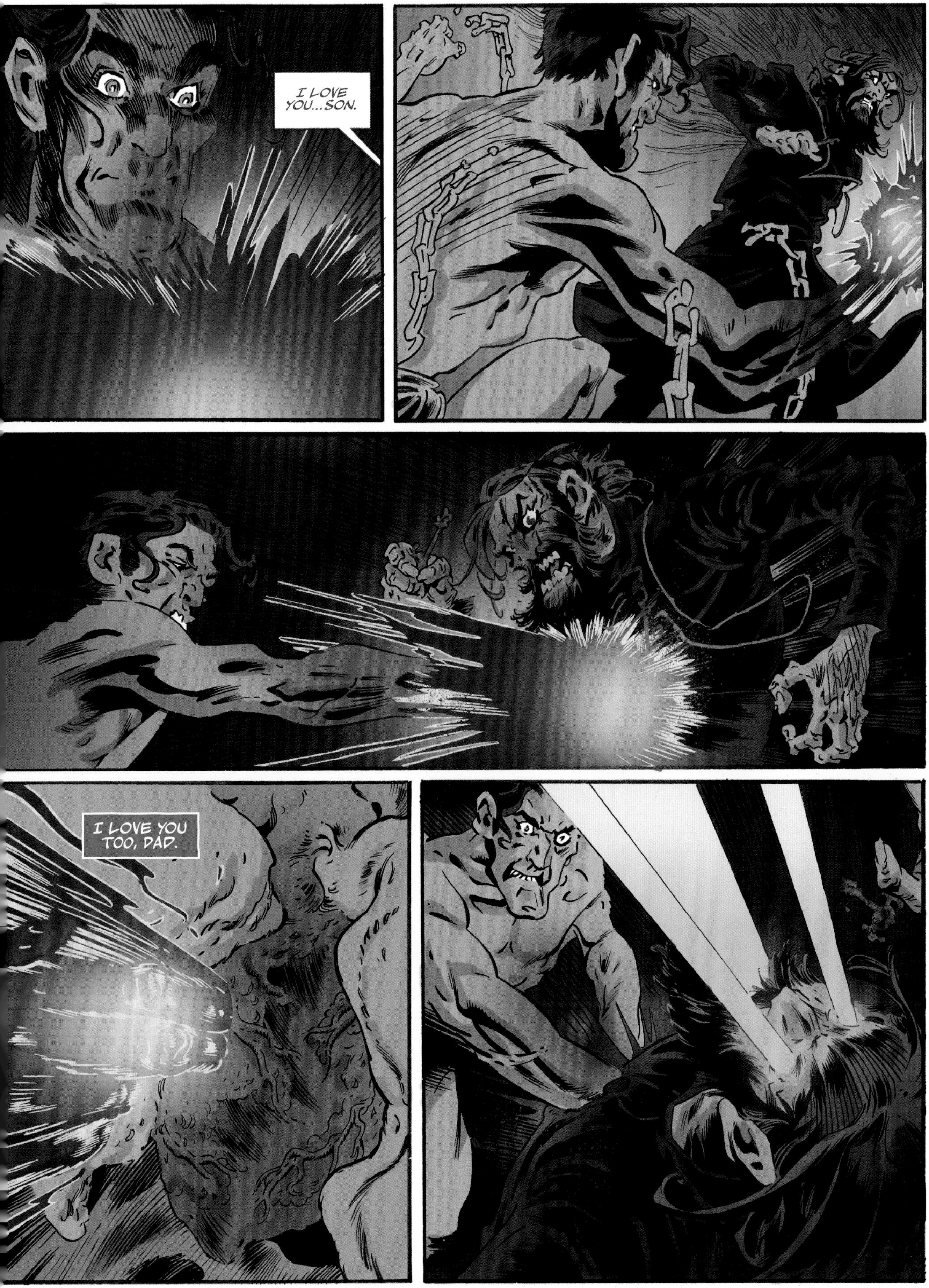
I LOVE YOU...SON.
I LOVE YOU TOO, DAD.

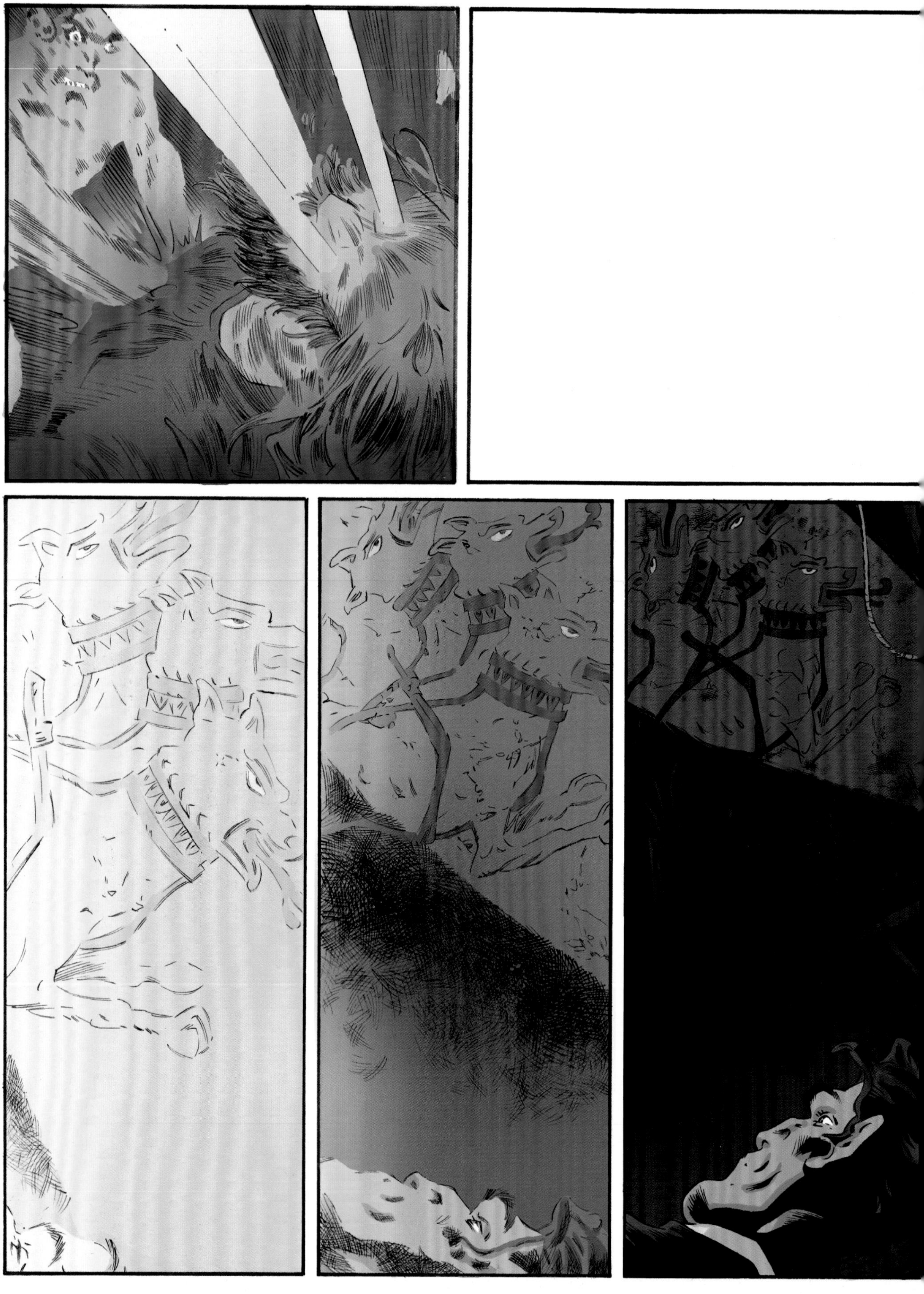

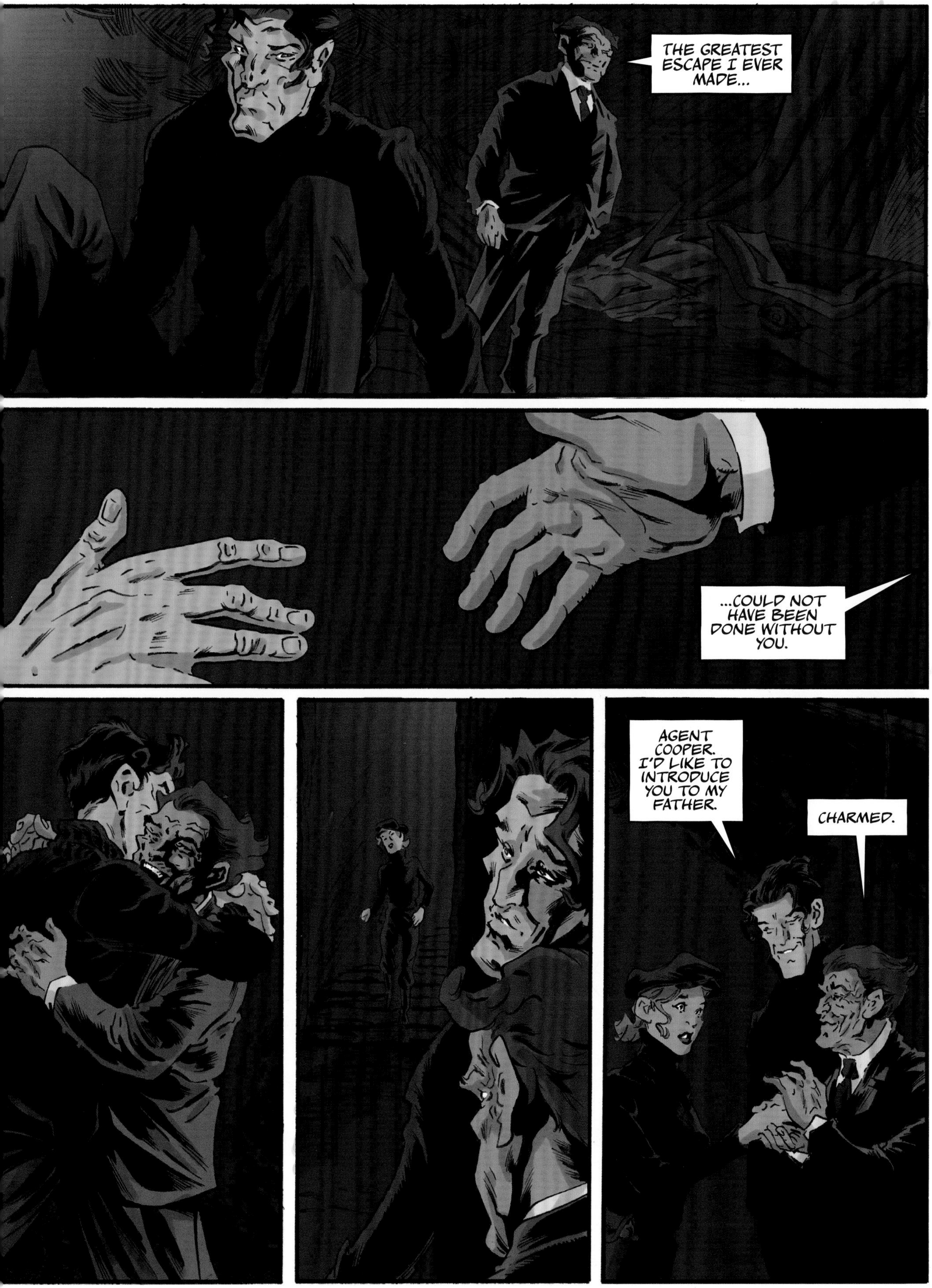
THE GREATEST ESCAPE I EVER MADE...
...COULD NOT HAVE BEEN DONE WITHOUT YOU.
AGENT COOPER. I'D LIKE TO INTRODUCE YOU TO MY FATHER.
CHARMED.

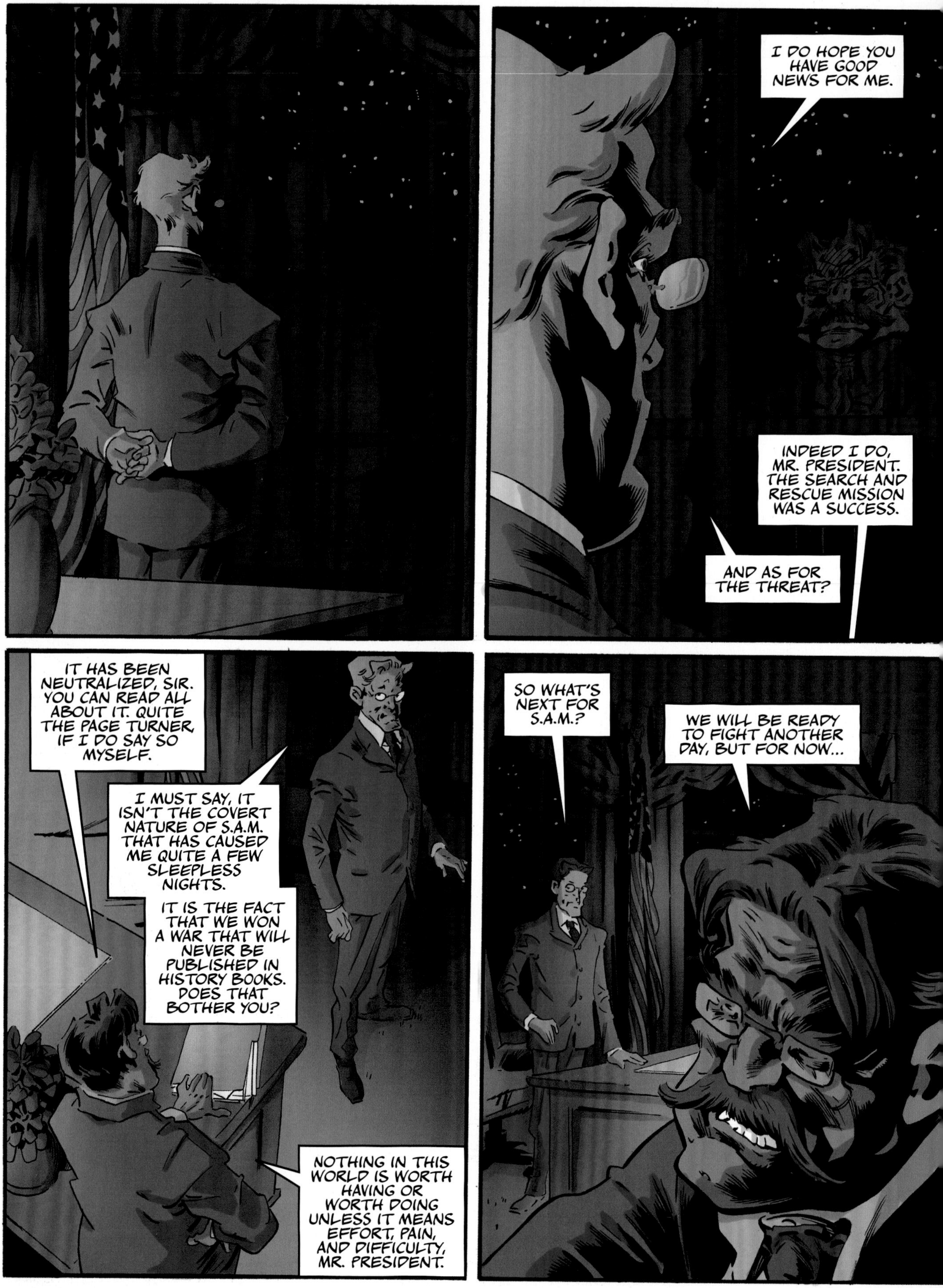
I DO HOPE YOU HAVE GOOD NEWS FOR ME.
INDEED I DO, MR. PRESIDENT. THE SEARCH AND RESCUE MISSION WAS A SUCCESS.
AND AS FOR THE THREAT?
IT HAS BEEN NEUTRALIZED, SIR. YOU CAN READ ALL ABOUT IT. QUITE THE PAGE TURNER, IF I DO SAY SO MYSELF.
I MUST SAY, IT ISN'T THE COVERT NATURE OF S.A.M. THAT HAS CAUSED ME QUITE A FEW SLEEPLESS NIGHTS.
IT IS THE FACT THAT WE WON A WAR THAT WILL NEVER BE PUBLISHED IN HISTORY BOOKS. DOES THAT BOTHER YOU?
NOTHING IN THIS WORLD IS WORTH HAVING OR WORTH DOING UNLESS IT MEANS EFFORT, PAIN, AND DIFFICULTY, MR. PRESIDENT.
SO WHAT'S NEXT FOR S.A.M.?
WE WILL BE READY TO FIGHT ANOTHER DAY, BUT FOR NOW...

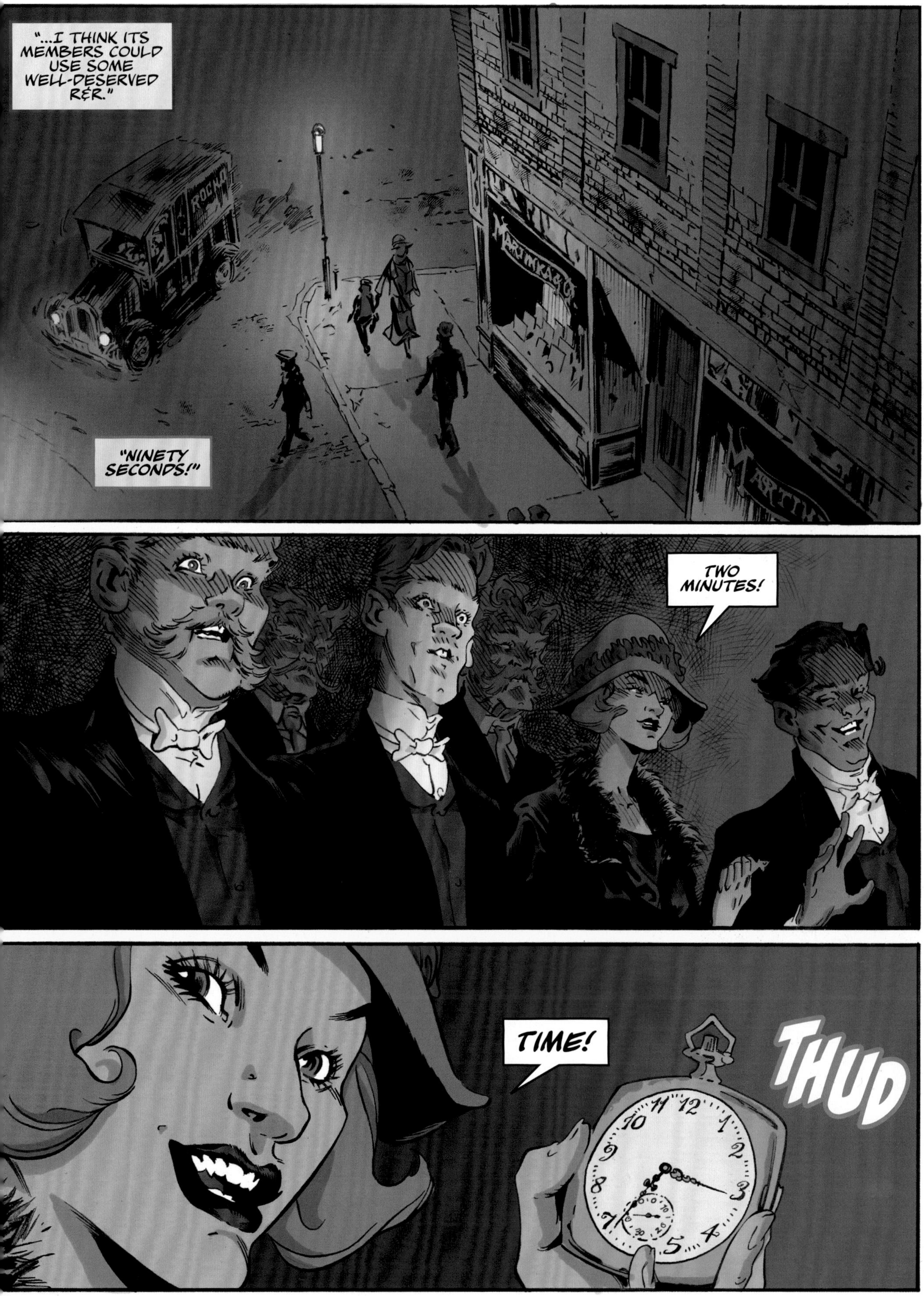
"...I THINK ITS MEMBERS COULD USE SOME WELL-DESERVED R&R."
"NINETY SECONDS!"
TWO MINUTES!
TIME!
THUD

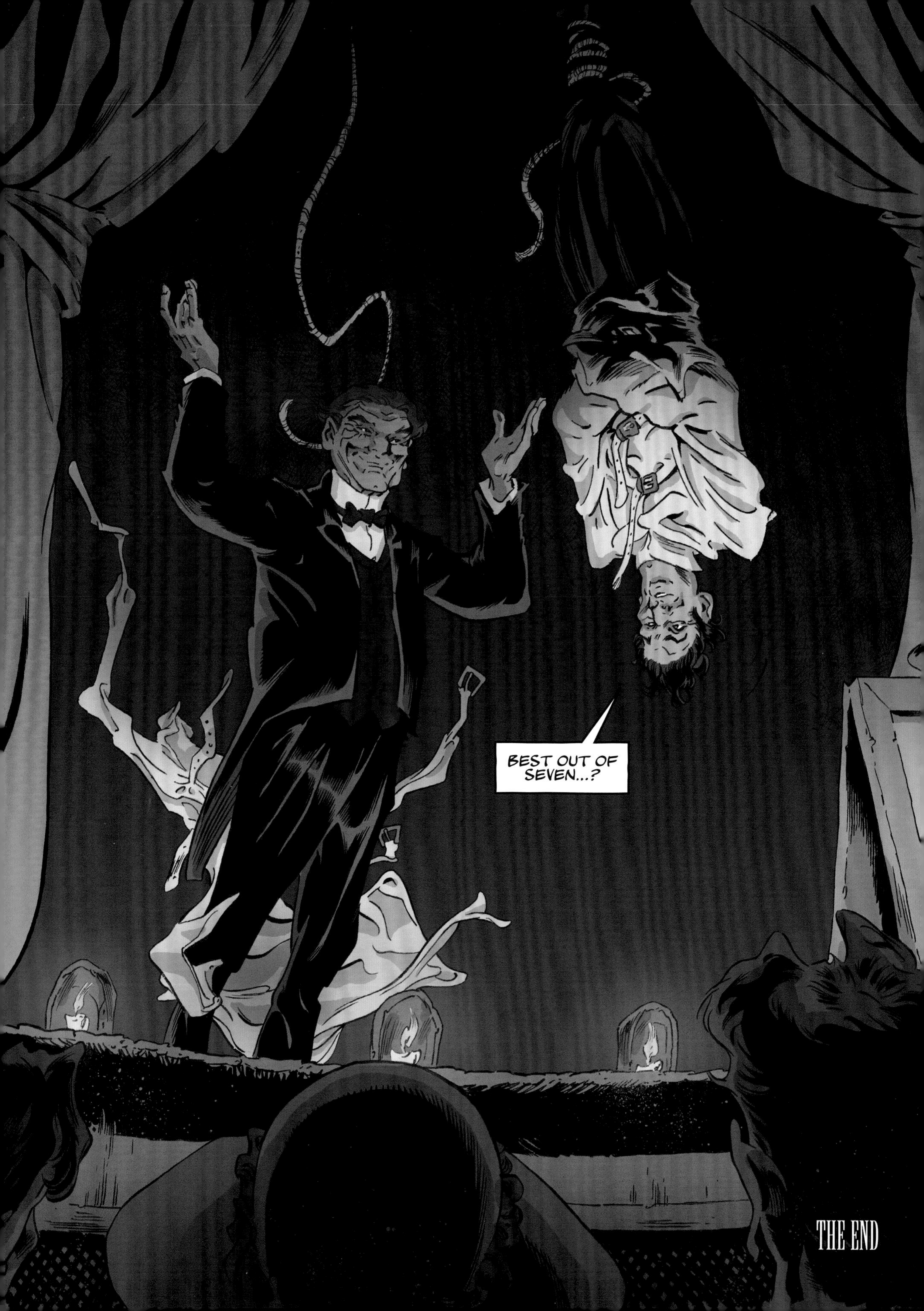
BEST OUT OF SEVEN...?
THE END

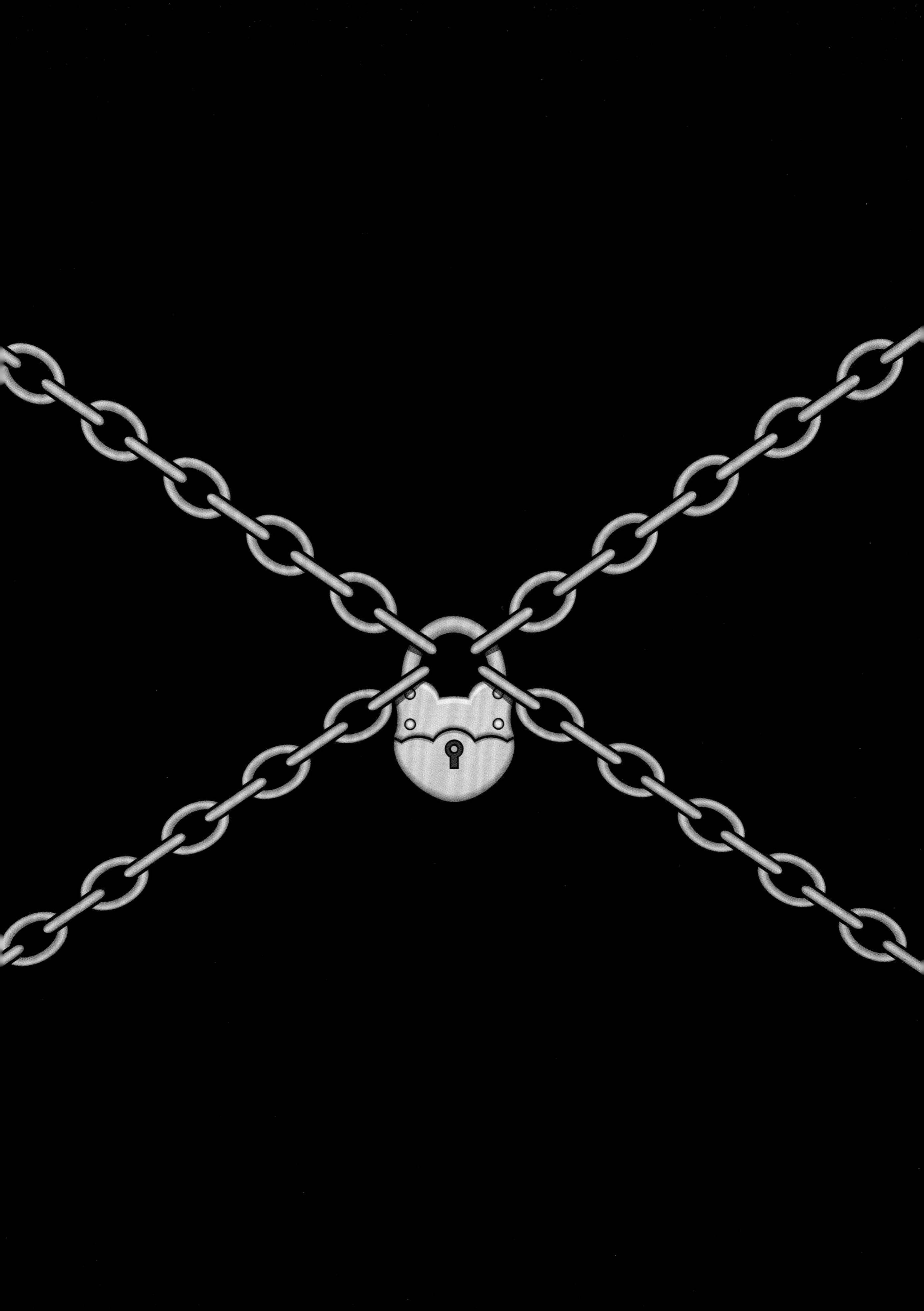

AFTERWORD

What you've just read is a passion project that was seven years in the making. Unbeknownst to many, this book experienced several false starts and a lot of rejection, and it was originally developed with a different artist. What you're about to read is the tale of the many people who made *After Houdini* possible—and how it almost didn't happen.

You see, making a comic book can be a complicated matter. Oftentimes it's not as simple as having a great idea and drawing it. Most comic books require an entire team of people to produce. More specifically in creator-owned comics, where the creators are not beholden to licensed properties and can create their own stories and characters, this starts with a collaboration between—at the very least—a writer and an artist.

This is where the complications begin.

Rarely can two people agree upon a shared idea and create a singular vision that—with a lot of hard work and a little luck—can resonate enough to attract the attention of a publisher (and eventual readers).

It's like attempting to capture lightning in a bottle.

The evolution of *After Houdini* started in the fall of 2011. I was in the process of pitching a completely different project to potential artists and getting nowhere. While attending New York Comic Con, I had the chance to meet writer Justin Jordan and artist Tradd Moore, creators of the popular Image Comics series *The Strange Talent of Luther Strode*. My friendship with both of them had started online, so it was great to finally meet in person.

It turned out that Tradd and I happened to have graduated from the same art school. When I asked him if he might know of any available artists, he said, "You should contact my old roommate, Kevin. He's super talented."

I sent Kevin Ziegler an introductory email with a link to some of my work and my intentions for our potential collaboration. He replied promptly, and we spent the next several months discussing a potential idea to work on. When none of my ideas were gelling with him, I finally asked him what he was interested in drawing.

On May 11, 2012, the seedling of *After Houdini* was planted.

The subject line of his email simply read "Houdini." In it, his ideas surrounding the iconic magician came pouring out in a lengthy stream of consciousness. He followed up with more emails containing several links that helped frame his intriguing concept. Embedded in one of these correspondences was a recommendation for a book titled *The Secret Life of Houdini*. I didn't know it then, but that book would serve as my primary inspiration for *After Houdini*.

Kevin's passion for the subject was evident, which got me super excited. I relayed my genuine interest in the idea and asked him to give me some time to shape it into something presentable. After two intense months of research and batting ideas back and forth with him, I was proud to send him the first issue of our story.

Pencils, inks, colors, letters, and book design for *After Houdini* #1 were completed on June 16, 2013. That same month, I attended HeroesCon in North Carolina and had the great fortune of meeting Kevin face-to-face for the first time. I had printed copies for the show, and we shared a table in Artists Alley. At one point during that weekend, Justin Jordan stopped by and thumbed through a copy.

"You bastard," he smirked. "I've been trying to get Kevin to draw me a full issue for years."

"Really?" I said. "I didn't know that."

"What's your secret?" he said. "How'd you get him to follow through?"

I shrugged. "I just asked him what he liked to draw."

Over the next several months I pitched the book to editors, both in person and via email. The pitch received a lot of compliments but was ultimately rejected. Turns out, unless you're Brian Wood, no one is interested in publishing your historical fiction comic book.

Kevin and I kept in touch. We'd regularly message each other, all the while trying to ignore the fact that we both had lost the momentum to produce the rest of the series on our own. Then we lost our colorist due to our lack of progress.

Ten months fell off the calendar, and Kevin and I were speaking less frequently. He had moved on to other work, and so had I. But I couldn't bring myself to completely abandon the wonderful adventure story that we had created, so I kept writing it.

By April of 2014, I had scripted 88 of 110 pages, with the remaining 22 in outline form. Around this time I came across a particularly interesting piece of comic book news: The illustrious publisher Penguin Books had established a graphic novel imprint called InkLit. I did some googling and came across contact information of one of the editors. With nothing to lose, I sent him a cold email inquiring about submitting a pitch.

Much to my surprise, the editor responded the very next day with, "You can submit it to me at the following email . . ."

Twenty minutes later, I sent him the first issue of *After Houdini*.

Did I think this was our big break? Abso-friggin-lutely. I was confident in the story and even more so in Kevin's art style. But with how these things typically go, I was sure to temper my expectations. I'm glad I did because after five agonizing months of waiting, the pitch was officially rejected on September 22.

Then, 2014 rolled into 2015. In this time, I'd managed to get two new series green-lit by the up-and-coming digital publisher MonkeyBrain Comics, and I'd added a third project titled *Skip to the End* to my schedule. Even so, *After Houdini* was never far from my thoughts.

In April, I received an unexpected email from the editor at Penguin, subject line: "Asking about After Houdini." He reached out to say he was now consulting for other publishers, not just Penguin, and wanted to know if I had placed the book. I wasn't ashamed to say that I hadn't. He informed me that a small publisher was preparing to launch a new graphic novel imprint, and he would run my pitch by them.

On July 26, 2015, our seedling of an idea began to sprout.

The editor wrote to say that Insight Editions was interested in publishing *After Houdini* under its comics imprint. Over the next two months, I was hit with a barrage of questions pertaining to the project's details.

How many pages is it?
What is your target audience?
Do you have a finished script?
Do you have any art beyond what you sent?
How many volumes were you imagining this would be?
Do you have written outlines for the proposed second and third volumes?

None of these questions scared me—not even the crazy idea that I might have to produce two additional volumes. I wasn't scared because my unwavering belief in the story had led me to that moment. I had come prepared.

On September 21, 2015, Insight Editions presented us with an official offer to publish *After Houdini*. Our seedling of an idea had finally planted roots.

Two months later, Kevin and I were having a conference call with the editorial staff. They all seemed very excited about the book, which put the winds back into Kevin's and my creative sails.

While Kevin was completing work on a fill-in issue for Dark Horse, I decided to focus on my end of *After Houdini*, so I continued writing the scripts, getting feedback, and incorporating notes from editorial. The editing process was fairly painless. All the notes I received were good ones that I happily made.

However, due to unforeseen delays on the Dark Horse project, Kevin wasn't able to return to *After Houdini* for four months.

Around this time, I had to finally come clean to editorial about serious production delays. Also around this time, Insight Editions brought on a new senior editor, Mark Irwin, who was to oversee the publisher's growing number of comic book titles. I was sure that this new editor with his impressive resume was going to cancel our book.

Even though Mark was now aware of how very behind schedule our book was, much to my surprise, he still believed in its potential success. The delays weren't good, but he went to bat for us and managed to push back the publishing date. Kevin now had a year to complete the book.

I should note that Kevin and I are friends. I am sure that he will read this, so he knows that everything I'm saying comes from a good place. I had the confidence that we were going to see this project through because he was the one that planted the seed of its promise into my head.

In early November 2016, a year after we signed contracts, I called Kevin to break the news that he was being asked by the publisher to step down from the project. As painful as this was for me to see happen, the reality is that he failed to meet the deadline.

But the book you hold in your hands could not have happened without him.

While all of this was unfolding, Insight's support of the book never wavered, so much so that they contracted me to write a second volume. For this, another artist named John Lucas, whose art graces these pages, was brought on. When Kevin stepped down, John was assigned to replace him, and boy did he have his work cut out for him. Due to their completely different art styles—samples of which accompany this essay—John was forced to start from page one. His distinct style eventually brought this book to life in a completely new way that has made not only me proud, but Kevin as well.

There aren't words that can sufficiently express my deep gratitude for Insight Comics' support, the commitment of my collaborators, and especially you, dear reader. Thank you for adding this book to your collection. In the end, this (back)story's happy ending could not have happened without you.

Jeremy Holt
Middlebury, Vermont
2018

AFTER HOUDINI
A COMIC IN THE MAKING

ORIGINAL ART
BY KEVIN ZIEGLER

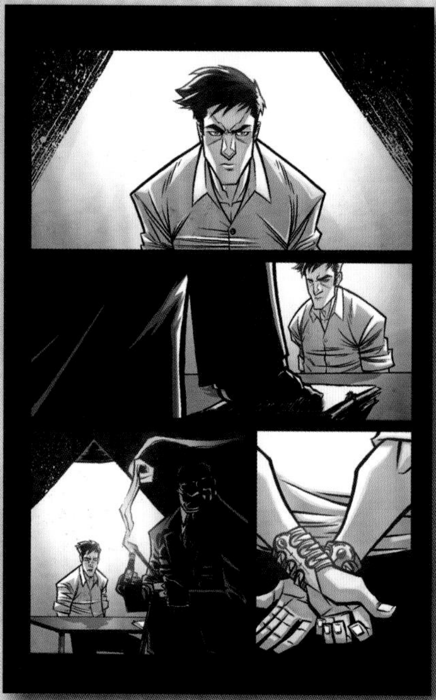

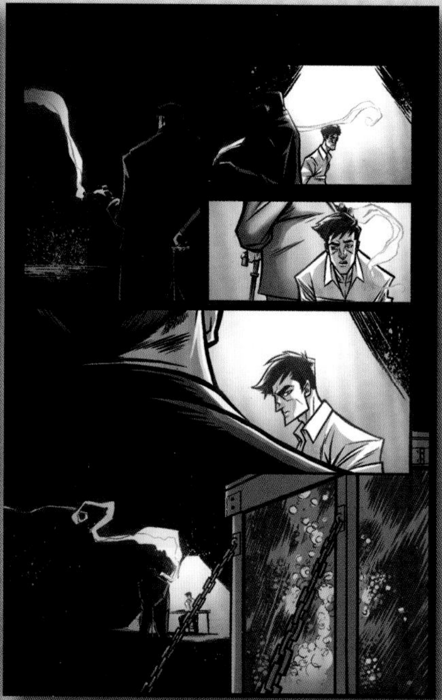

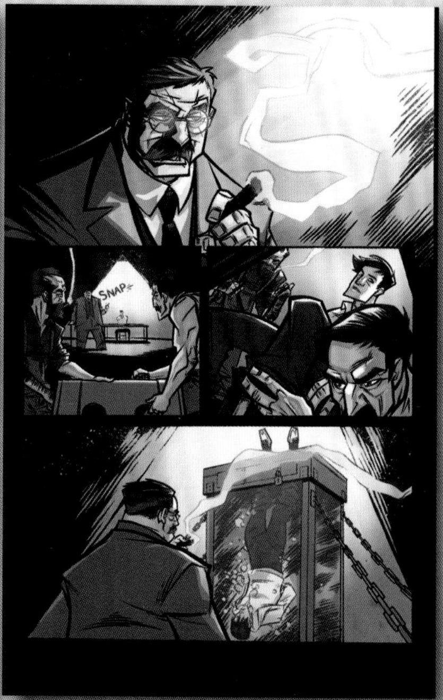
SNAP

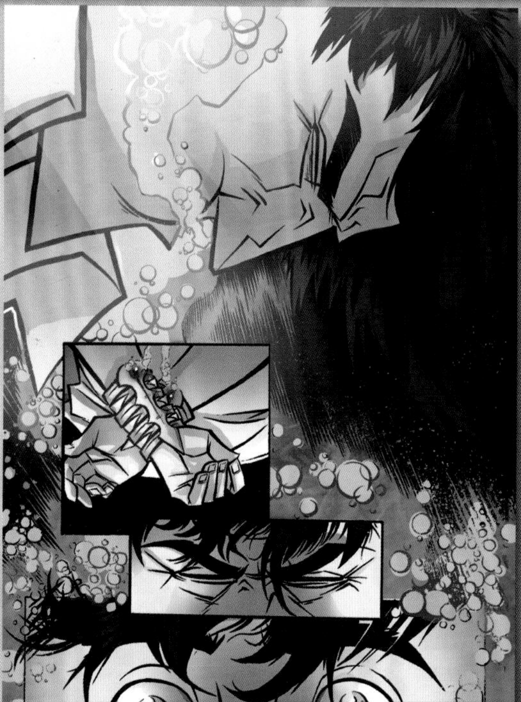

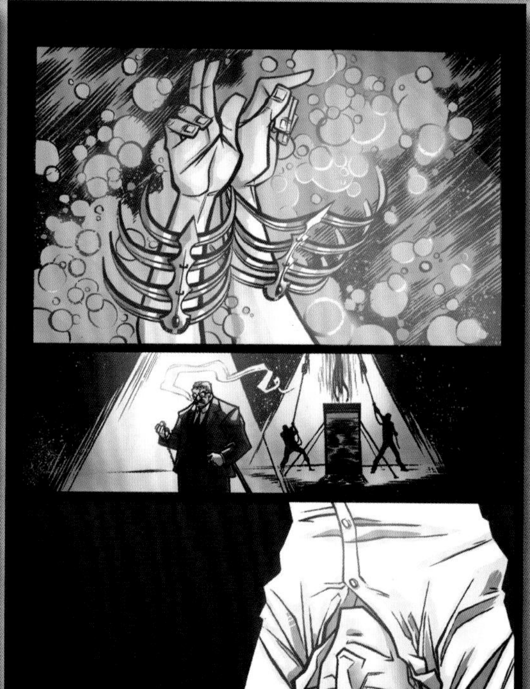

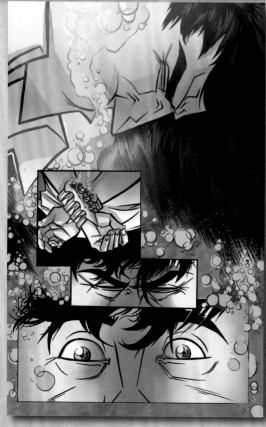

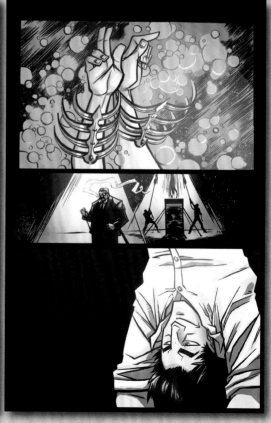

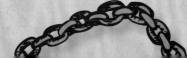

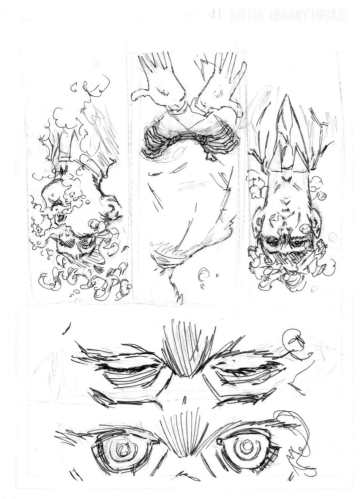

Page 21 • Layout Sketches

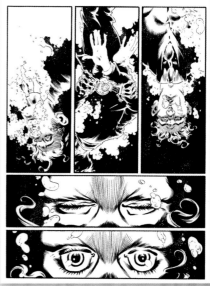

Page 21 • Inks

Page 21 • Colors

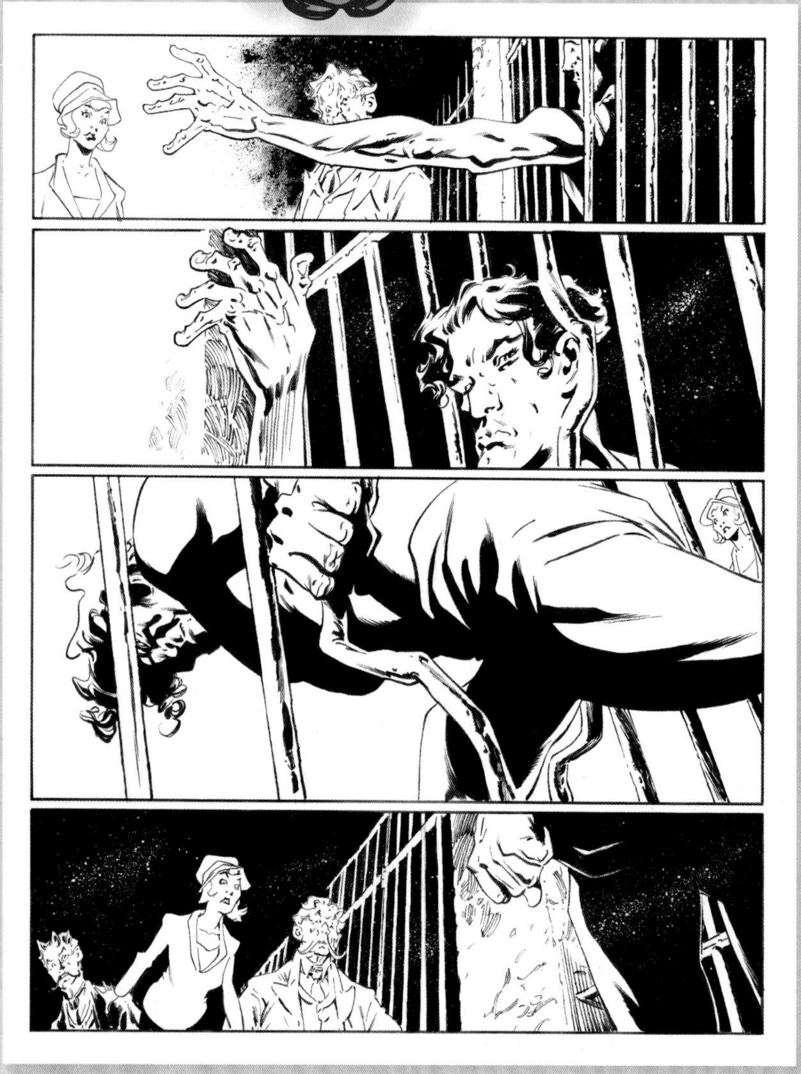

Page 52 • Inks

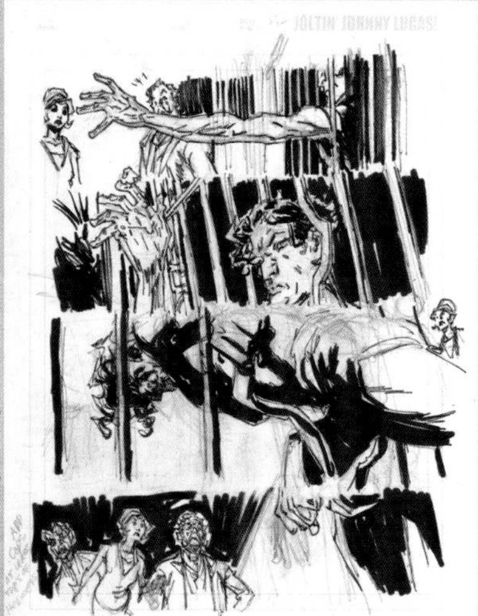
JOLTIN' JOHNNY LUCAS!

Page 52 • Layout Sketches

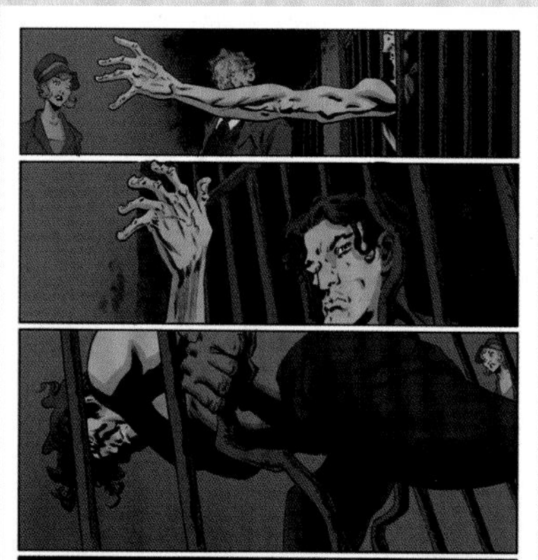

Page 52 • Colors

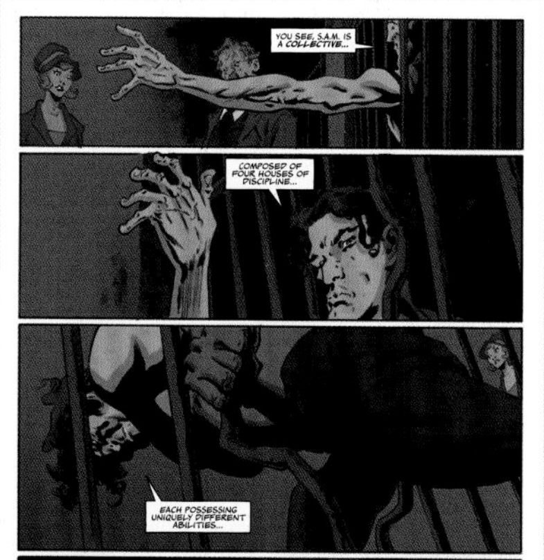
YOU SEE, S.A.M. IS A COLLECTIVE...
COMPOSED OF FOUR HOUSES OF DISCIPLINE...
EACH POSSESSING UNIQUELY DIFFERENT ABILITIES...
WHEN COMBINED, WE PROVIDE A COMPLEX DEFENSE NETWORK THAT IS PREPARED TO PROTECT ITSELF--AS WELL AS ITS ALLIES--AGAINST AN EQUALLY COMPLEX ENEMY.

Page 52 • Letters

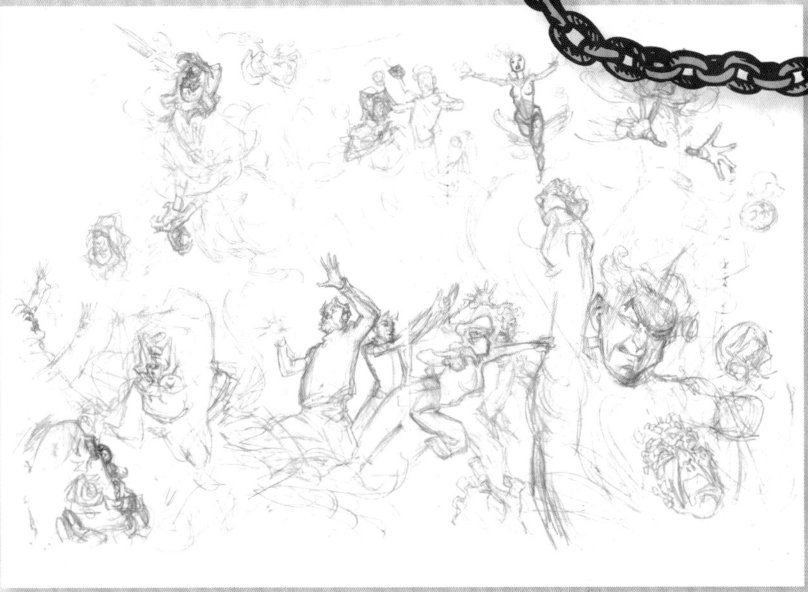
Pages 86–87 • Layout Sketches

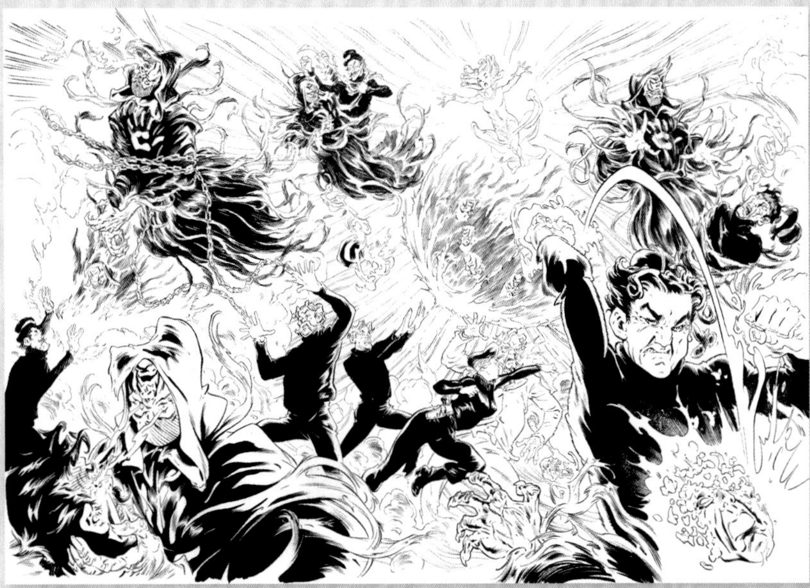
Pages 86–87 • Inks

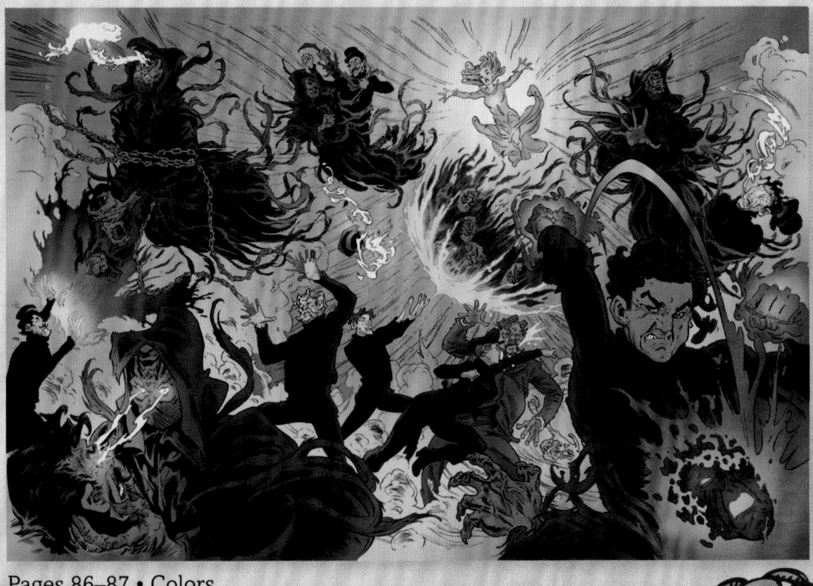
Pages 86–87 • Colors

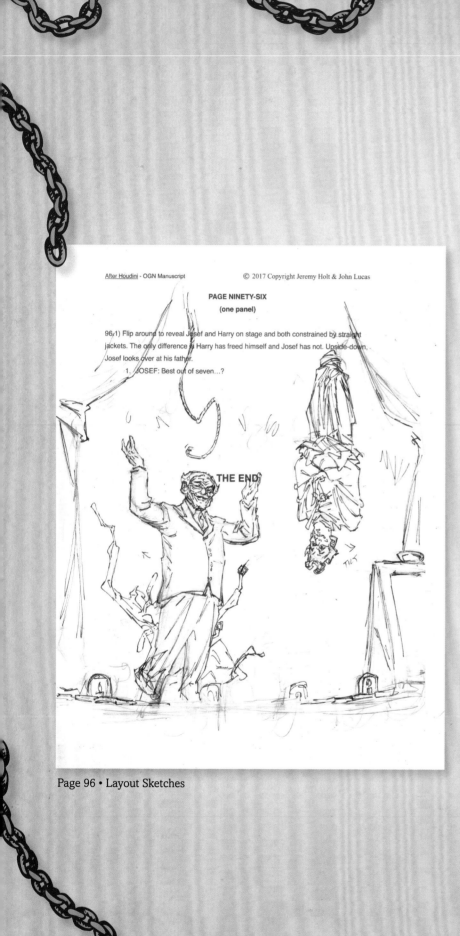

After Houdini - OGN Manuscript © 2017 Copyright Jeremy Holt & John Lucas

PAGE NINETY-SIX

(one panel)

96.1) Flip around to reveal Josef and Harry on stage and both constrained by straight jackets. The only difference is Harry has freed himself and Josef has not. Upside-down, Josef looks over at his father.

1. JOSEF: Best out of seven…?

THE END

Page 96 • Layout Sketches

Page 96 • Inks

Page 96 • Colors

BEST OUT OF SEVEN...?
THE END

Page 96 • Letters

A SNEAK PEEK AT
BEFORE HOUDINI

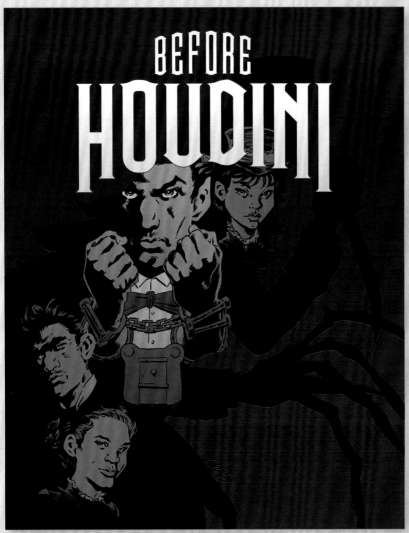

London, 1888. A shadowy killer stalks the streets of London, his appetite for blood unleashed upon the city's lower classes. To defeat him, MI6 turns to its most top-secret team: four teenage agents with extraordinary gifts—including a young American immigrant with a talent for illusion . . .

After Houdini began the story of Josef Houdini, son of the famous Harry Houdini—brilliant illusionist, acclaimed escape artist, and top-secret covert operative. Now we turn back the clock and meet Ehrich Weiss, a young man whose skill at picking locks is about to land him the adventure of his dreams and pull him into a war that will affect his life—and his son's—for years to come. This is the story of Ehrich's strange beginnings, from before he was a world-famous magician. Before he was a master of espionage. Before he was . . . Houdini.

Before Houdini available spring 2019!

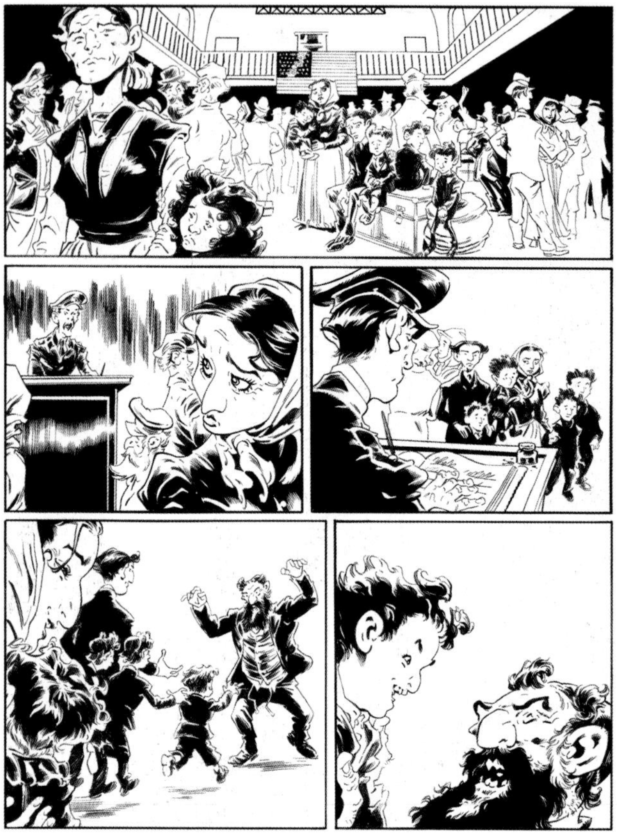

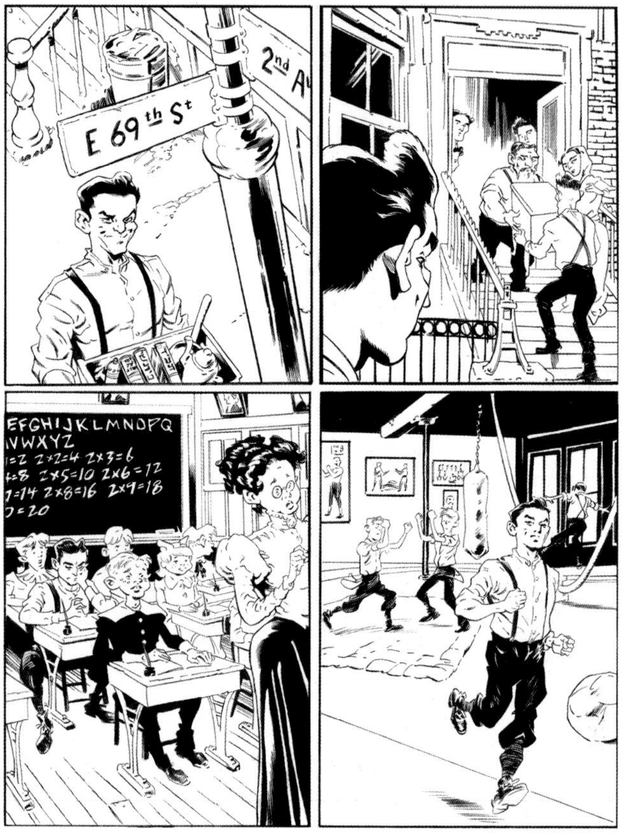

E 69th St
2nd A
EFGHIJKLMNOPQ
VWXYZ
2x2=4 2x3=6
2x5=10 2x6=12
2x8=16 2x9=18

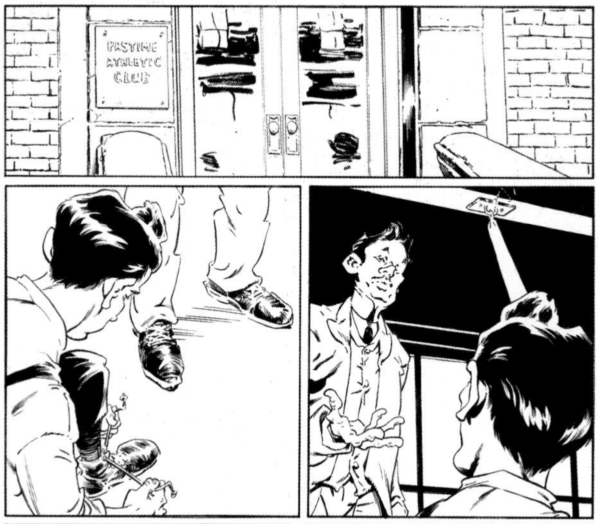

PASTIME ATHLETIC CLUB

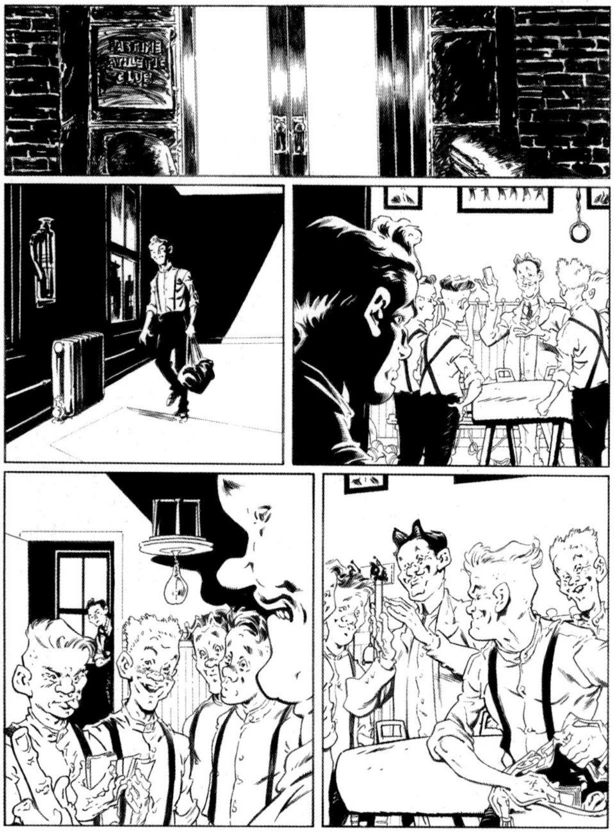

PASTIME ATHLETIC CLUB

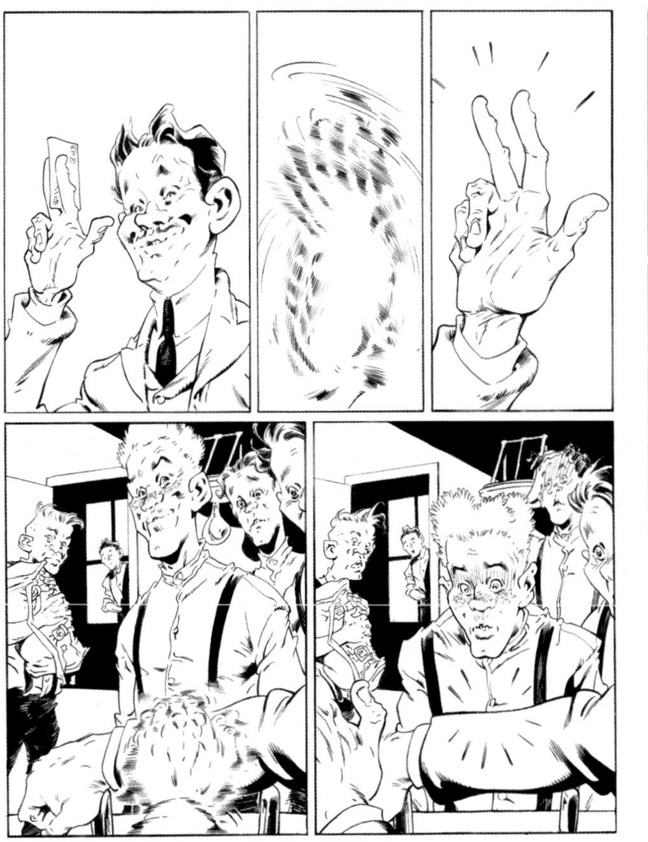
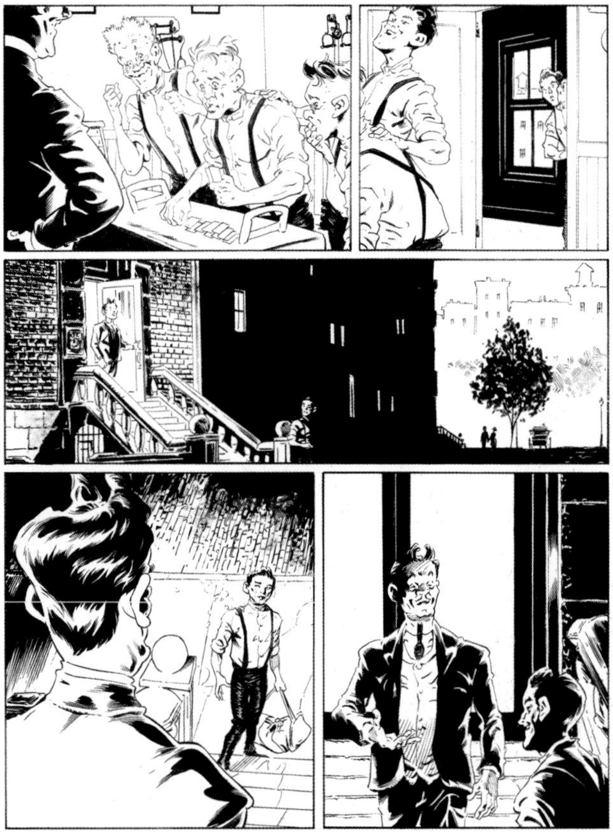
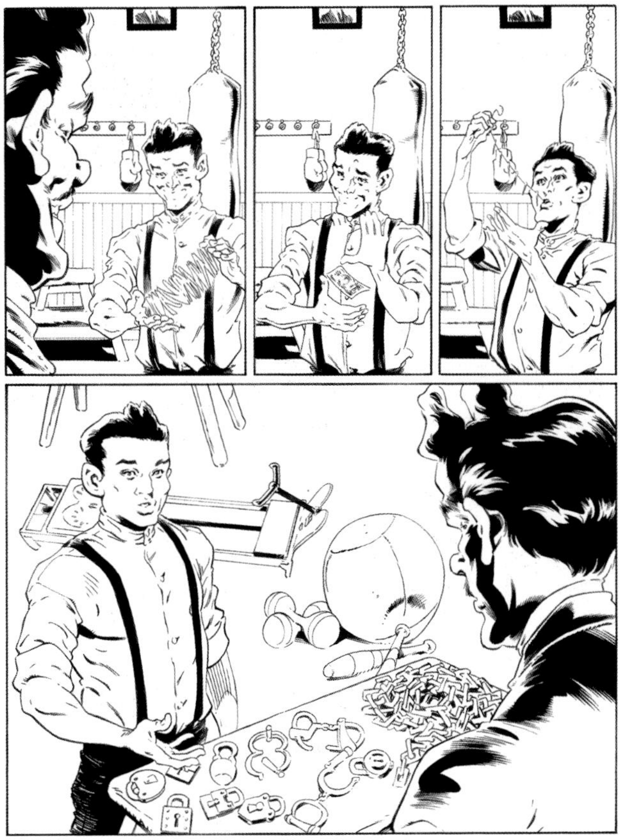
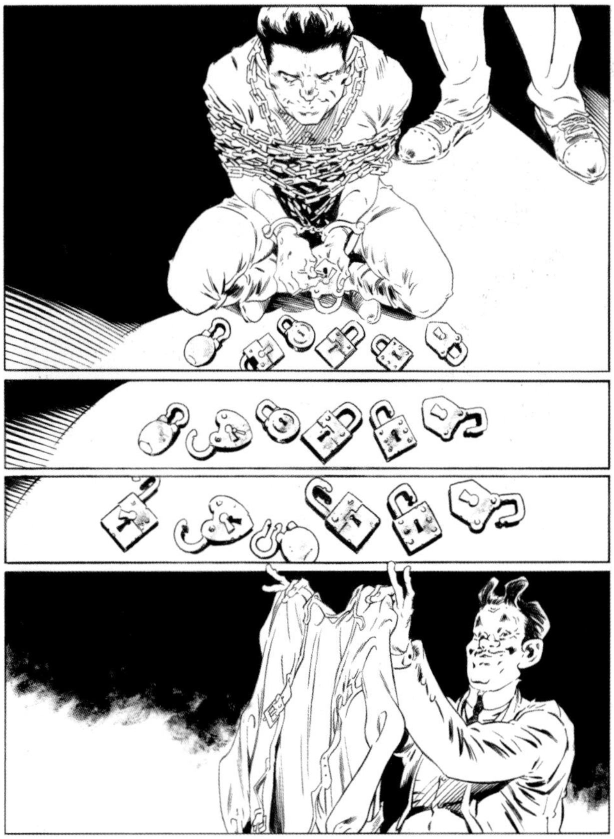

An imprint of Insight Editions
PO Box 3088
San Rafael, CA 94912
www.insightcomics.com

Find us on Facebook:
www.facebook.com/InsightEditionsComics

Follow us on Twitter:
@InsightComics

Follow us on Instagram:
Insight_Comics

Library of Congress Cataloging-in-Publication Data available.

ISBN: 978-1-60887-855-0

Publisher: Raoul Goff
Associate Publisher: Vanessa Lopez
Design Support: Amy DeGrote
Executive Editor: Mark Irwin
Assistant Editor: Holly Fisher
Senior Production Editor: Elaine Ou
Production Manager: Greg Steffen

ROOTS of PEACE
REPLANTED PAPER

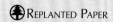

Insight Editions, in association with Roots of Peace, will plant two trees for each tree used in the manufacturing of this book. Roots of Peace is an internationally renowned humanitarian organization dedicated to eradicating land mines worldwide and converting war-torn lands into productive farms and wildlife habitats. Roots of Peace will plant two million fruit and nut trees in Afghanistan and provide farmers there with the skills and support necessary for sustainable land use.

Manufactured in China by Insight Editions

10 9 8 7 6 5 4 3 2 1